MW01103770

NO LONGER PROPERTY OF
KING COUNTY LIBRARY SYSTE

[JUL – 2016

The Confucian Cycle:

China's Sage and

America's Decline

By

William A. Taylor

Kenneth R. Taylor

The Confucian Cycle:
China's Sage and America's Decline
Copyright ©2015 William A. Taylor and Kenneth R. Taylor

ISBN 978-1622-879-61-8 HC
ISBN 978-1622-879-62-5 PBK
ISBN 978-1622-879-63-2 EBOOK

LCCN 2015946115

September 2015

Published and Distributed by
First Edition Design Publishing, Inc. in conjunction with Father's Press, LLC.
P.O. Box 20217, Sarasota, FL 34276-3217
www.firsteditiondesignpublishing.com

ALL RIGHTS RESERVED. No part of this book publication may be reproduced, stored in a retrieval system, or transmitted in any form or by any means — electronic, mechanical, photocopy, recording, or any other — except brief quotation in reviews, without the prior permission of the author or publisher.

The comments, opinions and viewpoints presented here are solely those of the authors as derived from their personal experiences and research.

Cover art by Jonathan Simpson and Mike Tyree.

Cover photographs used by permission. All rights reserved.

The Confucian Cycle

2,500 years ago, the Chinese sage, Confucius, observed that all governments follow a cycle: from unity, through prosperity to stagnation, then to collapse and anarchy.

He taught that when government officials sought personal power or wealth instead of taking care of the people, society lost the "Mandate of Heaven" and fell apart.

By "Mandate of Heaven," Confucius meant that God Himself had directed how society should work. Chinese history shows 15 or 20 collapses when government lost virtue and the country broke apart in civil war, but whenever the Chinese followed Confucius' rules, Chinese society worked well.

From his day to ours, civilizations all over the world have followed the same cycle Confucius observed. Today's United States is well into the "stagnation" phase and many observers predict a collapse.

But America has an advantage Confucius never imagined. Unlike the Chinese, America's voters have the power to replace their rulers and reform their government without armed revolution.

The Taylors' wide-ranging tour through history, culture, and modern news sheds new light on how the past both predicts the future and can be used to alter it for the better.

Dedication

We would like to dedicate this book to our mothers, both of whom were unimpressed by "the real me" of their sons, because "the real me" was a lazy bum. They took stern action to eliminate unacceptable childish behavior and replace it with acceptable adult behavior as rapidly as possible. Their efforts ultimately led to this book.

Acknowledgements

This book would never have been begun, much less completed, without the assistance and encouragement of Paul Waldschmidt. From its origins in articles published on Scragged.com, through years of revisions, rewrite, and editing, Paul's "third set of eyes" throughout has led to a vastly better work than it could have been otherwise.

John E. Taylor also provided extremely valuable editing review.

As one would expect, any errors or omissions are the fault of the authors, not the editors.

Table of Contents

Introduction

The true cause of national collapse seems to be elusive. Is it war? Nations which have collapsed had won wars in the past. Is it famine? There have always been famines, and a civilization of any strength survives them. Disease? Natural disaster? Political turmoil? All these catastrophes have been blamed for destroying once-great cultures; but catastrophes happen regularly, and usually don't do any permanent harm.

No, the underlying explanation for the collapse of great civilizations is rooted in something profoundly human, a phenomenon which we call the Pleasure-Pain Principle.

- All human beings seek to maximize their own personal comfort and pleasure
- All human beings seek to minimize discomfort and avoid pain

While people differ in their personal tastes with respect to what constitutes pleasure and what they regard as pain, some desires are pretty universal. In 1943, Abraham Maslow published *A Theory of Human Motivation* which proposed a hierarchy of human needs. Maslow pointed out that if a person is so thirsty that his body chemistry becomes unbalanced, *all* his energies turn toward finding water; other desires and needs are subordinated to the overriding need for water.[1]

Maslow argued that once our need for food, warmth, shelter, sex, water, and other bodily needs are satisfied, we become concerned

---

[1]   Maslow, Abraham "A Theory of Human Motivation", Psychological Review 50 (1943):370-96.

with "higher" needs such as the need to be respected and to have self-esteem. The two basic mechanisms by which people gain self-esteem are by amassing wealth or by amassing power.

By historical standards, nobody in America is really poor, particularly not government employees. There've probably been no deaths truly caused by starvation in the United States since the depths of the Great Depression, if then. With their basic needs satisfied, bureaucrats, like everybody else, turn to seeking pleasure by amassing money and power and minimizing pain by making sure that nobody can tell them what to do.

The same is true in the business world – business people are motivated to operate their businesses to gain wealth. As we hear every day, though, there is often a conflict between the needs of society and the greed of business people. In 1776, the same year Edward Gibbon produced the first volume of his masterwork *The Decline and Fall of the Roman Empire*, Adam Smith published *The Wealth of Nations* which explained how businessmen seek to fulfill their "higher needs" and benefit the entire society as a more-or-less accidental side effect of benefiting themselves.

Smith's book has been so influential that he's regarded by many as the founder of economics as an academic discipline. Although he's become the patron saint of free-market capitalism, he didn't believe that the best form of capitalism would be where businesses are allowed to operate entirely free from rules. He knew that *whenever* businessmen got together, greed would drive them to try to figure out how to raise prices to make more money without giving *any* societal benefits.

> "People of the same trade seldom meet together, even for merriment and diversion, but the conversation ends in a conspiracy against the public, or in some contrivance to raise prices."[2]

---

[2] Smith, Adam, *An Inquiry into the Nature and Causes of the Wealth of Nations*, (London, 1776)

The thought that business leaders might be greedy is an idea which most people find credible. To address this problem, Smith pointed out that the government's job is to write rules so that it's difficult to become rich without adding value to society. Bill Gates' wealth comes from selling a product which people voluntarily choose to buy. Adam Smith would approve of the immense wealth Windows and its offspring have brought to Microsoft as a company and to Bill Gates personally. In contrast, American sugar farming companies have become wealthy by persuading the government not to let us buy cheaper sugar from overseas; Smith disapproved of this tactic:

> "But though the law cannot hinder people of the same trade from sometimes assembling together, it ought to do nothing to facilitate such assemblies; much less to render them necessary."[3]

People have always tried to get favors and benefits from the government; Pres. William McKinley was shot in 1901 by a frustrated office-seeker who had been denied the government job he expected. Of late, however, our government has become so large, so complex, and has intruded into so many corners of our national life that businesses, parent groups, hunters, truck drivers, teachers, and many other interest groups find it worthwhile to band together either to protect themselves from damage inflicted by our government or to persuade government to give them money by one means or another.

What has this to do with the collapse of a civilization? Mr. Smith's characterization of business provides a complete explanation why societies collapse. Bureaucrats and functionaries who work around and for our government are as human as businessmen and are motivated in pretty much the same ways. If we can believe that businessmen always look for ways to raise prices and make more money at our expense, we ought to be able to

---

[3]   Ibid.

believe that government employees have the same basic motivations and that they look for ways to get more budget and power at our expense.

Taken as a whole, government employees behave no better and no worse than businessmen. They are no more selfish and no more altruistic. The difference is that if a businessman gets too greedy or neglects his customers, he'll go bankrupt. This market-based mechanism is what Adam Smith called the *invisible hand*: it smacks businessmen and their employees around. When businesses get too greedy or stop minding the store, customers go elsewhere and the business goes broke.

The economist Joseph Schumpeter spoke of the "creative destruction" of a properly functioning free market, in which once-great businesses that become lazy or corrupt lose their customers and are replaced by new upstarts with better products or service.[4]

Applying free-market principles to our economy has led to the wealthiest society mankind has ever known; people whom our bureaucrats classify as "poor" to justify their budgets aren't really poor. According to the Heritage Foundation:[5]

> The average poor American has more living space than the average individual living in Paris, London, Vienna, Athens, and other cities throughout Europe. (These comparisons are to the average citizens in foreign countries, not to those classified as poor.)
>
> Nearly three-quarters of poor households own a car; 31 percent own two or more cars.
>
> Ninety-seven percent of poor households have a color television; over half own two or more color televisions.

---

4   Schumpeter, Joseph. *Capitalism, Socialism and Democracy* (New York: Harper, 1975) [orig. pub. 1942], pp. 82-85

5   "How Poor Are America's Poor? Examining the 'Plague' of Poverty in America" report by the Heritage Foundation, August 27, 2007 available online at http://www.heritage.org/research/welfare/bg2064.cfm

Seventy-eight percent have a VCR or DVD player;
62 percent have cable or satellite TV reception.

There's a simple reason for such affluence - the prospect of corporate death forces companies to be efficient and effective. The more efficient and effective they are, the less their goods cost and the greater the benefit to every member of society. Businesses that can't keep up are replaced by those that can.

Unfortunately, there is *no* equivalent self-enforcing law of nature that ensures that a government employee will be dismissed for not working or that a government agency will have its budget cut if it messes up. As we know, the reverse usually happens.

Consider public schools. When teachers don't teach what they're supposed to, they get paid extra to teach summer school so kids can catch up. The worse job they do, the more money they make. If an agency manages to avoid solving a *genuine* problem long enough, a crisis may occur at which point the legislators generally shower the agency with money. For example, the CIA's budget was not cut in punishment for missing signs that 9-11 was coming or that the Soviet Union was about to fall apart, even though the agency's predictions have been incompetent and ineffective for longer than most of us have been alive.

We shouldn't disparage the motives of politicians; they have the same motives you and I do. There's no need to distrust the motives of bureaucrats either; their motives are all too plain. We *all* have the same desires that Abraham Maslow observed – to increase *our* personal status, wealth, and power regardless of the effect on society.

Although there is no "invisible hand" of the marketplace that adjusts the workings of government as it does business, governments, just like businesses, are in competition. A government that cannot or will not compete effectively faces a far more severe penalty than bankruptcy: it faces collapse of the entire society or civilization.

This book discusses well-documented warning signs of collapse that are all around us, telling us that our government is in urgent need of adjustment. In business terms, we are presented with *many* consecutive loss-making quarters and a plummeting share price. A company president in this situation needs to carefully examine the various divisions to find the root of the problem; this book helps each of us do that. After all, our founders gave us government "of the People; by the People; for the People." If We the People don't clean house, who will?

1 – The Burden of Bureaucracy

All nations, societies, and businesses have suffered from bureaucratic inefficiency ever since the Chinese invented bureaucracy some 5,000 years ago.[6]

Even though he had the power to order anyone executed at any time, the Emperor of China couldn't accomplish much by himself. He had to work through layers and layers of government employees to get anything done.

Massive projects such as the Egyptian pyramids or the Great Wall of China could only be completed using bureaucracy to organize thousands of workers. Reams of management and organizational theory have been ground out over the millennia, but no one has improved on a bureaucratic organization to handle repetitive tasks such as making sure that all dogs in the city are vaccinated or that births are duly registered with the government. The Chinese found the Imperial bureaucracy indispensable for maintaining roads, keeping the army paid, for collecting taxes, and for many other public purposes.

Fundamental problems with bureaucracy surfaced soon after its advantages were discovered – government employees are human beings just like you and me and sometimes serve their own interests instead of fulfilling the agency's mission.

---

6   Durant, William. *Our Oriental Heritage*, (New York, Simon and Schuster, 1954) p. 636 has a dynastic chart which starts with "Legendary rulers" in 2,800 BC, about 4,800 years ago. There are indications that Chinese rulers had well-developed organizational systems before that. The figure of 5,000 years is more or less traditional. In any case, the Chinese bureaucratic system is far older than the 200-year-old democratic form of government as practiced in America or communism which failed before reaching its first century.

The overlapping agencies of the Imperial government developed their own agendas over time. An Emperor's order might not be obeyed depending on how local officials felt about it. China was often called a "rope of sand" because pulling strings in the capital may or may not have any effect in distant provinces.

Chinese history explains a lot of what's going on in America today. American bureaucrats have the same ambitions and goals bureaucrats have had ever since bureaucracy was invented:

- Less work to do this year
- A bigger budget next year
- A comfortable retirement at the end

These desires aren't unique to government, of course. Only hard-core workaholics don't seek to get by with less work. Everyone would like to make more money next year without working any more, and we'd all like to retire comfortably as early as possible.

80% to 90% of the Chinese were farmers in Confucius' day, so bureaucrats were the only people who could achieve these goals. If farmers slacked off a bit, they'd have less to eat; and no matter how hard they worked, the land yielded only so much. To be able to retire, a farmer had to raise sons who'd take responsibility for feeding his parents when they could no longer work.

Bureaucrats had much richer opportunities to better themselves at public expense. Political maneuvering might get an official more subordinates to share the load or increase the budget in other ways. A lifetime of crafty manipulation could lead to a big department and enough accumulated wealth to support a lavish retirement.

These goals often conflict with citizens' interest. Over time, bureaucracies tend to run up government spending so much that society can't afford the cost.

Society collapses when government costs too much.

The Good Side of Government

Japan was bombed flat during World War II and repairing the infrastructure took years. In late 1945, General MacArthur sent a telegram to President Truman, "Send me bread or send me bullets." He had to feed the Japanese or shoot them; there was no food in Japan because the entire country had been bombed out.

As the Japanese struggled to put their infrastructure back together, I watched the government organize parades of men and women to carry gravel. Each one bounced along under two baskets hanging from a springy pole across the shoulders. Moving dirt by muscle power was the only way to fix the roads – all the trucks and bulldozers had been destroyed.[7]

The Japanese found that by working extremely hard, they could export about 15% of their annual GNP. On the minus side, they had to import 14% of GNP because Japan has almost no natural resources. They ran the entire country on a 1% margin.[8]

The Japanese government gave bureaucracies such as the Ministry of International Trade and Industry (MITI) vast power to influence businesses by allocating foreign exchange and granting or refusing import licenses. The bureaucrats set a vivid example of extremely hard work to help their society deal with the ongoing crisis. Most citizens followed their virtuous example. It took thirty years, but the Japanese economy grew to the point that many writers believed that Japan would rule the world economy.[9]

Japan's economy didn't grow because bureaucrats chose economic "winners." Venture capitalists who invest their own money get only one or two winners out of 10 investments; bureaucrats who "invest" tax money do far worse. To name but one example of bureaucratic frailty, MITI told Sony and Honda that their companies would never make it internationally. They were wrong.

---

[7]   Given WW II bombing damage, Japan was one vast shovel-ready project.

[8]   Taylor, William A, *What Every Engineer Should Know About Artificial Intelligence*, MIT Press (Boston, 1988) p 281

[9]   Vogel, Ezra, *Japan as #1: Lessons for America*, (IUniverse, 1979)

The Japanese government agencies helped a great deal, however, by setting an example of hard work and by managing logistics. Consular offices arranged meetings between Japanese executives and American mayors and governors who could locate new factories and do other favors.

They also urged businesses to share research. When the US Government required that tailpipe emissions be reduced starting with the 1975 model year, for example, the Japanese government helped automobile companies cooperate on research. The companies applied the new knowledge in different ways, but they didn't waste money duplicating research. In the US, in contrast, antitrust regulations kept Ford, GM, and Chrysler from cooperating. They each had to spend money duplicating the same research.

Since government employees were seen to be working very honestly and very hard, most people were motivated to serve society instead of serving themselves.

Once the economy took off, however, the crisis ended, motivation weakened, and human nature reasserted itself. Bureaucratic rot set in. The agencies decided that since the nation was doing well, they ought to build the agency instead of building the national economy. After a time, the people in the agencies decided that the agencies were doing well enough and started looking out for themselves.

As citizens saw government employees working less and serving themselves, they too became less virtuous. Japan has been stuck in economic stagnation since 1990. No leader has emerged who can inspire the bureaucracies to encourage the citizens by setting an example of sacrifice and virtuous hard work.

No one wants to endanger bureaucratic privilege by streamlining regulations which impose costs on businesses or, perish the thought, cut spending by reducing government employment. Citizens who see government employees serving themselves have less motivation to serve society. With everyone wanting to take out and no one wanting to put in, the economy stagnates until society collapses.

We see the same bureaucratic drag on the American economy.

The Washington Monument Strategy

Despite thousands of years of technical progress, modern American presidents suffer from the age-old tendency of government employees to serve themselves instead of the public. Most citizens resent the waste and corruption they see and expect their leaders to do something about it.

Two months after taking office, President Obama said, "The days of giving government contractors a blank check are over" and added that he planned changes that would save up to $40 billion a year.[10] I remember hearing every President since John F. Kennedy speak of cutting waste. It's far easier to speak eloquently about cutting government waste than to cut spending enough to save significant sums of money.

When Congress cut the Park Service budget in 1966, for example, the agency shut down the Washington Monument elevator. When my family visited, a Park Ranger explained that this was a cost-cutting measure and offered us a map so we could visit our representative's office and petition for "redress of grievances."[11]

We knew this ploy from living in Japan, whose bureaucracy makes ours seem simple. We refused the leaflet and walked up the monument on foot. Other tourists griped to their Congressman, though, and sure enough, Park Service funds were restored.

This game of saving trivial sums by annoying voters is known as the "Washington Monument Strategy."[12] It's bureaucracy 1.01. It's known and loved by every bureaucrat who cuts the library's hours and turns off streetlights while leaving government workers' salaries, pensions, and benefits untouched.

---

[10] "Obama orders federal contracting overhaul," *Associated Press*, March 4, 2009
[11] United States Constitution, Amendment I, ratified 12/15/1791
[12] O'Toole, Randal, *The Best-Laid Plans*, (Cato Institute, 2007) p 300.

Bureaucratic Neglect

Bureaucracies sometimes neglect their duty even when they aren't being pressed to cut costs. The New Orleans Levee District, which had the responsibility of maintaining dikes, dams, and other equipment to keep water out of the city, blocked a critical $427,000 floodgate repair in the months before Hurricane Katrina. They spent money on parks, docks, and leasing Bally's *Belle of New Orleans* floating casino for a party instead.[13]

The Levee District decided that leasing a casino was more important than fixing a floodgate, but all agency plans require money. Regardless of individual priorities, however, every agency employee agrees that the agency needs a bigger budget. The bigger government gets, the more government employees there are whose salaries cost more and who lobby for yet more money.

The Emperor and Culture Clash

Private bureaucracies can be wasteful too, as I found when I worked for a conglomerate called Gould in the early 1980s. The boss' name had too many y's and z's for me to pronounce, so I called him "Chairman Bill." Mao tze Tung had added so much glory to "Chairman" that people knew I meant the Chairman of the Board.

"Chairman" was my second choice. I called him "Emperor" at first because he ruled many independent business kingdoms. I encouraged my colleagues to increase sales so the Emperor could meet payroll more easily. I tried to travel cheaply because all expenses reduced our profit sharing pool. There are worse fates than being known for being tight with the Emperor's money.

Calling him "Emperor" was rooted in Confucian attitudes I'd learned while growing up in Japan. I'd lived in a structured,

---

[13] Brinkley, Douglas, *The Great Deluge*, (William Morrow, 2006) p 194. The book refers to "greedy scoundrels" who misused money that should have been used to prepare for storms.

hierarchical society based on the principle that every person owes obedience and loyalty to his or her superior. Every successful nation, culture, tribe, and business runs that way to a greater or lesser extent.

Powerful Japanese ruled subordinates, of course, but the Japanese had based their social structure on Confucius' teaching that every superior had a God-given responsibility to look out for their followers' wellbeing.

Weak people have no choice about obeying the strong. Powerful people have exploited weaker people throughout history. Confucian virtue lies in having the strong work to benefit all the people who depended on them.

In return for obedience, every Japanese boss had to look out for all employees. Every government official was obligated to look out for the citizens' welfare. This two-way loyalty was very strong – employees had lifetime jobs, did what they were told, and worked very hard. All workers knew they had to serve customers so customers would serve the business and payroll could continue.

I knew a college professor whose *kamikaze* flight had been scheduled near the end of World War II. He survived because the Japanese air force ran out of planes before he could crash into an American ship. Unlike Muslim jihadis who suicide to earn rewards in heaven, he and his *kamikaze* colleagues knew the war was lost. Their deaths would make no difference.

Why did they accept certain death and sacrifice themselves to no purpose? Their superiors ordered them to go. Disobeying orders would have violated Confucian virtue and disgraced the Emperor.

These attitudes carried over into business. There were no Japanese cars on American roads when I entered MIT in 1963. By the 1980's, Japanese workers' willingness to serve their employers by working hard to serve customers gained so much market share that American manufacturers demanded government help. The Japanese use the same word for "customer" as for "guest" and act accordingly.

My American colleagues weren't nearly as interested in serving the Emperor. Knowing that the Japanese were recovering from

World War II and that competition was coming, I urged my colleagues to help our Emperor increase sales and cut costs by traveling cheaply, turning off lights, and sharing equipment.

Our salesmen didn't call on companies that couldn't afford our products. Their job was to persuade customers that our products were more wonderful than the money in the customers' bank accounts. If they failed, we lost the sale.

Our job was to make products more wonderful through improvements and to reduce the price by cutting costs. The goal was to make our products more wonderful than money. Improvements made it easier for the Emperor to meet payroll by increasing sales; cost cutting contributed to our profit-sharing pool. What could be more virtuous than that?

One day, a middle manager told me, "Stop joking about the Emperor!" I was shocked. I wasn't joking, I was serious, but he thought I was making fun of the boss. The Emperor was owed honor because he had organized all of us into a team that offered products our customers wanted more than the money it cost to buy. His revenue covered my paycheck. What could be more virtuous than that? Why would anyone think I was joking?

In 5 words, this manager explained why American companies so often lose to Asian competitors. Americans aren't personally worried about taking care of the business they work for; they thought I was joking when I urged them to increase Imperial revenue and cut Imperial costs. Japanese firms for which I'd worked were full of people who focused on keeping their employers in business. Sales were far more important to individual Japanese workers than to Americans, so it was no wonder the Japanese were winning the economic war.

When I took the job, I'd sold the Emperor the right to tell me what to do. I'd accepted the obligation of doing whatever I could to increase income and cut costs. Calling him "Emperor" didn't get my point across, though, so "Chairman Bill" it was.

The Chairman and the Hammer

Chairman Bill was a skilled deal maker; he bought and sold divisions more often than lesser beings buy and sell cars. Shortly after he bought a very profitable division which fulfilled government contracts, the media reported that his division had been paid more than $100 for a hammer which could be bought in a hardware store for $2.98. It wasn't as bad as a $600 toilet seat or $3,000 coffee maker, but Chairman Bill's golf buddies teased him unmercifully about how they could show as much profit as he did if only they, too, could charge $100 for a $2.98 hammer.

Chairman Bill summoned his accountants and told them, "I don't care what it costs. If we robbed the government, I want to know and I'll take care of it. If we didn't rob the government, I want you to sign a letter saying we did everything right."

Having heard the magic words, "I don't care what it costs," the accountants swarmed into the military products business. Accountants don't often use words like "shock" or "amaze," but they admitted they were surprised by government accounting practice.

They found more than 20 cost categories associated with the hammer – marketing, travel, cleaning, general administration, and other items allocated to the hammer by formulas defined in the contract. The smallest line item was about $.23, the biggest $4.50 or so, but these items added up to the price Gould had charged. It would have been against the law to charge a penny less – and every single rule provided employment for the bureaucracy who wrote and enforced it.

Confucius Explained Bureaucracy

Americans know that our bureaucracy is out of control, but few realize that bureaucratic bloat goes back 5,000 years. The Chinese suffered from the same bureaucratic inefficiencies as we do and bureaucratic overload collapsed their society over and over.

Around 500 BC,[14] Confucius explained how society worked and why empires fall. Confucius taught that ordinary citizens had to obey orders but the government had to take care of the people. If people did as they were told and government sincerely looked out for their welfare, society would be stable and safe. Society kept the "Mandate of Heaven" when everybody operated by his rules.

By "Mandate of Heaven," Confucius meant that God Himself designed human nature so that societies could work in only one way. History demonstrates that Confucius' rules are as inescapable as Newton's laws of gravity. Societies that follow his formula of governance prosper, while societies that get too far from his path of virtue lose the "Mandate of Heaven and collapse."

A ruler's most important task was setting an example of virtuous behavior because citizens behave no better than their leaders. Every civil servant reported to the Emperor through the chain of command. Having set a good example and appointed the best people he could find, the Emperor's most vital task was terminating government employees who abused their positions. This encouraged survivors to be more virtuous. Confucius knew that the whisper of the axe is the only sure way to motivate a bureaucracy in a positive direction.

If the Emperor didn't enforce virtue, bureaucrats stole money, goofed off, and abused taxpayers. When people saw their leaders misbehaving, they cheated on their taxes. The Emperor raised tax rates to try to cover costs but higher tax rates made people work harder to avoid paying. As the bureaucracy wasted or stole more money, tax rates went up more and the army budget was cut to pay for "essential services." When the army became weak, people rebelled or the barbarians swept in and took over.

Confucius' rules aren't unique to him, of course. As President Obama put it, "No business wants to invest in a place where the government skims 20 percent off the top."[15]

---

[14] Durant, William. *Our Oriental Heritage*, (New York, Simon and Schuster, 1954) p. 636

[15] *New York Times* quote of the day, July 12, 2009

Half a millennium after Confucius, St. Paul wrote that God wanted people to obey government and pay taxes. Government should encourage virtue, punish the non-virtuous, and execute evildoers.[16] King Solomon made Confucius' point about the perils of non-virtuous kings and the benefits of virtuous rulers 500 years before Confucius:

> *"Woe to thee, O land, when thy king is a child, and thy princes eat in the morning! Blessed art thou, O land, when thy king is the son of nobles, and thy princes eat in due season, for strength, and not for drunkenness!"* **Ecclesiastes 10:16-17**

Confucius' ideas are known to work – society prospers when government rules virtuously.

When government lost virtue, society collapsed and war followed. The toughest warlord fought his way to the top, much as Mao tse Tung defeated Chiang Kai-shek in 1949. With bureaucracy reset to zero, the Confucian cycle of unity, peace, bureaucratic excess, collapse, war, and reunification begins again. Will Durant lists fourteen Chinese dynasties which fell apart when they lost the "Mandate of Heaven."[17]

Chinese history since Confucius can be seen as a series of foreign ideas such as Taoism, legalism, Buddhism,[18] Falun Gong, statism, and most recently communism and capitalism gaining influence - only to have China revert to Confucian principles when the new ideas don't work as well as expected.

Mao tse Tung promoted communism and millions starved. The Chinese switched to capitalism in the 1980's to keep people from rebelling. When the worldwide recession gave capitalism a black

---

[16]   Romans 13:1-10, I Peter 2:13-24
[17]   Durant, William. *Our Oriental Heritage*, (New York, Simon and Schuster, 1954) pp 636-637
[18]   Roupp, Heidi, *Teaching World History* (Sharpe, M. E., 1996) p 25 states that Buddhism traveled the Silk Road from India to China by "cultural diffusion." Confucius may have read Solomon's writings or other wisdom literature.

eye, the government started reviving Confucius' ideas even though most communist leaders had labeled Confucian rules "feudal."

Confucius is neither liberal nor conservative, neither modern nor feudal; he's practical and effective. Chinese keep returning to Confucius because 2,500 years of history show that his rules work.

Our constitutional republic is only 200 years old; the Chinese had at least three dynasties that lasted 300 years or more. Chinese leaders realistically argue that our system hasn't been tested long enough to know whether it works or not. Another reason not to introduce democracy is that they'd have to give up power, of course.

Emperors and Miscreants

Even though they declared that Confucius' other ideas were "feudal," the Chinese Communists kept the Emperor's power to chop heads if anyone got in their way. I learned that the Emperor's ability to hire and fire is fundamental to operating an efficient business. Chairman Bill personally reached down five levels to the bottom of Gould and fired me after a newspaper dug through 20 or 30 articles I'd written to find quotes to use to make him look bad.

Management had approved every word I'd published but our Emperor felt Gould would be better off without me. In contrast, the President of the United States can't even fine government employees who disobey him. Without ever hearing the whisper of the axe, why should bureaucrats pay attention to what the administration has been elected to do if they don't agree?

The American bureaucracy is even more of a threat to society than the Chinese equivalent because the President can't fire anyone. In China, no matter how expensive the bureaucracy became, an energetic Emperor could prune it back and restore virtue.

President Lincoln lived before the Civil Service Act of 1883 made it impossible to fire government workers. Having personally hired just about every Federal employee from the cabinet down to the lowliest letter carrier, he fired them when they didn't follow his policies. Lincoln would probably have lost the Civil War if he had had as little control of the bureaucracy as modern Presidents have.

How have we reached this sorry state of expensive ineffectiveness? Let's take a tour through our modern world and see.

2 – A Tale of Two Bureaucracies

Two cases of bureaucratic injustice received wide publicity in 2008. The way these incidents were treated shows the different mind-set between private companies and government bureaucracies:

- Tim Hortons coffee shop fired an employee for giving a screaming toddler a 16-cent donut hole.
- A child was taken from his home and his father was forced to leave when a refreshment counter employee accidentally gave the child alcoholic lemonade instead of what the father ordered.

These overbearing reactions were far out of proportion to the insignificant actions they were trying to correct. We'd be tempted to ask, "How can anybody be so stupid?" but bureaucrats, like most people, are pretty good at responding to incentives they're given.

We saw that when government pays $100 for a $2.98 hammer or $600 for a toilet seat, it's not because the people who did it are stupid. Instead of blaming the individuals, we should look at the incentives and procedures set up by the bureaucracies in which these people operate. There's a saying, "If you give me perverse incentives, don't be surprised when I act perversely."

These incidents support Confucius' observations about the nature of bureaucracy and show that his rules about how governments operate are as universal as Euclid's laws of geometry. It didn't matter whether people liked his formula, the next 2,500 years showed that society prospered when the majority followed his rules and always collapsed when people got too far from the path of virtue.

We see the same inevitability in the actions of Tim Hortons bureaucracy and the Child Protection Agency. We may not like what they did, but the universal laws of human nature make such blunders unavoidable in any bureaucracy.

Both unsatisfactory events happened when low-level people followed well-documented procedures. The different results of these bureaucratic blunders highlight the differences between the incentives in commercial firms and in government agencies.

Tim Hortons re-hired their employee after public protest, but there was no protest when the Child Protection Service (CPS) abused a child by removing him from a good home. A judge allowed the child to return home if the father moved out. The father was allowed back in his home after the story made national news, but there was no restitution for what the family spent defending itself from this misguided bureaucracy.

All bureaucracies are made of men and women who do their best to help their organization survive and grow. A business like Tim Hortons grows by persuading people to buy coffee and donuts; child protection agencies grow by convincing legislatures to fatten their budget and increase their staff. Child protection agencies do that by claiming, "There's a lot of abuse out there" and drawing families into their system. Hiring more bureaucrats makes them more important and makes it possible to wreak havoc on more families.

The people who made these decisions acted precisely as their managers expected. They operated rationally and sensibly given the rules handed down to them. Let's examine the details:

Tim Horton Firing

Reuters reports:[19]

---

[19] "Woman fired for giving 16-cent treat to toddler" *Reuters* May 8, 2008, see http://www.reuters.com/article/oddlyEnoughNews/idUSN0836799020080508

Nicole Lilliman, a single mother, said she was dismissed from a London, Ontario, outlet of the Tim Hortons coffee and doughnut chain after video cameras captured the 27-year-old giving a Timbit to a toddler.

... Tim Hortons said on Thursday that the firing was a mistake. "It was the unfortunate action of one manager who unfortunately made an overzealous decision, and thankfully we were able to rectify the situation," said company spokeswoman Rachel Douglas.

Tim Hortons has coffee shops all across Canada. Profitable fast-food chains minimize labor costs. The smarter store managers have to be, the more the chain has to pay them. A chain labors to define the manager's job to require neither initiative nor imagination because people with those abilities cost more than people who follow orders and go by the book. Writing "the book" saves money.

Teaching processes and procedures for everything turns each store into a small, rule-driven bureaucracy. McDonalds enrolls store managers in "Hamburger U" to learn how to run a McD's. The Tim Hortons book tells everything you need to know to run a Tim Hortons. If a manager runs "by the book," he needn't think. In fact, he *must* not think, or he'll get in trouble for not following the book.

Shoplifting and theft are death on stores - we've all seen signs threatening shoplifters with prosecution. Giving products away costs the same as shoplifting; give away product, you're fired. Ms. Lillman knew that she was in the wrong; she said, "I should have gone to my purse and got the change, but it was busy..."

Empathize with the store manager for a moment. When he reviewed the security video and caught Ms. Lillman giving away product, he fired her as the book said. He was paid to follow the book. He'd be in trouble if he didn't follow the book. He could've asked his boss, but that would have required thought and he's not paid to think. Expecting him to think, something the chain doesn't pay him to do and in fact teaches him not to do, would be unjust.

The story ended happily for Ms. Lillman. The public believed that calming a screaming toddler who was disturbing the whole store was worth 16 cents to the chain. They protested the firing and upper management re-hired Ms. Lillman.

Note that Rachel Douglas, the company spokesperson, used "unfortunate" to describe the manager's decision. It wasn't "wrong" because the book said she had to be fired. The manager is taught to follow the book, he's paid to follow the book, and that's what he did.

No matter how carefully you plan, it sometimes doesn't always work. Like any successful chain, Tim Hortons runs their stores rigidly and bureaucratically to keep costs down and guarantee the same customer experience in every store. If a job can be reduced to procedures requiring no thought or imagination, bureaucracy is the cheapest way to get it done.

One test of a bureaucracy is how it responds when the procedures don't work. Tim Hortons upper management passed this test, but only after public protest got their attention.

Retail bureaucracies do their best to define, teach, and enforce procedures that create a shopping experience that's pleasant enough that people will choose to come back while letting stores operate at a profit. We call this model "marketing and fulfillment."

The CPS bureaucracy operates differently because people rarely seek out CPS "services," it's the other way 'round. CPS finds victims and uses government power to force them to accept services. We call this "coercive intervention," a vastly different model from marketing and delivering a worthwhile customer experience.

Government-Sponsored Child Abuse

CPS-sponsored injustice had a different result as a *Detroit Free Press* April 28, 2008 article "Hard lemonade, hard price" reported:

> The way police and child protection workers figure it, Ratte should have known that what a Comerica Park vendor handed over when Ratte ordered a lemonade for his boy three Saturdays ago contained alcohol, and Ratte's ignorance justified placing young Leo in foster care until his dad got up to speed on the commercial beverage industry.
>
> Even if, in hindsight, that decision seems a bit, um, <u>idiotic</u>.[20] [emphasis added]

Christopher Ratte, a professor of archeology at University of Michigan, took his 7-year-old son Leo to a Tigers baseball game. A concession stand vendor gave Leo alcoholic lemonade by mistake. A guard noticed the bottle in Leo's hand and called the police.

A Detroit police officer interviewed Ratte at Children's Hospital where a doctor at the Comerica Park clinic had dispatched Leo – by ambulance! And we wonder why health costs are out of control. The Emergency Room resident who drew Leo's blood found no trace of alcohol, but the Child Protective Service (CPS) took him into custody anyway. It was two days before the state allowed Ratte's wife to take their son Leo home and nearly a week before Prof. Ratte was permitted to move back into his own house.

Leo Was Abused by Our Government

Removing a child from his home so that he cries himself to sleep in front of a television at CPS headquarters while his parents stand outside wondering if they'll ever see their child again is government-sponsored child abuse, pure and simple. Evil often results when unthinking bureaucratic apply their procedures to people.

---

[20]   "Hard lemonade, hard price" Detroit Free Press April 28, 2008, http://www.freep.com/apps/pbcs.dll/article?AID=/20080428/COL04/80428 0375/1081

The boy learned that his home isn't secure; the government can charge in and grab him at any time. Throwing an innocent father out of his own home as a condition of returning his child is an abuse of power but it's what the agency guidebook requires.[21]

When the mafia snatches a child and demands that we do what they want to get him back, we call it "kidnapping." What do we call it when government snatches a child from a good home and sets unconstitutional conditions for giving him back?

The police officer who interviewed Ratte said that her supervisor insisted on referring the matter to Child Protective Services. Federal law makes police officers "mandatory reporters"; they face fines and jail time if they don't report something which might be child abuse.

The CPS workers seemed to be more annoyed with the cop than with Ratte; they told him the whole thing was unnecessary as they drove Leo away. The *Free Press* explains, "But there was really nothing any of them could do, they all said. They were just adhering to protocol, following orders," just as the Hortons manager went by the book and fired Ms. Lillman.

We've heard this song before. Didn't we hang German bureaucrats for abusing people while "only following orders"?

The Ratte case gained overseas attention. In "Land of the Free?" the British journal *Economist* wrote:

> The American legal system also seems to have lost any sense of proportion. Christopher Ratte, a professor of archeology, recently tried to buy his seven-year-old son a bottle of lemonade at a baseball game. He was handed a bottle of Mike's Hard Lemonade, an alcoholic drink, by mistake. Officials

---

[21] Forcing an innocent man to leave his home is blatantly unconstitutional:
The right of the people to be <u>secure in their persons, houses, papers, and effects</u>, against unreasonable searches and seizures, shall not be violated, and no warrants shall issue, but upon probable cause, supported by oath or affirmation, and particularly describing the place to be searched, and the persons or things to be seized. (4th Amendment)

noticed the boy sipping the drink and immediately whisked him off to hospital. He was fine. But the family was condemned to legal hell: the police at first put the seven-year-old into a foster home and a judge ruled that he could go home only if his father moved out. It took several days of legal wrangling to reunite the family.[22]

There's another reason it's so difficult to untangle the web that shared the Rattes. Removing Leo into foster care started a federal revenue stream because the feds reimburse agencies when they remove children.

When two other relatives, one a licensed social worker and the other a foster parent, came to the CPS office and tried to take Leo into their care, CPS kept him in their chosen foster home. Giving him back to his family would have cut off the federal money.

The *Free Press* article about the Ratte case ended:

> Ratte and his wife have filed a formal complaint with the CPS ombudsman's office. "I have apologized to Leo from the bottom of my heart for the silly mistake that got him into this mess," Ratte wrote in the complaint. "But I have also told him that what happened afterward was an even bigger error, and I would like to be able to say to him that institutions, like people, can learn from their mistakes."

Bureaucrats don't learn from mistakes because nobody gets fired. Bureaucrats welcome mistakes – they blame lack of funds for anything that goes wrong and ask for more money to fund bigger and better mistakes next year. The worse job they do, the more children they abuse, the more money they get.

---

[22] "Land of the Free?" *Economist*, May 8, 2008
http://www.economist.com/world/unitedstates/displaystory.cfm?story_id=1
1332246

What will happen if the Rattes sue and win some money? CPS will gladly pay the money and ask for more from the taxpayers to cover the expense. They'll never reform their broken system to give back children who should never have been snatched because the feds cover their expenses and, according to "Child Welfare Financing: An Issue Overview,"[23] pay the agency an average of $750 per month extra as long as they are able to hang on to the child.

Any state agency will do almost anything to get federal funds because state politicians don't want to make their voters mad by raising taxes. The feds won't deny the agency money because of procedural errors; the more money the federal bureaucrats shovel out, the more money the agency can request from Congress next year.

Even if the courts rule that CPS violated the law in snatching and abusing Leo, they'll say that the error was due to overwork caused by lack of funds and ask for a bigger budget. The worse job they do, the more children they abuse, the more money they get.

Where Are the Protests?

When Tim Hortons corporate bureaucracy treated an employee unfairly by following the rules as written, media attention forced the bureaucracy to relent. When a government agency followed rules and removed a healthy child from a good family, it was child abuse. This is far worse than a questionable firing, yet where are the protests? Why hasn't protest forced the bureaucracy to reform – not just to give the child back, but to change the agency so that it doesn't trash families and abuse children?

On April 28, 2008, the *Detroit Free Press* quoted Don Duquette, a U-M law professor who directs the university's Child Advocacy Law Clinic. He said that the emergency removal powers of CPS, though

---

[23] *Child Welfare Financing: An Issue Overview.* Congressional Research Service, Library of Congress, April 6, 2005
http://digital.library.unt.edu/govdocs/crs//data/2005/upl-meta-crs-7687/meta-crs-7687.ocr

"well-intentioned", are "out of control and partly responsible for the large numbers of kids in the foster care system, which is almost universally acknowledged to be badly overburdened."[24]

We have a bureaucracy which experts say is "out of control" and is "universally acknowledged to be badly overburdened." Everyone familiar with the system knows it's out of control and that it damages children and families, yet there are no protests.

Each child is worth $750 per month more than he costs the agency, so why is anyone surprised? Bureaucrats respond to the market they see no matter how strange their actions seem to people who don't understand their market. The more children they grab, the more money they get.[25]

Unjustified child removal traumatizes children and fills their parents with a burning sense of having been abused. Is it sound public policy to turn good parents into enemies of government? In Chinese history, people rebelled when the government took too much of their money away or the court system became too corrupt. Will Americans rebel if the government takes too many of their children away? Or will they respond by having fewer children?

As far back as 1989, the page-one article "Child-Abuse Charges Ensnare Some Parents In Baseless Proceedings" in the *Wall Street Journal* reported that two-thirds of children who were removed from their homes as a result of child abuse interventions turned out not to be abused at all. Abrupt removal is always traumatic for a child and constitutes abuse 2/3 of the time. This means,

---

[24] "Hard lemonade, hard price" *Detroit Free Press* April 28, 2008, online at http://www.freep.com/apps/pbcs.dll/article?AID=/20080428/COL04/80428 0375/1081

[25] "Florida Shifts Child-Welfare System's Focus to Saving Families," *New York Times*, July 25, 2009, reports a welcome change in approach. "Ordinarily, federal aid is determined by how many children are in custody. Florida asked to receive a flat fee that it could spend on counseling and other aid instead of foster care when it wished. The shift was seen as fiscally risky — an increase in foster children would not bring more money — but it has paid off." The *Times* doesn't seem to think it odd that state agencies are paid according to the number of children whom they remove from their homes.

mathematically, that our government abuses twice as many children as parents do.

Where are the protests? If people would protest an unjust firing from a coffee shop, you'd think they'd protest the unjust kidnapping and abuse of a child, but you'd be wrong. Why?

There are no protests because people believe that protesting government abuse is futile. If you "can't fight city hall," what chance have you against a state bureaucracy? Vaclev Havel, who led the Czechoslovakian people in their rebellion against Soviet-imposed tyranny, found it hard to persuade people to oppose government-imposed abuse.

When Havel started protesting against his government in 1978, he wrote "The Power of the Powerless," which warned against "the attractions of mass indifference" and the "general unwillingness of consumption-oriented people to sacrifice some material certainties for the sake of their own spiritual and moral integrity."[26]

Havel believed that abuses of tyrants such as Stalin, Saddam Hussein, the Iranian mullahs, or Osama bin Laden couldn't continue unless free people went along with them in the name of "peace," "accommodation," or "diplomatic engagement." He said, "We can talk to every ruler, but first of all it is necessary to tell the truth."

Americans have constitutional rights to freedom of speech and to "petition our elected representatives for redress of grievances." Federal law criminalizes saying anything about a child abuse action, even if you're innocent. CPS workers threaten their victims with jail for telling anyone how they've been abused by the government.

Mr. Havel spent years in prison for criticizing the regime, but his efforts led to mass protests that eventually brought down the government in 1989. Why do journalists and citizens in countries that supposedly protect freedom of the speech and of the press go along with such blatant abuse of families by government agencies?

---

[26] Havel, Vaclav, "The Power of the Powerless," (Routledge, 1985) p 38, quoted in "Tyranny and Indifference," *Wall Street Journal*, Dec 20, 2111, p A17

People protested because they knew that Tim Hortons would respond to protest. Tim Hortons cares more about selling coffee than about following rules. People realized that upper management knew that they'd go out of business if the company lost its customers' confidence. That meant that protests would lead to action.

Being "helped" by our government is like being run over by a bus. Even if you're rightfully in the crosswalk, you'll get squashed like a bug and there's nothing you can do about it. CPS agencies are funded by tax money whether they please "customers" or not. A government bureaucracy doesn't care about anything other than following rules and getting a bigger budget next year. Whether they do evil or help people is irrelevant to the agency as a whole.

Maybe enough voters will become disgusted with the child abuse that our government commits in our name and instruct their legislatures to cut CPS back, but don't count on it. In the meantime, if you're the parent of young children, you'd better pray that CPS doesn't notice you. Get on their radar, and you're toast.

Bureaucracies Blunder Now and Then

We've seen how two bureaucracies achieved unacceptable results by following standard procedures. As the Chinese discovered soon after they invented bureaucracy thousands of years ago, standardization is the best, most economical way to organize large numbers of people so that what they do is predictable and uniform.

Standardization is essential because it's too expensive to make up brand-new solutions for each problem. This is particularly true in government because governments are the largest organizations we have. Unfortunately, standardization can't cover every situation that arises in the real world. Every bureaucracy needs a way to tell the leadership when procedures fail.

Negative publicity told Hortons management that their procedures had failed and they re-hired their employee. They had to undo their mistake because the money that supports the bureaucracy comes directly and voluntarily from the public. The government forcibly takes the tax money that supports the CPS bureaucracy so they don't have to respond constructively to mistakes.

As the rest of this book demonstrates, all large organizations require bureaucracies. The sort of bureaucratic evil exemplified by Child Protective Services is all too common; our government bureaucracy is out of control for reasons that will be explored later.

Adam Smith wrote[27] that there's a limit to how incompetent or evil a business can get. When management and labor become too inner-directed, they lose sales and the business goes bankrupt unless the government gives them public money.

Unfortunately, no one has found a way to ensure that government agencies fulfill their missions. They needn't make anyone happy because people are forced to deal with them. When CPS took Ratte's son, he had to play by their rules to get his child back. Their immunity from constraints of efficiency or even effectiveness leads to unbounded government growth.

Confucius Explained Why

The mechanisms by which bureaucrats expand their empires, increase budgets, and get more power differ from case to case, but there are many common elements. Confucius noted the forces behind bureaucratic growth in his rules for ordering society:

- Children have a duty to serve and obey their parents
- Wives have a duty to serve and obey their husbands
- Citizens have a duty to serve and obey the government

---

[27] Smith, Adam, *The Wealth of Nations*, 1776

- Government has a duty to serve the welfare of the people.

If any of these rules broke down – that is, children stopped obeying parents, families split apart, people defied government, or government officials sought power or wealth instead of taking care of the people – civilization lost the "Mandate of Heaven" and collapsed.

Confucius was a serious student of history, a respected scholar, thinker, and government advisor. The historian Will Durant dates Confucius' life as 551-478 BC.[28] In 500 B.C., China was by far the most civilized nation on earth and had already been civilized for thousands of years. His insights came halfway through China's 5,000 years of history.[29]

The Chinese bureaucracy was essential to society because bureaucracy was the only way to maintain roads, collect taxes, keep the Grand Canal   from silting up, and fund the army. It has survived in pretty much the same form from day one until today.

Over the millennia, Chinese society collapsed many times as the government violated the rules, lost the "Mandate of Heaven," and fell apart. Each new ruler quickly learned the value of the bureaucracy and restarted the bureaucracy in more or less the traditional form.

A number of legendary rulers governed China from 2,800-2,200 BC, when the Hsia Dynasty took power. Two more dynasties came and went by the time Confucius was born.[30] He had records of preceding dynasties that had fallen apart and knew how his own government operated. He understood the effect of government on the lives of the people and derived his simple, pragmatic rules from his studies of history.

---

[28] Durant, William. *Our Oriental Heritage*, (New York, Simon and Schuster, 1954) p 636
[29] Ibid., p 636. The figure of 5,000 years is more or less traditional.
[30] Ibid., p 636

Confucius didn't invent the rules; he called himself "a transmitter, not a maker."[31] He merely observed and described self-evident rules that were already in place, much as Isaac Newton documented laws of gravity that had always existed.

Other wise men have recognized the importance of one or another of Confucius' rules. For example, Jewish law said that when a son persistently disobeyed his parents, "all the men of his city shall stone him with stones, that he die."[32] There was no rule for stoning disobedient daughters. Nobody wanted to waste a uterus because children were everyone's old-age pension.

Becoming a Religion

It's easy to see why emperors would elevate Confucianism into a state religion – Confucius taught that God Himself wanted citizens to obey government. What better endorsement could a ruler want?

Emperors preferred to forget that Confucius taught that the rule most likely to fail was the rule about government looking out for the people. They also forgot his observation that the Emperor was personally responsible for all government officials' behavior.[33]

Confucius taught that the ruler's main job was to set a good example and that his second-most important task was appointing honest officials. Having authority over every government employee, the ruler had to find government officials who defrauded the people

---

[31] Confucius, *Analects*, VII, i
[32] Deuteronomy 21:18-20
[33] The idea of personal responsibility is strong in some Asian cultures. When the Watergate scandal broke, my Japanese friends were shocked that Mr. Nixon hadn't made it clear that he expected his subordinates to follow the law. Mr. Nixon should resign, I was told, because he didn't teach his followers virtue.

and literally cut their heads off to encourage others to be more virtuous.[34]

History since Confucius' writings supports his arguments as thoroughly as the years that preceded him. Chinese history shows many collapses when government failed to keep order and the country broke apart in civil war, but whenever the Chinese followed Confucius' rules, Chinese society remained stable and relatively safe.

Competing Ideas

As Confucius' ideas spread, skeptics such as the legalists pointed out that relying on the ruler to appoint virtuous officials was too risky. An incompetent or non-virtuous ruler could destroy society. They argued that historical records proved that virtue always ran out, greed took over, and society fell.

Legalists argued that perfect laws would make up for the inadequacies of less virtuous leaders. Americans who talk about "original intent" revere the "perfect law" ideal.

The legalists were correct in saying that virtue always ran out, but were wrong in asserting that perfect laws would preserve society against non-virtuous leaders. Even if someone could write perfect laws, imperfect judges would interpret and twist the laws. Society either prospers on human virtue or falls apart without it, just as Confucius said.

The legalists correctly observed that virtue isn't natural to people. It must be taught through constant teaching, pleading, and example. Instilling virtue is so much work that virtue runs out when teachers and parents get lazy. The legalists' observation was correct but their solution was wrong-headed.

---

[34] Niccolo Machiavelli gave another reason for rulers to try to be virtuous. "... it is still to be feared lest they [the people] may conspire in secret, from which the prince may guard himself well by avoiding hatred and contempt, and keeping the people well satisfied with him..." *The Prince*, That We Must Avoid Being Despised and Hated

Legalists argued that laws should rule instead of men. They believed that common citizens were not intelligent enough to rule themselves. Citizens had to be guided by an aristocracy whose actions were based on well-understood laws.

Most legalists had little faith in commerce. They saw that businessmen could harm society by pursuing their own selfish interests, and anticipated Adam Smith by millennia. This faction argued that the government ought to nationalize all businesses, monopolize trade, and prevent unjust concentration of wealth.

They didn't understand that competitors keep businesses from being too exploitative if government keeps businesses from colluding. They also overlooked the fact that only virtue enforced from the very top could keep bureaucrats backed by government power from exploiting the people. They didn't see that large businesses could help protect people from government via "checks and balances."

The legalists disagreed with Confucius so vehemently that when Shih Huang-ti unified China around 220 BC, his legalist prime minister persuaded him to order Confucius' books to be burned. Having the books banned by the Emperor made them more precious, of course; scholars died as martyrs to preserve them.[35]

The next Emperor realized the value of Confucius' teaching about the necessity of citizens serving rulers. He rescinded the ban and turned Confucianism into a state religion.

From time to time, the Chinese try new ideas for a century or two only to return to Confucian ideas about how governments maintain the "Mandate of Heaven." Confucius' emphasis on virtue has proven correct every time. The legalists, the Taoists, the Fascists, the Buddhists, the Communists, and many other reformers forgot that even if they could write perfect laws and set up perfect systems, those laws would be administered by imperfect men.

History has shown repeatedly that the ruler's character and the government officials' honesty and industry are of extreme

---

[35] Durant, William. *Our Oriental Heritage*, (New York, Simon and Schuster, 1954) p 675

importance. Confucius' emphasis on personal virtue turns out to be the most important factor in whether society survives or not regardless of the political system in which rulers operate.

Confucius defined "virtue" broadly. He taught, for example, that the government should not only concern itself with honesty, public morality and setting the best possible example; it should also emphasize politeness because we become what we do. He taught that government should pay close attention to the kinds of music people hear because music affects morality as well as behavior.[36]

> "Benevolence is akin to music and righteousness to good manners."[37]

Pete Seeger, whose songs stirred up opposition to government policies during the Vietnam War, often echoed Plato, "Rulers should be careful about what songs are allowed to be sung."[38]

The Confucian Cycle

Chinese history demonstrated that governments run in cycles. Some powerful warlord unified the country, acquired the "Mandate of Heaven," and established a dynasty.[39] As generations went by, government became more and more corrupt to the point that the infrastructure started to collapse because someone stole the road maintenance money and the army was weakened by dishonest

---

[36] "Let me write the songs of a nation, and I care not who writes its laws." - attributed to many, including both Plato and Napoleon Bonaparte.

[37] Durant, William. *Our Oriental Heritage*, (New York, Simon and Schuster, 1954) p 673

[38] "Bolshie with a banjo," *Economist*, Feb. 1, 2014, p 24

[39] My friends who travel in China tell me that many Chinese citizens think of Mao Tse Tung as the equivalent of George Washington – he fought many wars for the sake of unifying his country. Any collateral damage along the way was an unfortunate manifestation of the longstanding rules of omelet-making – ya gotta break eggs.

contractors and suppliers. As transportation became less efficient, the economy shrank which led to less government revenue.

No government employee wants to give up perks,[40] of course, so there'd be even less money spent on roads, then they'd steal even more from the army budget. When the army got weak enough, the barbarians would attack or outraged taxpayers would rebel. Having lost the "Mandate of Heaven," civilization fell.

The same pattern holds outside China. The Duke of Olivares, prime minister of Spain AD 1623-43, tried to overcome a decline in Spain's power with massive tax increases and a centralization of power. The result was regional revolts all across the Spanish empire by 1640. Instead of reversing Spain's decline, Olivares plunged the Spanish economy into a three-century abyss.[41]

The Roman Emperor Diocletian, who ruled from AD 284 to 305, stripped power from the elected government. He held off the barbarians, but his tax increases crippled the economy. People complained that there were more tax collectors than taxpayers and that the land tax consumed about one-third of a farmer's output. Such heavy taxation destroyed people's loyalty to Rome.[42]

Diocletian's successor Constantine (AD 306-33) realized that the Roman bureaucracy had become unmanageable, so he moved the capital to Byzantium leaving the bureaucrats behind. The Roman Empire split into Eastern and Western halves for more efficient administration, but the bulk of the bureaucracy remained in the West.

---

[40]   "Unions vs Taxpayers" *Wall Street Journal* May 14, 2009 p A17 explained how unionized government workers use political clout to stop budget cuts and direct funds to their agencies. "The average public sector worker earned 46% more in salary and benefits than comparable private-sector workers."

[41]   "The Pessimist Persuasion," *Wilson Quarterly*, Spring 2009 p 66

[42]   Ibid.

Rome and the Western Roman Empire collapsed in 410 AD,[43] but Byzantium, which was also known as Constantinople, survived another thousand years until it was conquered by the Ottoman Turks in 1453 AD. Moving the capital reset the bureaucracy and put off the final collapse by a thousand years.

The bureaucracy grew back after Constantine moved the capital, of course. It became so lavish that the word "Byzantine" describes a particularly complex and impenetrable bureaucracy. It's hard to be certain of details after a major invasion, but records suggest that for the last hundred years before the fall, bureaucrats diverted money for maintaining the walls around the city to other things.

The Cycle in Detail

Confucius saw that there was a clear pattern of cycles, through which civilizations lost the "Mandate of Heaven" over time:

Anarchy – China fell apart into varying numbers of small states that jockeyed for power much as medieval France and Germany broke into many competing statelets until one ruler conquered the others. Periods of chaos lasted between 75 and 500 years.

Unity – The toughest, smartest, luckiest warlord took over. People were tired of anarchy and were willing to pay taxes to a central ruler whose victory proved he had the "Mandate of Heaven."[44] The more vigorously the new Emperor and his successors enforced virtue by controlling the bureaucracy, the longer the dynasty lasted. This brought a flurry of public works

---

[43] Edward Gibbon reports that the army budget was spent on "essential services" as Rome fell: "A large portion of public and private wealth was consecrated to the specious demands of charity and devotion; and the soldiers pay was lavished on the useless multitudes of both sexes, who could only plead the merits of abstinence and chastity."

[44] For all the veneration he receives as the founder of modern China, Mao Tse Tung failed to found a hereditary dynasty. Lack of a clear line of succession forces the Communist Party to go through the perilous process of choosing a new top dog every ten to fifteen years rather than having the government remain stable for an entire lifetime.

such as roads and canals that lowered transportation costs. This improved economic efficiency, helped the economy grow, and increased tax revenue. It was easy to spend all the extra money, of course, but cutting spending when tax revenue fell was much more difficult.

Greed – Prosperity made everyone think that the nation had become invincible. Bureaucrats, judges, and other government employees are as human as anyone else – they're always trying to get more perks. When the emperor took his eye off the ball, corrupt officials multiplied so that too much money was wasted on administrative costs and roads, canals, and the army went downhill. This shrank the economy, reduced government revenue,[45] and set a bad example for citizens. Society eventually lost the "Mandate of Heaven" and collapsed into anarchy, either due to conquest from outside or from internal rebellion.

China had gone through this cycle two or three times before Confucius so he believed that society can recover from a collapse.

Recovery may be peculiar to China, however. Neither the Eastern Roman Empire nor the Western half recovered. Spain is recovering from the weaknesses imposed by the Duke of Olivares but isn't nearly as powerful as it was when he raised taxes to arrest its decline. The Soviet Union has not recovered from its collapse although it might. The East German government disappeared into a reunited Germany. Recovery may be unique to Chinese geography. That is even more reason for Americans to try to avoid collapse.

---

[45] "Man is not free unless government is limited. There's a clear cause and effect here that is as neat and predictable as a law of physics: As government expands, liberty contracts" – Ronald Reagan's farewell address. In a speech of Sept. 7, 1973, he said, "History makes it plain that unless restrained, government proliferates to a point where its cost bankrupts the people at the same time it robs them of their freedom."

The End of the Cycle

History and Confucius agree that the only cure for bureaucratic excess is collapse. The cancer overwhelms the patient and both die.

Confucius observed that there's no natural limit to the human greed, whether of government employees, businessmen, or you and me. No bureaucrat sees how mismanaging his own personal rice bowl can make a difference, but all the little thefts, mismanagement, waste, earmarks, bribes, regulations, restrictions, campaign contributions, and other costs add up.

Society can't function when government overhead gets too great. The size of the Chinese economy in Confucius' day was fixed because the Chinese deliberately decided not to allow technical progress.   This limited government revenue.   If government spending grew beyond that, society fell apart.

The virtuous cycle started over when the bureaucracy reset to zero after a period of anarchy. Just as a ruined farm must lie fallow a while before it can be productive, Confucius observed that several generations of chaos taught people not to expect government to take care of them and taught them to look out for themselves again.

China has been called a "historian's paradise"[46] because Chinese court officials wrote down everything that happened. Confucius lived halfway through a 500-year period of disorder which followed the collapse of the Chou Dynasty and had access to the records of three earlier dynasties.

Will Durant lists fourteen dynasties which unified various portions of modern-day China.[47] Combining these with the three dynasties before Confucius gives a total of 17 major ruling families, and many other kingdoms controlled parts of China during periods of collapse. These kingdoms and nations all fell apart when virtue ran out and they lost the "Mandate of Heaven."

---

[46] Thorndike, Lynn, *A short history of civilization*, (Appleton-Century-Crofts, 1948) p 240
[47] Durant, William. *Our Oriental Heritage*, (New York, Simon and Schuster, 1954) pp 636-637

Confucius' laws hold true across cultures, peoples, and businesses. King Solomon's kingdom split when his son ignored Confucius' rule that government should serve the people and expected the people to serve him instead.[48] This indecent also illustrates Confucius' concern for strong families and for a ruler setting an example of virtue across generations. As succeeding Israelite kings became less and less virtuous, the nation of Israel declined and the people were carried off to captivity.

China, Rome, Byzantium, ancient Israel, Persia, Athens, General Motors, RCA – great civil and business empires follow the cycle described by Confucius and fall. While modern technology may make us think that it can't happen here, human nature hasn't changed. A bureaucrat with a writ is just as dangerous whether arriving by horse, sedan chair, limousine, or e-mail. You're just as dead whether a spear or a nuclear bomb kills you.

The next chapter explains how our leaders are losing the virtue needed to keep government employees in check. Without vigorous imposition of virtue from the top, the American bureaucracy is imposing greater and greater costs on society. Our economy can't grow fast enough to keep up with government spending, taxes, and the cost of meeting government regulations. When we can no longer afford to pay the cost of our government, our society will collapse.

---

[48]   II Chronicles 10:1-19 ~ 975 BC

3 – The Confucian Cycle in America

During the 2,500 years from Confucius' day until the 1950's, the amount of farmland limited the size of the Chinese economy. The economy and tax revenue both peaked once an energetic Emperor fixed the roads and restored the Grand Canal. There was no way to make the economy bigger thereafter, so the government couldn't get more money through economic growth.

When government lost virtue, government employees started wasting or stealing money so there were fewer resources available to repair the Great Wall, feed soldiers, or maintain roads and canals.

The only cure for greed was to force the bureaucrats to be virtuous, which virtuous Emperors did. When they let dishonest or incompetent government employees multiply, however, they had to raise taxes. This hurt the economy, which reduced revenue. Government raised taxes even more, which hurt the economy more. A virtuous emperor could cut spending and keep costs in line with the economy, but bureaucracy always "won" in the end by becoming so expensive that society collapsed.

The Problem of Controlling Government

America's Founders knew that it's impossible to build a perfect government with imperfect government employees. George Washington is claimed to have said, "Government is not reason; it is not eloquent; it is force. Like fire, it is a dangerous servant and a fearful master."[49] James Madison wrote:

> But what is government itself, but the greatest of all reflections on human nature. If men were angels, no government would be necessary. If angels were to govern, neither external nor internal controls on government would be necessary. In forming a government which is to be administered by men over men, the great difficulty lies in this: you must first enable government to control the governed; and in the next place oblige it to control itself.[50] [emphasis added]

Government can control people; the difficulty lies in "oblig[ing] it [government] to control itself." Our Founders hoped that citizens would control government by electing virtuous leaders, as the legalists had hoped that perfect laws could stabilize society. Similarly, Confucius wrote that government would remain stable until virtue ran out, at which point a crash became inevitable as people rebelled or the barbarians invaded.

Greek, Roman, and American history show that non-virtuous leaders cheat on elections by padding voting rolls or by miscounting ballots. Once in power, crooked rulers use the force of the state to neutralize citizens who give them trouble.

Our Founders, remembering that armed colonists were essential to defeat the British, required an armed citizenry to make it easier for citizens to enforce virtue from the bottom up. The American Constitution gives citizens the right and the obligation to arm themselves against government oppression as the American revolutionaries had armed themselves to resist the British:

---

[49] Mary Baker Eddy attributed this statement to Washington in 1902, but there is no proof of its origin. The statement is true no matter who said it, of course.

[50] Madison, James, *Federalist 51*

A well-regulated Militia, being necessary to the security of a free State, the right of the people to keep and bear Arms, shall not be infringed.[51]

The purpose of the 2nd Amendment was explained best in 1914:

"Where the people fear the government you have tyranny. Where the government fears the people you have liberty."[52]

England had centuries of experience with armed citizens. In 1252, Englishmen were required to own a bow and arrows. The Archery Law of 1363 required archery practice on Sundays and forbade all sport that took up time better spent on war training.[53]

Today, Swiss and Israeli army veterans keep automatic weapons and ammunition in their homes. Early Americans were also expected to arm themselves and were supposed to organize local militia so that they could mobilize to protect themselves from oppression or invasion. The Militia Act of 1792 required Americans to organize into armed companies and to buy their own weapons.

Virtuous governments need not fear armed citizens, but non-virtuous governments generally try to disarm their people. Vigilant, virtuous citizens can keep elections honest and control government, but it's not clear whether American voters have enough virtue to enforce virtue on their leaders.

The men who wrote the Constitution knew that successful societies operate on virtue and had no confidence that kings would stay virtuous over time. The Constitution gives the federal government relatively few powers. It reserves most power to the

[51] United States Constitution, 2nd Amendment. The Right to Keep and Bear Arms is often abbreviated "RKBA."

[52] John Basil Barnhill, *Barnhill-Tichenor Debate on Socialism*, As It Appeared in the National Rip-Saw. Saint Louis, Mo.: The National Rip-Saw Pub. Co., 1914, p 34

[53] Alley, Steve, et al., *The Traditional Bowyer's Bible*, Lyons Press, (Guilford, Ct, 2008) p255

state governments and to the people in the hope that the people would force government to be virtuous.

The Constitution won't work without virtuous citizens:

"Our Constitution was made only for a moral and religious people. It is wholly inadequate to the government of any other."[54]

The major issue in any democracy is whether voters will take responsibility for themselves and force government to leave them alone or whether they want government to provide for them by taxing "someone else." Athenian democracy collapsed when voters gave themselves too many benefits and weakened their society.[55]

The American Founders knew about these long-term problems with democracy. Their Constitution tried to protect minorities such as property owners from majorities such as tenants. They hoped that well-armed, virtuous citizens would resist when government became oppressive or raised taxes too high.

While they agreed with Confucius in saying that society can't operate without virtue, they disagreed with him about the source of virtue. Confucius thought virtue had to flow from the top down because common people could never be virtuous.

The American Founders knew that kings and emperors always lost virtue and hoped that virtue would flow from citizens up to government. They enshrined the Right to Keep and Bear Arms (RKBA) so that citizens could enforce their right to rebel against tyranny.

As noted in Chapter 2, Confucius also recognized the right of rebellion, but since the idea of armed citizens was unthinkable, total rebellion and foreign invasion were the only limits on government power. The Founders, in contrast, hoped that elections and armed

[54] John Adams in a letter to officers in the Militia of Massachusetts, 11 October, 1798
[55] Robinson, Charles Alexander, *Athens in the Age of Pericles*, (University of Oklahoma Press, 1959) pp 19-20

citizens would force government back to virtue before full-scale rebellion became necessary.

Government and Economic Growth

If the Chinese had permitted innovation by new businesses, the economy could have grown beyond the limits set by agriculture. Gunpowder and large ocean-going ships are two of many technologies they could have pursued to increase economic activity. Expanding the economy would have increased government revenue and lessened the damage done by bureaucratic theft and waste, at least until theft and waste outran economic growth.

Chinese philosophers had less faith in business virtue than in government virtue. In arguing that businessmen abandoned virtue and pursued their own interests to the harm of society, they anticipated Adam Smith[56] by millennia. Unfortunately, they missed Mr. Smith's insight that business greed could bring huge benefits to society if the rulers channeled greed properly.

Some anticipated Karl Marx and argued that government ought to nationalize all businesses, monopolize trade, and prevent unjust concentration of wealth.[57] Scholars were suspicious of businessmen who dealt with tangible products, and their horror at bankers who profited by shuttling numbers on an abacus knew no bounds.

Confucius had little use for merchants or bankers who were concerned with filthy money;[58] he suspected that speaking of merchants' "virtue" was a contradiction in terms. This attitude is echoed in many modern Western scholars and politicians' suspicion of "Big Business." Enough of his anti-business attitude permeated Chinese thinking that China effectively refused to allow technical innovations to change their society.

---

[56] Smith, Adam, *The Wealth of Nations*, 1776
[57] Durant, William. *Our Oriental Heritage*, (New York, Simon and Schuster, 1954) p 675-676
[58] "For the love of money is the root of all evil" – I Timothy 6:10 ~ 50 AD

Over the years, the Chinese invented movable type, paper money, the magnetic compass, and many other cutting-edge discoveries, but refused to develop these inventions further. Since the Chinese wouldn't allow new technology to expand their economy, Chinese society was more susceptible to "death by bureaucracy" than an economy that grows as businessmen are able to innovate.

Nobody really understood the business cycle until Adam Smith published *The Wealth of Nations* in 1776. He explained how businessmen benefit everyone as a side effect of benefiting themselves.[59]

Smith's book has been so influential that he's regarded as the founder of economics. Although he's the patron saint of free-market capitalism, he didn't believe that businesses should be allowed to operate without rules. He agreed with the Chinese legalists that businessmen usually lacked virtue:

> "People of the same trade seldom meet together, even for merriment and diversion, but the conversation ends in a conspiracy against the public, or in some contrivance to raise prices."[60]

Smith pointed out that government's job is to write and enforce rules so that it's hard to become rich without adding value to society. In saying that government should oppose businesses that gouge the public, Smith echoed Confucius' view that the Emperor had to strike down government employees and businesses that gouge the public.

---

[59] It's been said that capitalism harnesses human greed to benefit society whereas communism harnesses human altruism. The fact that capitalist economies grow faster than communist economies suggests that there's more greed available for harnessing than altruism. Government must write rules to make it impossible to get rich without benefitting society. This requires vigilance and virtue – the greedy keep thinking of ways to get rich without adding value.

[60] Smith, Adam, *An Inquiry into the Nature and Causes of the Wealth of Nations*, (London, 1776)

Smith saw that government and business balance each other. If government made it hard to become rich without adding value, greedy businesses benefit society, like it or not. Greed was made virtuous through the magic of appropriate government regulation.

Bill Gates is wealthy because people choose to buy his products. Adam Smith would approve of his immense wealth because society benefitted from his innovations. American sugar farmers, in contrast, became wealthy by persuading government to keep out cheaper sugar from overseas;[61] Smith disapproved of this sort of theft:

> "But though the law cannot hinder people of the same trade from sometimes assembling together, it ought to do nothing to facilitate such assemblies; much less to render them necessary."[62]

Adam Smith would see high import taxes on sugar as government having "facilitated assemblies" of sugar growers to help them raise prices to gouge the public. Market forces should drive prices down, benefit consumers, and punish inefficient producers that don't pay enough attention to customers. Inefficient sugar producers can't go bankrupt because the government keeps efficient sugar producers out of the market.

Adam Smith warned of unions, management, or any other group that had enough political power to persuade government to pass laws that let businesses charge excess prices for their goods or bail out a company that should die. Society suffers from crony capitalism when non-virtuous businesses conspire with government officials to make greed profitable without benefiting society. Being ripped off by crooked businessmen or bureaucrats is bad enough. It's worse when the crooks work together.

---

[61] Clawson, Marion, *Policy directions for U.S. agriculture: long-range choices in farming and rural living* (Johns Hopkins Press, 1968) p 182

[62] Ibid.

Unfortunately, bailing out losing businesses has become common in the US, from Chrysler in the 1980s to Amtrak, the airlines, big banks, and struggling automobile corporations of today.

Smith also said that government shouldn't "render them [business combines] necessary." He believed businessmen generally get together to conspire to raise prices. When laws make it hard to make a profit, however, businessmen band together in organizations like the US Chamber of Commerce to lobby against the laws.

When businessmen join together to change burdensome laws, it's easy for them to also pursue less virtuous changes. It would be better for government not to threaten businesses or citizens to the point that they join together to defend themselves from government.

Government Growth and Societal Collapse

The American economy grows if government permits technical innovation, the tax code lets investors make money starting new businesses, banks can lend to risky ventures, and startups can raise growth capital in the stock market. Unfortunately, the governmental drain on the American economy grows faster than the economy can grow. In 1849, the cost of the Federal government was about 2 percent of the American economy. The government had about 25,000 employees, 80% of whom worked for the post office.[63]

This chart shows the fraction of the economy consumed by government expenditures from 1979-2007.[64] The government's piece of the pie grows steadily. The economy grew enough to cover spending growth during the boom years of the early 1990's, but government grows faster most of the time.

---

[63] *Historical Statistics of the United States, Colonial Times to 1970* (Washington DC, US Census Bureau, 1975) series Y308, Y314

[64] U.S. Department of Commerce, Bureau of Economic Analysis, National Income and Product Accounts Tables 1.1 and 3.1

The Interstate Highway System was a good investment; improved transportation efficiency led to economic growth that increased government revenue. As construction projects multiply, however, government spending drains resources and provides no benefit. People who profit from government spending fight so hard to keep their favorite programs going that it's hard to cut back.

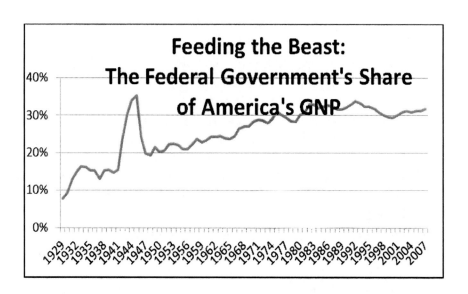

Chinese Infrastructure

After Emperor Shih united China, he initiated a flurry of highway and canal building.[65] His investment in transportation led to economic growth in China as the highway system did here. The Emperor also connected the many walls along the northern frontier into what became known as the "Great Wall of China," one of the few man-made artifacts that's visible from outer space.

---

[65]   Durant, William. *Our Oriental Heritage*, (New York, Simon and Schuster, 1954)

Building the wall took ten years and cost countless lives. Anticipating Mao Tse-Tung's reeducation camps by millennia, Shih exiled his political opponents to the wall and worked them to death.

The Chinese have always been players on the international stage whether their presence was recognized or not. As Will Durant put it:

> "...it [the wall] was the ruin of one generation," say the Chinese, "and the salvation of many." It did not quite keep out the barbarians, as we shall see, but it delayed and reduced their attacks. The Huns, barred for a time from Chinese soil, moved west into Europe and south into Italy. <u>Rome fell because China built a wall</u>.[66] [emphasis added]

The Great Wall reduced the manpower needed to keep the barbarians out, freeing soldiers and money for other uses. It diverted at least one horde, the Huns, who attacked Rome instead. Like most military projects, "cost was no object" because the Emperor didn't care how many of his enemies were worked to death.

The Great Wall couldn't do the job alone, of course, it had to be backed up by the Chinese army. The Tartars came through in 1550 and the Manchus crossed it unopposed in 1644.

> As a defense system, the wall ultimately failed, not because of intrinsic design flaws but because of the internal weaknesses – corruption, cowardice, infighting – of various imperial regimes.[67]

The Great Wall of China saved a lot of tax money that would have to have been spent on the army. Government investments should generate a measurable payback of some kind. This requires

---

[66] Durant, William. *Our Oriental Heritage*, (New York, Simon and Schuster, 1954) p. 695
[67] "Up Against the Wall," *Smithsonian Magazine*, August 2008, p 35

virtuous decision-making. As virtue runs out, government spending benefits society less and less.

As we'll see later, most worthwhile infrastructure investments in the US have already been made. Environmental impact statements, lawsuits, and other activities that increase cost and reduce payback hold up what's left. Government investments in American infrastructure don't pay off as well as in the past, and many lead to a net loss.

Regulating the Economy Drains Resources

Taxation is one cost of government. What corporations and individuals pay to follow regulations is another.

The US Congress writes vague laws that allow bureaucrats to write rules which have the force of law and then rely on the courts to supply interpretations. Legislators claim credit if something good happens. When anything goes wrong, they blame faceless bureaucrats. In turn, the bureaucrats blame lawmakers for not giving them enough money to get the job done.

In the early days of the American republic, courts ruled that Congress could not delegate rule-making authority to the executive branch of government. As late as 1892, our Supreme Court ruled

> That Congress cannot delegate legislative power to the President is a principle universally recognized as vital to the integrity and maintenance of the system of government ordained by the Constitution.[68]

Despite such rulings, Congress has been delegating legislative power to federal agencies since 1887, starting with the now-defunct

---

[68] *Field v. Clark*, 143 U.S. 649

Interstate Commerce Commission.[69] Congress gave the ICC power to specify shipping charges for various types of freight. The Federal Trade Commission in 1914 extended the idea of having the executive branch of government write, interpret, and enforce rules.

Nobody kept track of federal rules in the early years. In July 1933, President Roosevelt issued regulations concerning petroleum usage. The Panama Refining Company sued on the grounds that government inspectors had exceeded the scope of his first order which had been changed by a subsequent order. By not challenging the President's power to regulate but merely questioning the manner in which he did it, the Panama Refining Company admitted that the 1892 Supreme Court ruling was a dead letter and that the President had the power to regulate the economy.

In 1934, the Supreme Court chastised the President for giving inadequate notice of federal orders – the government couldn't find the original order despite an all-out search. Formal documentation of federal regulations began on March 14, 1936. The well-organized Chinese bureaucrats would have sniffed in contempt.

The Federal Register Act passed in 1935. Since then, the *Federal Register*, which records all the rules, has grown obese. In 1976 alone, various federal agencies issued 12,578 pages of rules; in 2001, the number of new pages nearly doubled.[70]

There are more than one hundred federal agencies with subagencies and departments under them, and they complete about four thousand five hundred new rules annually according to the Office of Management and Budget.[71]

Writing rules benefits government agencies – they hire more people to write, track, and enforce rules. This pushes up the cost of doing business, shrinks the economy, and reduces tax revenue.

This chart shows how government payrolls have grown over time compared with manufacturing. Manufacturing jobs pay much

---

[69]   Skrzycki , Cindy, *The regulators: anonymous power brokers in American politics* (Rowman & Littlefield, 2003) p 28

[70]   Ibid., pp 27-28, pp 32-33

[71]   Ibid., p 28

better than most other jobs. The loss of jobs that pay so much income tax in favor of government jobs that consume tax revenue is depressing from the standpoint of maximizing government revenue. All these federal employees work together to multiply their pay, privileges, and pensions, of course.

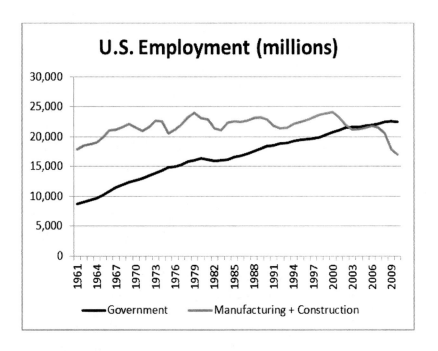

It's nearly impossible to fire a government employee, so they don't have to work very hard. There are hard-working bureaucrats, but it appears that what most of them work on is ways to increase their budget by putting more burdens on citizens.

For example, US citizens spend tens of thousands of man-hours filling out their tax returns every year instead of boosting the economy. *Forbes Magazine* estimated the cost of compliance with IRS regulations at $200 to $300 billion per year.[72]

---

[72] "Taxpayer Heroine," *Forbes Magazine*, March 16, 2009, available online at http://www.forbes.com/forbes/2009/0316/013_taxpayer_heroine.html

The *Wall Street Journal* estimated that the total cost of federal regulation was $1.75 trillion in 2008, about 14% of national income. This is on top of the 21% federal tax burden. Thus, the federal government consumes one out of every three dollars earned in the United States.[73] State and local exactions come on top of that.

The *Economist* estimates that government health care regulations cost the economy $169 billion more each year than they return in benefits.[74] Those dollars are taken out of the economy just as surely as if the government had spent them.

Anyone wanting to put up a building has to spend a great deal of time and money getting permission to build on his own land. All this paper shuffling represents pure cost. The regulatory burden on the American economy is growing, even beyond the growth of formally-recognized government spending.

> Regulations affecting the cost of housing are particularly painful for taxpayers.
>
> Caldwell Baker says that, in 2006, $155,000 would buy a home in Houston suitable for a "corporate middle manager" – a four bedroom, two-and-one-half bath 2,200 square foot home with a large family room and two-car garage in a nice neighborhood. The same house would cost more than twice that much in Portland, close to four times that much in Boulder, and more than eight times as much in San Jose. Such huge variations in the cost of housing from city to city did not exist 50 years ago, and today they are mainly due to artificial housing shortages caused by land-use planning.[75]

Anything that increases costs reduces economic activity and reduces government revenue. Governments hate to cut spending, so politicians usually increase tax rates. Higher taxes reduce the

---

[73] "The Regulation Tax Keeps growing", *Wall Street Journal*, Sept 27, 2010 P A17
[74] "Of horses' teeth and liberty." The *Economist*, Oct 25, 2007
[75] O'Toole, Randall, *The Best-Laid Plans*, (Cato Institute, 2007) p 111

incentive to work and make tax evasion more worthwhile. As in ancient China, revenue goes down when tax rates become too high.[76] Our society will collapse when we can no longer afford our government.

This isn't because bureaucrats, planners, or politicians are evil, it's because they're human beings who respond to incentives just as you and I do. Considering the many pots of money hidden in the billions and billions that our politicians give away, it's surprising that government functions at all.

The Turning Point

Bureaucrats always want more money regardless of the needs of society. This is the heart of the Confucian problem. Our bureaucracies grow in the same ways Chinese agencies grew, but American agencies invented a new twist which helps them grow even faster.

Senator Daniel Patrick Moynihan (D-NY) wrote about a new bureaucratic *modus operandi* which he called the "professionalization of reform." He listed situations where the bureaucracy thought up problems for government to solve rather than responding to problems identified by others. In an article written for the fall 1995 issue of *Public Interest*, Sen. Moynihan explained how he had documented this phenomenon in the first issue of *Public Interest* in 1965.

After serving as Assistant Secretary of Labor for Policy Planning and Research under both Presidents Kennedy and Johnson, he discussed the expansion of social services during his tenure.

> "The most interesting thing about all this sudden
> expansion of social services was that it had behind it,
> nothing like the powerful political pressure and long-

---

[76] Laffer, Arthur B. "The Laffer Curve: Past, Present, and Future." June 1, 2004, see http://www.heritage.org/research/taxes/bg1765.cfm

sustained intellectual support that produced the great welfare measures of the New Deal – Social Security, Unemployment Insurance, Public Welfare, Public Housing. The massive political support and intellectual leadership that produced the reforms of the thirties simply did not exist; yet the reforms were moving forward.

"The Johnson War on Poverty was the most dramatic example of professionalization. It began with various initiatives designed to help the Appalachian region. Again, the Department of Labor was much involved on behalf of workers, but with little involvement from workers themselves.

"War on poverty was not declared at the behest of the poor; just the opposite. The poor were not only invisible ... they were also for the most part silent. John F. Kennedy ventured into Appalachia searching for Protestant votes, not for poverty."[77]

Sen. Moynihan describes an expansion of the Confucian problem. Instead of waiting for demand from citizens and taxpayers as they had during the New Deal, the "professionals" sought bigger budgets and opportunities to solve problems they themselves had identified but for which there was no citizen demand.

What's worse, the professionals set up rule-bound bureaucracies that are involved directly in the lives of individual people. As we'll see, when bureaucrats do "what comes naturally" and apply rigid rules to people's lives, their actions can result in great evil.

The Common Thread

No matter what bureaucrats may want to do, they need money. The natural goal of every agency is the same – maximize budget and

---

[77] Moynihan, Daniel Patrick. "The Professionalization of Reform," *Public Interest*, Fall of 1965

power.[78]   This natural bureaucratic growth causes the Confucian collapse.

We were in decent shape as long as legislators funded projects that voters desired. Once our House and Senate let bureaucrats fill in the details of new programs, bureaucrats wrote the rules to maximize costs so they could keep begging Congress for more money. This short-circuited the "separation of powers", starting our rapid slide into the abyss of the Confucian cycle.

The "Great Society" programs also weakened society by providing an alternative to work. A woman no longer needed to insist that a man get a job to support her before letting him get her pregnant.

Moynihan was vilified for "blaming the victim" when he wrote about increased fatherlessness in the black community. Like Confucius, he recognized that weak families were a danger to society. He also believed that people should work for a living instead of relying on government handouts. When someone asked him, "Why should I work if I am going to just end up emptying slop jars?" he replied,

> "That's a complaint you hear mostly from people who don't empty slop jars. This country has a lot of people who do exactly that for a living. And they do it well. It's not pleasant work, but it's a living. And it has to be done. Somebody has to go around and empty all those bed pans. And it's perfectly honorable work. There's nothing the matter with doing it. Indeed, there is a lot that is right about doing it, as any hospital patient will tell you."[79]

By warning of the risks of weaker families and pointing out the honorable nature of all work, Sen. Moynihan touched on Confucius'

---

[78]   O'Toole, Randall, *The Best-Laid Plans*, (Washington DC, Cato Institute, 2007) p 298

[79]   "In Their Own Words" *US News and World Report* (May 26-June 2, 2008)

rules for ordering society. Moynihan realized that if too many families broke apart or too many people collected government handouts instead of working and paying taxes, society would be at risk.

He favored the War on Poverty because he didn't realize that bureaucratic processes are not suitable for managing people's lives. He didn't see that this new opportunity for increased budgets carried the seeds of the destruction of society. Welfare programs lead to too many citizens becoming dependent on government by letting them add "work" to their lists of forbidden four-letter words.

He missed the danger to society when bureaucrats extend their power by thinking of new tasks to perform.

The Bureaucratic Growth Imperative

Sen. Moynihan realized that bureaucrats get status and power by having more people work for them, just as in business, but he seems not to have recognized the danger of bureaucratic growth. The only way a business can get more people working for it without going broke is to increase sales, but bureaucrats get budget increases through political action. Nobody wants to deal with the DMV or the EPA or the TSA; agencies grow by asking politicians to pass more rules so that people have to deal with them, like it or not.

This is not a new phenomenon. Thomas Jefferson listed a number of governmental abuses:

> He [the British King] has erected a multitude of
> New Offices, and sent hither swarms of Officers to
> harass our people and eat out their substance.

The Federal Government establishes New Offices all the time – EPA, FDA, Homeland Security, Department of Education – whose officers harass us, take power from our local representatives, eat out our substance, and make us pad through airports in our stocking feet.

As Sen. Moynihan pointed out, bureaucrats try to think of new "problems" to solve but not all bureaucrats are creative enough to invent new rules so that more people have to come to them. A lesser bureaucrat's strategy to get more money is by demonstrating that his people are overworked and that he needs more subordinates.

I had a friend who needed a government agency's approval. "It only has to go through four people," he told me. "Each of them can handle my application in about ten minutes. Why has it taken a month to get to the second guy?"

I explained that in order to justify a bigger budget for his boss, each bureaucrat had to act hopelessly overworked. Each one had to keep enough papers on his desk to look busy. Assuming that each paper took an hour and that 50 applications made the desk look "full enough," each bureaucrat had to hold each application for a week and a day. If it took 200 applications to fill a desk enough to look busy, the delay would have to be five weeks per bureaucrat.

My friend didn't believe me, but sure enough, his application took five months to traverse four bureaucrats.

Bureaucrats will do anything they can get away with to get more money and power. This isn't unique to government; don't businesses take extraordinary steps to get more money? With businessmen, we call it "marketing" or "gouging," with bureaucrats, it's "pork," "kickbacks," "earmarks," "campaign contributions," or whatever term we use for political self-dealing.

Sugar growers and ethanol brewers ally with bureaucrats to pass rules that help businessman raise prices and give bureaucrats new rules to enforce. The *Economist* reported:[80]

> But rules relating to health, safety, the environment and national security have multiplied. Some of these are necessary, but many are not. For example, by one estimate, American health-care regulations cost $169 billion a year more than they yield in benefits, and lead to 7m Americans not being

---

[80]   "Of horses' teeth and liberty." The *Economist,* Oct 25, 2007

able to afford health insurance. By another estimate, measures to keep terrorists off airplanes cost lives by prompting people to drive instead of fly, which is nine times more dangerous.

And even the worst regulation usually heaps benefits on a small group, while its costs are widely spread. The beneficiaries thus lobby hard to keep each rule, while its victims do nothing. The late Mancur Olson, an economist, predicted that <u>interest groups will grow in number until they cause their host society to slip into economic decline</u>. [emphasis added]

All rules, no matter how stupid, costly, or ineffective, benefit someone, if only the bureaucrat who got paid to write them.

To sum up: Congress has given agencies rule-making power with the force of criminal law. The agencies can influence their agendas by thinking up new problems to solve. Our regulatory mechanisms benefit the bureaucrats who think up new rules to enforce, not those who live under them.

It's difficult to estimate the total cost of complying with all the government rules and regulations. As of 2002, the Office of Management and Budget estimated the cost as between $520 and $620 billion, while other estimates went as high as $843 billion annually.[81] This is broadly consistent with the *Wall Street Journal* estimate that regulatory costs had grown to $1.75 trillion by 2008.[82] When government takes too much out of the economy, society collapses.

---

[81]   Skrzycki , Cindy, *The regulators: anonymous power brokers in American politics* (Rowman & Littlefield, 2003) p 49

[82]   "The Regulation Tax Keeps growing", *Wall Street Journal*, Sept 27, 2010 P A17

Regulation Drives Corruption

The more complicated and costly regulations get, the more opportunities for regulators or politicians to profit by doing favors. This is especially true of bank regulations that deal directly with money.

Banking and investment are so important to commerce and offer so many opportunities to gain wealth or damage the economy that all governments regulate these industries closely. Financial regulation is supposed to reduce fraud and avoid the "boom and bust" cycles which occur every 20 to 30 years no matter what we do.

The United States suffered a "Savings and Loan" crisis in the late 1980's and early 1990's during which 747 banks failed in spite of the regulations that were in place at the time. Profit seeking bankers made high-risk loans backed by deposits in government-insured savings accounts. When interest rates were higher than banks were allowed to pay, savers took money out of the banks, putting them at risk of failing. Many banks engaged in questionable practices to attract money to support their loan portfolios.

Lincoln Savings and Loan collapsed in 1989. The federal government paid about $3 billion to savers whose accounts had been federally insured. Charles Keating, the president of the bank, was accused of fraud. The investigation found that he had donated $1.3 million to five senators who became known as the "Keating Five."

Lincoln Savings had been under investigation by the Federal Home Bank Loan Board (FHBLB), one of many government agencies who share overlapping responsibility to manage banks. The FHBLB believed that Lincoln Savings had more "high risk" loans than permitted. Examining the books after the collapse proved them right. Unfortunately for taxpayers, the FHBLB ended the investigation without taking action against the bank shortly after Mr. Keating's "donations" to the five senators.

In talking to reporters, Keating said, "One question, among many raised in recent weeks, had to do with whether my financial support in any way influenced several political figures to take up my cause. I want to say in the most forceful way I can: I certainly hope so."

Despite months of investigation by a legislative committee, Mr. Keating's statements about why he gave the money, and the head of the FHBLB charging that the senators had "subverted the regulatory process," not one of the Keating Five was found to have broken any laws. They claimed it was normal "constituent services."

Sen. McCain said, "I have done this sort of thing many times." People who write our laws are careful not to forbid their practice of selling favors in return for campaign contributions or jobs for relatives. They see nothing wrong in being paid to help us deal with the bureaucratic tangles they've created by the laws they pass.

We see similar favors when the administration grants waivers from Obamacare to many well-connected companies, unions, and other organizations, including the State of Maine.[83] Although this isn't technically against the law because the 1,200 page law explicitly lets the government grant such waivers, the administration's practice of allowing favored organizations to ignore the law makes a mockery of the concept of equal justice.

The Importance of Bank Regulation

People have been suspicious of money lenders for centuries. Mohammad banned charging interest on loans. The Catholic Church banned interest charges in 1311. History has shown, however, that allowing interest on loans helps the economy grow.

> Civilizations that eased the ban on moneylending have grown rich. Those that have retained it have stagnated. Northern Italy boomed in the 15th century when the Medicis ... found ways to bend the

---

[83] Drew Armstrong, "Maine Wins First Waiver to Health Insurance Premium Rules," *Bloomberg News*, March 8, 2011. Instead of 80%, Maine insurers selling policies to individuals will have to spend only 65 percent of premiums on patients, with the rest going toward profits and administrative costs.

rules. ... As Europe pulled ahead, the usury-banning Islamic world remained mired in poverty. In 1000 Western Europe's share of global GDP was 11.1% compared with the Middle East's 8.6%. By 1700 western Europe had a 13.5% share compared with the Middle East's 3.4%.[84]

The *Economist* explains that the invention of banking accounts for most of Europe's much more rapid economic growth. *The Great Depression: A Diary*[85] illustrates the importance of banking in a modern society. It contains notes by Benjamin Roth, a lawyer who practiced in Youngstown, Ohio, during the Depression. When the banking system froze up, the entire economy froze up because sellers lost confidence that they'd be paid:

> Oct. 16, 1931
> Business is being operated in crazy-quilt fashion. <u>No one will accept checks and nobody has cash</u>. The wholesalers, most of whom have their offices in other cities, refuse to deliver merchandise to the stores except C.O.D. cash. p 31 [emphasis added]

> Oct 17, 1931
> The financial situation would be ridiculous if it were not tragic. Everybody demands cash – no checks are accepted. The Truscon Steel Co. paid its employees with checks drawn on a large New York bank and the local banks refused to cash them. The check may be good today and bad tomorrow. Even certified checks are regarded suspiciously. p 32

Business was at a standstill because nobody knew which banks could honor checks on any given day. A bank might be strong one

---

84   "The dangers of demonology" *Economist*, Jan 7, 2012, p 60
85   Roth, Benjamin, with James Ledbetter, *The Great Depression: A Diary*, Public Affairs, (New York, 2009)

morning and collapse in the afternoon. Most banks were healthy and honored checks drawn on them but nobody knew which were good. In the end, only about 20% of all American banks failed, but enough sellers lost money that people became fearful.

Rumors are damaging in times of uncertainty. Depositors will leave their money in a bank if they know it's OK, but if they suspect trouble, they'll demand it all. A bank has limited cash on hand; no bank can survive a "run" of hordes of depositors wanting cash *now!*

Banks are linked together, so trouble in any bank spreads through the banking system at the speed of rumor. Bear Stearns and Lehman Brothers collapsed over a weekend. Bankers left Friday afternoon without a care in the world and arrived Monday morning to find the doors padlocked.

People are so suspicious of banks and banks are so important to the economy that they have to be regulated. Congress created the Federal Deposit Insurance Corp (FDIC) in 1933 to keep the financial system from seizing up again. The law said that the federal government would guarantee all bank deposits. Savers wouldn't worry about losing money, so they'd be less likely to panic and cause a run.

With the FDIC in place, the federal government became the "lender of last resort." The government can stop a crash by funding troubled banks. Having abandoned the gold standard in 1934, the government can print as much money as it needs, overnight via computer if necessary. Dealing with the increase in the money supply is put off for another day.

Protecting savers from risk causes "moral hazard." Savers know they'll be bailed out and have no incentive to look closely at a bank's finances. This tempts bankers to make risky loans with high returns. Extra profits make bosses look good and lead to large bonuses, but risky deals destroy a great deal of value when things go wrong. Creating a "moral hazard" where bankers think, "Heads I win, tails the taxpayers lose" is a recipe for disaster.

Once the FDIC put taxpayer's money at risk, regulations were written to limit the risks banks took on. The Federal Home Bank

Loan Board (FHBLB) investigated Lincoln Savings because the agency thought the bank had too many risky loans.

As the FHBLB had suspected, some of these loans were failing. As gamblers will, Charles Keating doubled his bets and took on even more risk. If his extra-risky loans had paid off, he'd have looked like a financial genius. His plan to save his bank would come unglued if the FHBLB forced him to unload risk too early, so he paid five senators $1.3 million to stop the investigation. His loans cost the taxpayers hundreds of millions when his bank went bust.

Mr. Keating's investments would have made money if banking regulations had let him wait long enough. Homes in his "Estrella Mountain Ranch" sold well after being transferred to new owners in 2005.[86] Once government stood behind banks, however, government took over the job of managing bank risk because savers didn't care anymore. The Keating Five gave citizens the impression that government rules apply only to those who can't pay to avoid them.

Questionable government behavior flows down to all levels of society. Lack of virtue shows in such situations and leads citizens to assume that government is corrupt. Senators who accept campaign contributions in return for letting banks take huge risks give police officers who fix traffic tickets the justification of thinking, "Everybody's doing it, why not me?"

Meddling in the Market

Politicians accepting bribes to let bankers get away with evading regulations is bad enough, but it's worse when politicians pass laws that allow the government to meddle directly in the banking business. Unintended consequences often keep laws that are intended to stabilize or increase the economy from having the desired effect.

---

[86] *Estrella Exploratorium puts focus on area's rich history,* available online at http://www.azcentral.com/news/articles/2008/09/12/20080912wv-exploratorium0912.html

Benjamin Roth[87] noted that lawmakers try to prevent crashes:

> Jan 9, 1937
> Each time in a depression new theories and "New Deals" are tried out but rarely do they seem to change the basic structure of the economic cycle.

As Economist John Kenneth Galbraith put it, "The foresight of financial experts was, as so often, a poor guide to the future,[88]" and, "The only function of economic forecasting is to make astrology look respectable." We voters let politicians keep trying to manage the economy despite their dismal record of non-accomplishment. Sometimes they try to keep banks from taking risks that will upset the economy; at other times, they pass laws requiring banks to take risky actions that seem to be socially desirable.

The Way Mortgages Were

Bankers say, "Any fool can lend money, the trick is getting it back." Over the centuries, bankers evolved reliable formulas to set loan limits and interest rates to make sure they'll get paid.

Years ago, when a couple applied for a home mortgage, for example, banks limited the maximum loan to between 3 and 5 times the husband's salary. If that plus the down payment wasn't enough, the seller had to drop the price or wait for a buyer with more money.

Any money the wife earned could be used to pay the loan back faster. This reduced risk and might earn the couple a lower interest rate. Her pay wasn't counted when setting the maximum loan, however, because wives were expected to stop working when they had children.

---

[87]   Roth, Benjamin, with James Ledbetter, *The Great Depression: A Diary*, Public Affairs, (New York, 2009)

[88]   Galbraith, John, *The New Economics at High Noon*, p 269

This changed in 1975, when the Equal Credit Opportunity Act required that a wife's income be included when evaluating mortgage applications.[89]

Two-income couples could pay higher prices for houses. Just as colleges increased tuition when student loan programs made more tuition money available, sellers started the "housing bubble" by increasing prices as soon as the government made more mortgage money available. It wasn't long before one income couldn't afford much house at all, which forced more women into the work force.

Women going to work nearly doubled the supply of labor, so the price of labor fell. The more the price of labor fell, the harder it was for fathers to provide by themselves. This put more pressure on wives to go to work. When they did, wages dropped even more – it' well known that middle-class incomes have stagnated since the 1970s.

Basing mortgages on two incomes also increased the risk of default. A non-working wife could go to work if her husband lost his job, but a mortgage depending on two incomes was at risk if either husband or wife became unemployed or fell ill.

Then the government decided that evil racist bankers weren't lending enough money to minorities. They started fining banks for "redlining," that is, refusing mortgages in minority neighborhoods. When that didn't create enough minority homeowners, bank examiners evaluated loan portfolios to make sure there were enough minority mortgages and fined banks that weren't "cooperating."

The Housing Bubble Grows, and Pops

This might have worked if banks had kept mortgages instead of selling them because losses came out of the bank's profits. This

---

[89]   Warren, Elizabeth & Tyagi, Amelia, *The Two-Income Trap*, Basic Books (New York, 2003) p 29

made bankers careful. On Sept. 30, 1999, the *New York Times* wrote:[90]

> In a move that could help increase home ownership rates among minorities and low-income consumers, the Fannie Mae Corporation is <u>easing the credit requirements</u> on loans that it will purchase from banks and other lenders.
>
> The action, which will begin as a pilot program involving 24 banks in 15 markets -- including the New York metropolitan region -- will <u>encourage those banks to extend home mortgages to individuals whose credit is generally not good enough to qualify for conventional loans</u>. Fannie Mae officials say they hope to make it a nationwide program by next spring. [emphasis added]

Lending money to borrowers with bad credit increased the risk of mortgages not being repaid. The *Times* foretold the coming crisis:

> In moving, even tentatively, into this new area of lending, Fannie Mae is taking on significantly <u>more risk</u>, which may not pose any difficulties during flush economic times. But the government-subsidized corporation <u>may run into trouble in an economic downturn, prompting a government rescue similar to that of the savings and loan industry in the 1980's</u>. [emphasis added]

The *Times* explained how the government's desire for more minority homeowners could bring down the entire housing market:

> Fannie Mae, the nation's biggest underwriter of home mortgages, does not lend money directly to

---

[90] "Fannie Mae Eases Credit To Aid Mortgage Lending", *New York Times*, Sept. 30, 1999

consumers. Instead, it purchases loans that banks make on what is called the secondary market. By expanding the type of loans that it will buy, Fannie Mae is hoping to spur banks to make more loans to people with less-than-stellar credit ratings.

Fannie Mae didn't write mortgages; it bought mortgages from banks that originated them. The government was saying they'd buy much riskier loans than before. As they became able to unload risky loans, banks offered mortgages to people with No Income, No Jobs or Assets, the infamous NINJA loans. Given that banks could be fined for not lending to enough minority borrowers, banks cut lending standards even more. Is it any wonder that so many minority homeowners were unable to pay off their mortgages?

Instead of crowing about their 1999 disaster prediction, the *Times* let the *Independent*, a British paper, explain what happened:[91]

What is the proximate cause of the collapse of confidence in the world's banks? Millions of improvident loans to American housebuyers. Which organizations were on their own responsible for guaranteeing half of this $12 trillion market? Freddie Mac and Fannie Mae, the so-called Government Sponsored Enterprises which were formally nationalized to prevent their immediate and catastrophic collapse. Now, who do you think were among the leading figures blocking all the earlier attempts by President Bush – and other Republicans – to bring these lending behemoths under greater regulatory control? Step forward, Barney Frank and Chris Dodd.

In September 2003 the Bush administration launched a measure to bring Fannie Mae and Freddie Mac under stricter regulatory control, after a report

---

[91] "Democrat fingerprints are all over the financial crisis" *Independent*, October 3, 2008

by outside investigators established that they were not adequately hedging against risks and that Fannie Mae in particular had scandalously mis-stated its accounts. ... Yet Barney Frank and his chums blocked all Bush's attempts to put a rein on Raines [the director of Fannie Mae].

The government's attempts to manage the home mortgage market pumped money into housing. Home prices rose further than they would have without government help. Increasing the number of minority homeowners relaxed lending standards and more loans went into default. Fannie Mae and Freddie Mac, the agencies which bought bad loans, ran up more than $150 billion in taxpayer losses.

Opinions differ on whether government meddling caused the "housing bubble" and the economic collapse, of course.

When addressing the 40th-anniversary breakfast of the Association for a Better New York, for example, Mayor Michael Bloomberg said, "It's not the banks that created the mortgage crisis. It was, plain and simple, Congress who forced everybody to go and give mortgages to people who were on the cusp ... They were the ones that pushed the banks to loan to everybody, and now we want to go vilify the banks because ... It's easy to blame them."

Former Mayor Koch, said, "I want to see somebody ... punished criminally. There's something wrong with a kid who steals a bike going to jail and someone who steals millions paying a fine."[92]

Mayor Bloomberg alluded to the government's fining bankers who didn't make enough loans to minorities. When they ran out of qualified minorities who wanted to buy, banks lent to people who didn't qualify. This led to huge losses. Mayor Koch, on the other hand, believes that crooked bankers bent the rules and deliberately sold bad loans to the government.

Both mayors are correct – banks made riskier loans than they would have preferred to make. They sold suspect loans to the

---

[92] Mayor Bloomberg and Mayor Koch's statements were reported in "Protesters force cafe layoffs as biz drops," the *New York Post*, November 2, 2011

government because the government was willing to buy them and because the banks knew the loans were ticking time bombs. Losses make citizens believe that both government and business are corrupt. This view of government makes citizens more likely to cut corners and less likely to promote social good.

Banking is only one example of an area where regulations offer opportunities for bribery and other forms of chicanery. We've seen regulatory disasters in mining safety, oil drilling, keeping Bernie Madoff from selling Ponzi investments, and many more. The more government regulates, the more opportunities for the non-virtuous to get rich at our expense.

Most people are tempted to cut corners to better themselves at the expense of others. This drove Confucius to emphasize the need for the government to set good examples and to punish vice publicly. Unfortunately, as the next chapter shows, the Chinese approach to trimming the bureaucracy and instilling virtue in government employees can't work in present-day America.

4 – Our Invincible Bureaucracy

The Chinese have centuries of experience managing far-flung organizations filled with individuals who'd rather look out for themselves than watch out for the best interests of the taxpayers who pay the bills. China has been called a "rope of sand"[93] because most Chinese were more loyal to their families and towns than to the Emperor.

The central government's problem in working its will on day-to-day governance was summed up as, "The mountains are high, and the Emperor is far, far away."[94] Given the distances and the impossibility of communicating faster than a horse could run, local officials had great latitude in managing affairs to suit themselves.

The Chinese ruling elite knew that capital punishment was the best way to send a message strong enough to lead to virtuous action. It got people's attention. During the short interval while you had everybody's attention, you could make a few points about virtuous behavior before people forgot your message and got back to normal.

The Chinese shared a long land border with the Mongol hordes to the north, so it's no surprise that they'd glorify military heroes more than we do. Sun Tzu,[95] their greatest warrior-hero, has even gained traction in modern America.

The story goes that before Sun Tzu became famous, he told the emperor he could teach the emperor's concubines military drill in a few hours. This would prove that he was worthy to command the

---

93   Hansard, Thomas, *Hansard's Parliamentary Debates* (Cornelius Buck, 1862) p 76
94   State University of New York College at Oneonta, Boston College. Center for East Europe, Russia, and Asia, *Asian Thought & Society* (East-West Pub., 1998) p 15
95   Sun Tzu *The Art of War*, said to have been written around 500 BC, roughly contemporary with Confucius (Dover Publications, 2002)

---

army. The Emperor told him to go ahead. The general divided 180 of the prettiest women into two platoons and appointed the Emperor's two favorite concubines as platoon leaders.

When he explained the drum signals that meant "right face," "left face," and "march," the women laughed. When he ordered a maneuver, the women ran in all directions and laughed harder.

After the second try, the general had the two platoon leaders kneel and chopped their heads off for failing to maintain order in their commands. Knowing that the general was serious, the women drilled as flawlessly as well-trained troops.

The management techniques of "kill one to regulate hundreds" and "kill a chick to warn the monkey" are not unique to China. The French say, *"pour encourager les autres,"*[96] which can mean "It's good to put heads up on poles to encourage the others to be virtuous." The British shot Admiral Byng for refusing battle and losing the island of Minorca to the French in 1756.[97]

The classical Chinese management approach is coming back:

> "BEIJING, July 10 — China executed its former top food and drug regulator on Tuesday for taking bribes to approve untested medicine, as the Beijing leadership scrambled to show that it was serious about improving the safety of Chinese products."[98]

Shooting miscreants is the fastest method of encouraging virtuous behavior. There are other techniques in the leadership toolbox, of course, but setting a good example and writing mission statements take longer to reach the time-servers at the bottom of the pyramid.

---

[96] Voltaire, *Candide*. The quote is "Dans ce pay-ci, il est bon de tuer de temps en temps un amiral pour encourager les autres." "In this country it is good to kill an admiral from time to time, to encourage the others."

[97] Osborn, Sarah Byng et al., *Political and Social Letters of a Lady of the Eighteenth Century, 1721-1771* (Dodd, Mead & Company, 1891) pp 112-113 Admiral Byng was the lady's brother.

[98] *New York Times,* July 11, 2007

The late lamented bureaucrat wasn't necessarily whacked for taking bribes. The *New York Times* wrote that the execution took place "as the Beijing leadership scrambled to show that it was serious about improving the safety of Chinese products." A few Chinese citizens dying from poisoned food may not seem such a big deal when you've got 1.3 billion people who're doing their best to get around your "one child" policy, but times changed faster than bureaucrats can.

China has always been overcrowded. The perceived value of a human life is low enough that offing a bureaucrat or two to solve a problem wouldn't be seen as out of line.[99] The Chinese people were losing faith in the integrity of their food supply, which would be bad politics. Far worse, Americans were threatening to cut off Chinese imports, which would have been bad for business. Losing a bureaucrat or two is no big deal, but losing money, that's serious.

Regardless of the effect of this message on Chinese government employees,[100] the Chinese sent us a message that they were serious about drug safety. They know that Americans value individual lives more than they do and they know that actions speak far louder than bureaucratic platitudes. What better way to make a point than

---

[99] Woodruff, Charles, *Expansion of races*, (Rebman company, 1909) p 46 put it thus "We often wonder why the killing of Chinese soldiers was so quickly forgotten – it made no impression. A million Chinese could be killed and the loss would not be felt in that sodden, gelatinous, inelastic mass – indeed the Empire would be benefitted. Safety for foreigners can only be obtained by ever-present force. Chinamen are cheaper than beasts of burden and cost less to feed, and are even far cheaper than engines."

[100] The Chinese proverb, "food is the people's sky" underscores the importance of a reliable food supply to the Chinese, but "Baby formula recall in China after infant death," *Telegraph.co.uk* 13 Sept. 2008 suggests that the message not to sell poisoned food didn't get through to domestic manufacturers.

selecting someone to take the blame and blaming him? Trimming a bureaucrat reduced spending and taught virtue at the same time.[101]

We'll never know whether this official really took bribes or not – the Chinese decision-making process and justice system are opaque. The real message might have been, "Bribes are OK but don't poison customers who can shut us out of a big market."

Enforcing virtue by decapitation carried risks: fearful bureaucrats might assassinate the Emperor. One reason the Imperial Palace in the Forbidden City has so many bedrooms is that the Emperor needed many different places to spend the night.[102] Only the eunuchs who brought his chosen concubine to the bedchamber knew where he was.[103]

The Revival of Confucianism

Chapter 2 noted that the history of China can be regarded as a series of outside ideas such as Buddhism, Taoism, and most recently, Communism and capitalism, gaining influence for a century or two only to fall away as Confucian ideas recover their traditional sway.

Communism claims to be atheistic in the sense of denying that God exists. In the early years of Mao Tse Tung's revolution, Communist leaders had difficulty accepting Confucian ideas – Confucianism had become a religion centered on ancestor worship mixed with Emperor worship and was denounced as "feudal."

---

[101] In any organization, cutting head-count is the only way to cut costs. Monitoring travel, cutting magazine subscriptions, and adjusting thermostats save a few bucks, but real cost savings require reducing head count by fair means or foul. Cutting pay across the board works, but when you cut people's pay, they're still around to fight you. Anybody you get rid of can't fight back. On the national level, rulers know that merely defeating enemies leaves them alive to attack again. That's why the gallows is the first servant of the state.

[102] "Forbidden No More," *Smithsonian Magazine*, March 2008 pp 80-90

[103] Turnbull, Stephen, Reynolds, Wayne, *Ninja, A.D. 1460-1650* (Osprey Publishing, 2003) p 63 documents another approach to thwarting assassination. Japanese castles had "nightingale floors" which had small metal springs under the floorboards to make noise when someone stepped near the ruler's bedroom.

The people at the top of the Chinese hierarchy are quite pragmatic, however. Having noted that most Chinese have a deep sense of religion, the leaders realized that in denying religion, they'd given up a useful tool for motivating the population. Confucius' teaching that God Himself wanted people to obey government helps people feel good about doing what they're told. The religious carrot balances the stick of being fired at will.

The Communist Party is sponsoring a Confucian revival. Confucius' 2,500 year old ideas are being promoted ever so carefully as a well-tested model of governance which is better suited to China than democracy with its mere 200-year pedigree.

> "Confucianism has quietly come back," said Joseph Cheng, a political scientist at the City University of Hong Kong, "and the communist leadership has been exploiting it to help fill the ideological vacuum and improve morality. It is a low-key revival, but it suits their needs to find a new cohesive force at a time when Marxism is dead but democracy is absent."[104] [emphasis added]

Marxism had to go when the Chinese realized 20 years ago that the younger generation was infected with western ideas about democracy and economic prosperity. In the summer of 1989, a group of students occupied Tiananmen Square in Beijing, put up a copy of the Statue of Liberty, and demanded that the ruling elite convert to democracy. The leadership sent the army to crush the unarmed students with tanks.

Having suffered a challenge to their authority, the party decided that the best way to keep people from rebelling was to let them get

---

[104] "Forget Tianamen, thus spake Confucius" *Asia Times Online,* June 3, 2009

rich.[105]   Marxism meant that the masses could never become rich; Marxist control of the economy was gradually replaced by economic freedom. My friends who commute to China tell me that the Chinese coast is the most capitalistic region on the face of the earth.

Democracy is absent from China in that no tyrant wants to give up power by granting power to the people. Allowing Confucian teachings about obeying the government to reclaim its former place in Chinese hearts is a practical step towards maintaining stability.

> China watchers say President Hu Jintao believes that rampant consumerism has left an ethical vacuum that could be filled with Confucian values of honor and decency. In a recent lecture titled "The Socialist Concept of Honor and Disgrace", he extolled Confucius's "eight virtues", such as plain living and public service, and warned of his "eight disgraces", like pursuit of profit.[106]

Confucius never understood market forces or the role of profit. In Western theory, profit measures how well the business is run and provides money for investment in new projects or to attract investment to expand the business.

Individual Chinese are greedy enough that Confucius' ideas about the evils of profit won't stop them trying to become wealthy. Hopefully, though, they will learn to distinguish "virtuous profit" which is the reward of serving the public by providing goods and services people want to buy from "evil profit" which comes from gouging the public as American sugar and ethanol producers do.

---

[105]   This is a variant on the Roman idea of "bread and circuses" to keep the mob at bay. The Chinese are cleverer than the Romans were. Rome went bankrupt supplying bread and circuses at no cost to the recipients. Instead of funding giveaways, Chinese rulers make people pay for their own entertainment and force them to work to earn wealth. Chinese have life and pursuit of happiness, but no liberty. 2 out of 3 might be good enough.

[106]   "Forget Tianamen, thus spake Confucius," *Asia Times Online*, June 3, 2009

Reviving Confucianism allows the government to combine the carrot of everyone getting rich with the traditional Confucian teaching that everyone has a duty to obey the government and practice virtue. This allows the government to describe increasing material wealth as a reward of exercising the virtue of hard work and serving customers instead of letting business engage in the naked pursuit of profit regardless of virtue.

Horatio Alger would approve, but the fact that business leaders appear to be willing to bribe government inspectors to let them sell poisoned infant formula[107] doesn't bode well for "virtuous profit" taking hold without forceful enforcement from on high. The government will probably have to execute some number of corrupt businessmen along with corrupt bureaucrats to communicate an appropriate standard of commercial virtue.

The revival of the Confucian notion of virtuous behavior doesn't affect the stick part of government power, of course. The Communists have always been quick to shoot anyone who didn't follow their directives. Capital punishment was used primarily to consolidate Communist power during Mao's career, but as people have become more and more aware of government corruption, the Communist party has executed the occasional bureaucrat to suggest that they're trying to instill virtue.

By happy coincidence, getting rid of corrupt bureaucrats is precisely what Confucius advises virtuous rulers to do. Few businessmen were influential enough to need killing in Confucius' day, but the party won't have any trouble extending the principle of management by forced horizontal retirement to non-virtuous businessmen.

In addition to reviving Confucianism at home, the Chinese government is funding more than 300 "Confucius Institutes" at universities worldwide.[108] Communism has lost its appeal in the

---

[107] "Tainted Baby Formula Blamed In Chinese Kidney Cases," *Wall Street Journal*, September 12, 2008

[108] "A message from Confucius," *Economist*, Oct. 24, 2009, p 10 of a special report on China

United States and in China.[109] The Chinese government realizes that selling Confucianism might influence American thought. Confucian teachings on peace and harmony are an important part of the image the Chinese government desires to project abroad.

The Untouchables

In contrast to Chinese practice, American civil service regulations combined with the power of government employee unions mean that it's nearly impossible to get rid of any government employee, no matter how incompetent, venal, or unproductive.

We often see politicians promising more responsive, consumer-oriented bureaucracies as they reduce "waste, fraud, and abuse" particularly when running for re-election. We see union leaders complaining that government employees are not the sharpest tools in the drawer because they're underpaid: if only we'd raise their wages, we'd get better government workers. The conventional wisdom is that government employees are barely competent if not incompetent.

Conventional wisdom could hardly be more wrong. Our bureaucrats are in fact very, very good at what they do, which is gaming the system to increase their budgets, and they're getting better at it all the time. Their increasing level of bureaucratic professionalism and competence is a serious threat to our national health: we'd be much better off if most government minions were truly as incompetent and clueless as we tend to think they are.

To the Victor Went the Spoils

Our Constitution mandates three branches of government: Legislative, Judicial, and Executive. The President and Vice-

---

[109] Communism is alive and well on liberal college campuses, of course. There's a joke going 'round that the Chinese no longer send their best students to the US because they were coming back as socialists.

President have detailed eligibility requirements, even down to the oath of office they must swear. It's strange that the bureaucrats with whom citizens interact the most hardly appear in the Constitution at all.

The federal bureaucracy is part of the Executive branch which answers to the President, but each agency is created, funded, and given rule-writing authority by a separate act of Congress. There are no direct Constitutional requirements which federal employees must fulfill and the President can't shut down a department if Congress insists that he spend money on it.

When our nation was founded, there were many jobs to fill – customs officers, lighthouse-keepers, tax collectors and "revenue agents" of various kinds, postmasters and mailmen. Since these posts all answered to the President, it seemed logical for him to hire and fire them at need. Early Presidents generally sought the best person for the job regardless of politics.

This changed with the election of President Andrew Jackson in 1829. He believed he had a mandate to make sure that all levels of government carried out the policies he'd been elected to implement, and what better way to accomplish this than by appointing his political supporters to government jobs? He sacked the current officeholders and started from scratch, giving his political operatives nice cushy positions of publicly-funded ease.

This became standard practice. The "Spoils System" turned out to be good management for a while. Abraham Lincoln used the Spoils System to excellent effect during the Civil War. Even though many Americans opposed the war or wanted to end it with a compromise, he appointed people who agreed with him. He made sure that the entire federal government pulled his way and achieved complete victory in the Civil War.

Much of Lincoln's preserved correspondence is from people asking for government jobs; he often complained about the burden to his friends. As irritating and time-consuming as this was, though, Lincoln recognized the importance hiring and firing held to accomplishing his goals. If he hadn't been so careful to make sure that his people were in all positions high and low, he'd have lost the war.

There are inherent problems with making appointments on a purely political basis: you can wind up with crooks who only pretend to agree with your goals. Ulysses Grant is remembered as a great general, a man who loved his country, and a personally honest man, but a dreadful President because of his lousy judgment in making appointments. The scandals that rocked his administration made Bill Clinton look like a piker.[110] Following Grant's retirement, President Hayes was elected on a platform of clean government. His administration botched the reforms and he didn't run for re-election.

The Civil Service is Born

Americans were disgusted by corruption in government appointments, but it took an assassination to start the Civil Service.

President Garfield followed Hayes, and we'll never know what reforms he might have put in place. Four months into his administration, Charles Guiteau shot him, taking out his anger at not receiving a government job. Between the scandals of Grant's appointees and the assassination of Garfield over the same issue, the American people had had enough.

The Pendleton Civil Service Reform Act of 1883[111] created the bureaucracy we have today. No longer could Presidents appoint

---

[110] Bunting, Josiah, *Ulysses S. Grant* (Published by Macmillan, 2004) p 1 The author believes it unfair that Grant was blamed for the sins of his appointees but the Chinese have always known that the buck stops at the top.

[111] The act didn't affect state or municipal employment. Fish, C. R., *The Civil Service and the Patronage* (Longmans, Green & co, 1905) p 157 said, "It is here that the function of the spoils system becomes evident; the civil service becomes the pay roll of the party leader; offices are apportioned according to the rank and merits of his subordinates, and, if duties are too heavy or new positions are needed, new offices may be created." Mr. Fish neglected the possibility that a new office might be created to give a favored subordinate a no-show job from which he could serve his patron's interests full-time.

government staffers except at the very top. Ordinary workers were selected via the United States Civil Service Commission, which created a battery of scientific aptitude tests and examinations. It's illegal to expect any sort of political favor from a government civil servant or to make any political demand on them at all. The goal was to remove politics from government employment and let the best-qualified people have the jobs.

Politics *is* Human Nature

That's not what happened. In a very real way, politics is human nature writ large. How many people do you know who are truly apolitical? Any at all? Almost everyone leans toward one party or another. People who aren't affiliated with a party still have views on political issues. By removing the power of the President to hire and fire civil servants, reformers didn't remove politics from governance, they removed *control* of politics from governance.

Andrew Jackson was right – the president wins office on whatever platform he runs on and has a theoretical mandate to try to put them into place. Over the last few decades, however, it's become almost impossible to change the direction of the bureaucracy regardless of the electoral success of the President. How can we hold the President responsible for what government workers do when he can't appoint them, promote them, demote them, or fire them?

Ronald Reagan's platform called for the elimination of the Department of Energy. He won in a landslide; if ever there was a mandate, he had it. The Department of Energy is still around. What sort of chief executive can't shut down one of his lesser divisions?

The Buck Stops Here Occasionally

Corruption occurred in the old days of the Spoils System but there were limits to bureaucratic misbehavior. In a very real way, the President was personally responsible for the behavior of the bureaucrats because he appointed them all. Their actions reflected on him and he had the power to dismiss any of them at any time.

Today, in contrast, federal agencies don't answer to anyone. How many times did the CIA "adjust" intelligence – first to suit what they thought President George Bush wanted and later to make him look foolish? There was nothing he could do about it.

The culture of the civil service is so entrenched that Congress and the media apply its rules even where they don't legally apply. Remember the ruckus over Mr. Bush's firings of Justice Department attorneys? Supposedly there was political influence in this action.

Of course there was – attorneys are political appointments! The President has the right to sack them just as he can demand the resignation of cabinet secretaries or the Attorney General. Past Presidents haven't been shy about this – Bill Clinton fired all the attorneys when he took office, including two who were investigating his involvement in Whitewater. Scandalous? Only when Mr. Bush did it.

The Constitution places the authority to enforce the laws in the hands of the President. Attorneys who do the actual investigations and prosecutions answer to the President, including their hiring and firing. It's not possible to investigate and prosecute each and every crime across the fruited plain. We've always had the doctrine of "prosecutorial discretion," where not everything gets chased down. The President is elected by the people with a mandate of whatever he ran on; what's wrong with putting his mandate into play?

If we elect a Democratic president, we expect the Justice Department to spend a lot of time investigating polluters, big businesses, and discrimination. That's what Democrats promise, and when elected, they have every right to do it.

Similarly, it's nonsense to expect Republicans to have the same emphasis; they chase down corrupt labor unions, the Mafia, and terrorists, just as they promise. If the American people want a change in approach, they can change Presidents at the next election.

If this is true for prosecutors, it should be true all up and down the corridors of power. Modern Presidents are emasculated by the power of untouchable bureaucrats.

The opposition of the State Department bureaucrats to everything President Bush tried to do is legendary. President Bush could replace the Secretary of State or the Director of the CIA but given the opposition to his firing the attorneys, he couldn't reach down into the cubicle farm and throw his problem children out the door. President Lincoln would have lost the Civil War if he had had as little control of the Federal bureaucracy as Mr. Bush had.

Term Limits for Bureaucrats

This brings up another limit to bureaucratic power and corruption under the appointments system. No matter how successful a President or how popular his policies, sooner or later there'd be a President from the opposite party. In the days of the Spoils System, that meant an immediate replacement of the entire bureaucracy from top to bottom – bureaucrats had what amounted to term limits.

A President is in office for four years. He might get re-elected to another four. With luck, his vice-president might be elected president and leave some officials in place, for a total of twelve years.

There have been few runs of the same party holding the Oval Office much beyond that. As term limits are supposed to prevent people from being "professional politicians," the old-fashioned spoils system prevented people from becoming "permanent bureaucrats." If it's a good idea for politicians to return to the real world every now and again, how much more so is this true for the bureaucrats whose actions more directly affect ordinary folks?

The Taxpayer-Funded Big-Government Lobby

Government growth shows that our government workers are highly skilled. When you think a bureaucrat's incompetent, you're almost certainly wrong because you're looking at the wrong measure. You're acting like a consumer – this DMV agency makes me wait hours in line, that IRS auditor is aggressively harsh, the TSA makes silly rules that don't help security and inconvenience everybody.

If any of those agencies were private businesses, they'd be out of business. There's a good reason McDonald's rarely has long lines – if the line is too long, customers go to Burger King and the Golden Arches lose sales. McDonald's management makes sure this doesn't happen: managers get fired if sales drop. Companies must provide a service that people want for a reasonable price, or they lose business. A truly rotten company goes bankrupt, and vanishes.

Government agencies never die. The DMV and IRS have just as many "customers" no matter how lousy or inefficient they get. Nobody chooses to deal with the EPA, TSA, or any other agency. The incentives which apply to employees of private companies – the business has to make money or I get laid off, so the product or service I provide actually matters – don't apply to government.

An ambitious private company worker can get ahead in any number of ways, but the simplest path to promotion is by increasing sales – that is, by bringing more money into the company. Capitalism forces ambitious, greedy people to get ahead by providing something people want badly enough to spend money to get it – the product has to be more wonderful than money or it won't sell. This harnesses greed to the common good, converting greed to virtue as if by magic. Unfortunately, nobody has figured out an equivalent incentive for government employees.

Government agencies don't increase in size by serving customers well because people don't deal with them by choice. Nobody deals with the government unless they have to. Therein lies the key to getting ahead as a bureaucrat: lobby for laws or regulations or write rules to force more people to deal with you. An ambitious bureaucrat furthers his or her career by growing the size of government, all in the "public interest" of course. That's why the number of rules is exploding – writing rules is a bureaucratic profit center.

If you can't create a new department, you can always get your people to work slower. That makes lines longer. When your victims get mad enough, they'll demand that politicians do something about it. You'll give the politicians the usual swindle about not having enough people. The politicians can't fire you; the only thing they can do is give you more people. The worse job you do, the more money you get. Nirvana!

By allowing, nay, requiring, permanent, untouchable career civil servants, the Civil Service Act created a sizable, lavishly funded, and powerful force whose goal is expanding the power and reach of government *regardless of need*. The more things which are regulated, the more bureaucrats are required to issue, interpret, and enforce the regulations. The more species that can be listed as endangered, the more bureaucrats are needed to protect them.

This means more government jobs and more high-ranking, well paid bureaucrats with posh pensions and other benefits. It's nice to move up the ranks by taking your boss's job; it's even nicer not to have to, by creating a whole new department to be the boss of, and leave your old boss in charge of his. Then the two of you can work together to make work for each other.

In the days of the Spoils System, it wasn't worthwhile for a talented bureaucrat to expand the system. Come the next election, his new position fell to someone from the opposite party. The fruit of his labors would go to his political enemy. This was a good reason not to grow government! Today's incentives are the exact opposite.

A quick look at the size of our federal budget and the employment graphs earlier reveals that our bureaucrats are, in fact, very good at doing what their incentives push them to do: grow the size of government. Since the Civil Service Act eliminated the two restraints on bureaucracy and Sen. Moynihan's "professionalization of reform" allowed bureaucrats to set their own agendas, the total spending of government has done nothing but grow. The only time it slips down, slightly, is after the peak of a war; but soon it's back on the upward trend.

President Reagan was elected to cut the size of government; he failed, although he did slow the growth. President Clinton was elected promising new government programs; he succeeded. Why might this be?

Unintended Consequences

The Founding Fathers designed our system of governance with checks and balances throughout. They knew that human beings seek power, so they made sure that when the President tried to grab too much power, there'd be judges and the Congress to grab it back. With the three branches of government scrambling for control, they hoped that people would be left alone most of the time.

The concept of an unaccountable bureaucracy never occurred to the Founders. There were bureaucracies in their day, of course. The word comes from French, showing how French kings had multiplied officers, and the British were no different. In all cases, however, the king held power over each and every member of the bureaucracy. If a civil servant fouled up too badly or got too big for his britches, the king could not only throw him out of office or throw him in jail, he might even have his head, just like the Emperors of China.

Louis XIV's treasury minister, Nicholas Fouquet, discovered this when the king became angry that Fouquet could afford to throw more lavish parties than the king could; he ordered Fouquet arrested and imprisoned until his death. Voltaire memorably described the abrupt nature of this stroke: "On 17 August at 6 in the evening, Fouquet was King of France; at 2 in the morning, he was nobody."

One can only imagine how carefully King Louis' other ministers watched their backs for a long time to come. Our Founders were familiar with Fouquet's fate as well. The situation of today where no one has much control over government agents would have confounded the authors of our Constitution as well as Confucius.

With power should come accountability. Thanks to the Civil Service Act, there is no accountability for the actions of the hundreds of thousands of government workers who collect salaries from the taxpayers. Nobody – not the Congress, not the President, not even the courts – can remove bureaucrats from office, no matter what they do, no matter how they abuse the public, as long as it's not a crime. Even if a bureaucrat loses his job from having committed a crime, he generally keeps his pension. Is this not truly a form of tyranny?

For many years, lovers of small government have moaned, "If only we had a Republican president and Republican Congress! They'll slash and burn the government down to size!" We've tried that over the past decades. How'd it work out?

At one time, elimination of whole government departments and programs was part of the official Republican Party national platform. After 34 years during which we've had 20 years of Republican Presidents, this plan is gone without trace. The targeted departments are still merrily turning taxpayer money into ashes. Our most recent Republican president added another – the Department of Homeland Security – which is ridiculed as utterly incompetent if not corrupt.

Back to the Confucian Path

Confucius believed that the best way to persuade government employees to be virtuous was drastic cuts. There are other ways, of course, and it's possible that a simple remedy might help.

Consider the effect of one simple change: give the President the power to fire one employee from each department per week. The President could use this power to get rid of the incompetent or to weed out those who opposed his policies; that one soul would be an example to the rest as with the Chinese system.

With this tiny improvement, the President might be able to implement his promises. Bureaucrats are acutely sensitive to the whisper of the axe, but to nothing else. If the President had this power, he'd hardly ever have to use it. Just knowing that papa could spank would mean that he very seldom had to.

This operates on the same theory as "Mutually Assured Destruction" (MAD). The fact that America and Russia could obliterate each other meant that they didn't have to – each side always backed off before stomping the other's trip wires.

The Coming Collapse

As Confucius pointed out, there's a limit to the overhead a society can stand. When government takes too much out of the economy, the economy collapses and we start over. An economic collapse would be bad enough, but what if our education system falls apart so badly that we can no longer maintain our technology?

Our farms make lavish use of petroleum-based fertilizers and complex machinery. If we lose too much technology and have to go back to muscle-powered farming, half of our population will starve.

That's the origin of the Chinese curse, "May you live in interesting times."

The only possible "interesting times" in ancient China were war, famine, or plague. China was so large and travel so slow that it was possible that an interesting catastrophe far away wouldn't affect you. To an ancient Chinese, the only thing worse than "interesting times" was "May your life be exciting," which meant you'd be in the middle of it when catastrophe came. Our society is so tightly integrated that if the collapse comes, our lives will become exciting indeed.

The American electorate has the power to demand that the bureaucracy be trimmed back so that we can avert the catastrophe if we choose to do so. Our government is spending far more than we can afford, but bureaucracy isn't the only problem.

Our society is considerably more complex than Chinese society was. The Chinese bureaucracy was the only entity with the power and influence to cause spending to grow beyond what society could handle. Unlike China, we have a host of other entities such as labor unions, pensioners, welfare recipients, and businesses seeking favorable tax treatment which help boost social costs.

The next several chapters discuss some of these other cost centers. As government has become more powerful, various groups forge alliances with the bureaucracy and with greedy politicians to benefit themselves at public expense.

These hordes of non-virtuous, self-centered actors are more worried about taking out than putting in. Their lack of virtue is just as damaging to society as lack of virtue in the bureaucracy. Confucius would be appalled, but he'd understand that human greed manifests itself anywhere it finds opportunity.

5 – Bridges to Nowhere

Trying to increase government revenue by raising tax rates makes people work harder not to pay. The best way to raise tax revenue is to make investments that create more action because the power to tax gives government a piece of everybody's action. Growing businesses pay more taxes and government profits from its investment.

This virtuous cycle has operated for thousands of years. The Emperor Shih Huang-ti, who unified all of what is now considered China around 230 BC, some 250 years after Confucius, built highways from his capital to the far-flung outposts of his empire.[112] As with Roman roads and President Eisenhower's Interstate Highway System, his primary goal was efficient military transportation to secure his rule. Reduced transportation costs increased economic activity and increased tax revenue as a welcome side effect of his military preparations.

Later Chinese infrastructure added water transport. Freight moved on the 650-mile Grand Canal between Hangchow and Tientsin and on 25,000 miles of smaller canals. The Grand Canal was started around 300 AD and was completed by Kublai Khan, the emperor who hosted Marco Polo.[113]

Grain shipments via the Canal supplied famine relief. The decreased probability of starving gave citizens another reason to remain loyal to the government. Operating and maintaining the Grand Canal gave the bureaucracy something constructive to do.

---

[112] Durant, William. *Our Oriental Heritage*, (New York, Simon and Schuster, 1954) p 696
[113] Ibid., p 778

The Canal was a two-edged sword – people felt entitled to low-cost grain shipments from distant places. Hungry citizens contemplated rebellion when bureaucrats stole so much of the dredging fund that the canal silted up or a natural disaster damaged the canal.

American infrastructure has benefited us both economically and politically. Government investments not only knit our nation together, they reduced transportation costs, increased overall economic activity, and contributed to national wealth and prosperity.

When New York Governor De Witt Clinton proposed the Erie Canal between Albany and Buffalo in 1807, people criticized his project as "Clinton's Ditch." People 250 miles from Buffalo in eastern Michigan were so convinced of the benefits the "Ditch" would bring, however, that they named the Clinton River and the town of Clintonville in Clinton's honor before the canal opened in 1825.

The cost of shipping a ton of grain from the Midwest to New York City dropped by 75% once freight could go all the way by water. Farmers and manufacturers sold products eastward, giving city people better food and other goods at lower cost.

As transportation costs fell, businesses served larger markets. Traffic exceeded estimates and the government received far more tolls and tax revenue than anticipated. The increased revenue paid for more improvements. This virtuous cycle continued for a century as railroads and highways replaced the canal.

The first transcontinental railroad opened in 1869. Like the canals, it reduced transportation costs and increased tax revenue at first. As with the automobile business, however, government regulation, management mistakes, and union featherbedding increased and nearly put the railroads out of business. The Staggers Act of 1980 removed enough of the regulatory burden that freight railroads can operate profitably and benefit society once again.

Building better roads also increased corporate profits. My grandfather owned a bottling plant in Winston-Salem, NC, in the early 1900s. Trucks went 80 miles to his Charlotte distributor. His profits went up noticeably when the government paved the road.

The new road saved driver time and truck maintenance as well as fuel. The government collected more tax on his increased profits than it lost on reduced fuel taxes.

Our Interstate highway system started by President Eisenhower has 4% of the nation's public roads but it carries 40% of highway traffic and 70% of truck freight.[114] These highways pull traffic from lower-capacity roads and reduce delays. Economic activity increased so much from increased transportation efficiencies that government received more in taxes than it cost to build the highways.

From Profit to Loss

New roads, canals, and other transportation infrastructure usually increased economic efficiency during most of the 20th century, but not always. Geography does not provide unlimited opportunities for profitable infrastructure investments but there is no limit to the desire of contractors to profit by building infrastructure.

Consider hydroelectric dams. There are only so many rivers in America, and essentially all the suitable ones were dammed by the 1960's. Similarly, our canal, road, and rail networks are now so extensive that very few additional infrastructure investments would show a profit.

For example, the 374 km canal between the Tennessee and Tombigbee rivers, known as Tenn-Tom, was known to be a money-loser because there was so little need for it. The people who wanted to build it fudged the cost / benefit analysis and President Nixon cut the ribbon to start construction in 1971. A later analysis reported:

---

[114] Statement of Rodney E. Slater, Federal Highway Administrator, before a Southern California Earthquake Hearing chaired by Senator Dianne Feinstein, April 4, 1994, http://testimony.ost.dot.gov/test/pasttest/94test/Slater1.pdf p 3

For example, to justify the canalization of the Missouri the ACE [Army Corps of Engineers] predicted 12m tons of traffic annually, while today it carries 1.8m tons – a 85% shortfall. Maintenance costs are 1.7c/ton-mi compared to under a tenth of a cent on the Mississippi. And the Tennessee-Tombigbee canal built in the 1980s at a cost of $2b on the basis that it would carry 27m tons is carrying 1.7m tons – a 93% shortfall. Maintenance costs are 1.1c/ton-mi. The Ten-Tom costs $16m/yr to maintain. If it had been commercially financed investors would expect say 8% return on capital ($2b x 0.08) or $160m so it would need to generate $176m to break even. In fact based on the average fuel tax user fee the barge operators on the canal pay less than $0.5m, so it is $175.5m or 99.7% away from break even. <u>The fees charged are a tiny gesture, pocket money, relative to the costs.</u>[115]

Four systems – the Mississippi, Ohio, and Illinois rivers and the Intra-Coastal Waterway – carry 570m tons or 90% of the total 630m tons of traffic on America's interior waterways. Similarly these four oldest systems carry 230b of the total 255b ton-mi. They cost $220m to maintain or 0.086c/ton-mi. That is 2.5 times the user fees paid which average 0.035c. Only the busiest leg of the system, the Lower Mississippi, comes near to recovering even operating costs in user fees. <u>The rest of the US canal system is a gigantic rip-off of taxpayers</u>. 16 waterways have operating costs over 1c/ton-mi, which is 30 times what users pay. Seven of these have costs over 10c/ton-mi or 300 times operating costs. [emphasis added]

---

[115] "WET BOONDOGGLE: Canals with Few Barges" *Toll Roads Newsletter*, Issue 48, April 2000, p 18 http://www.tollroadsnews.com/node/2645

"Pocket money" is a polite way to say that the cost/benefit analysis was a total crock; the contractors and politicians who wanted the money lied like rugs. The canal has so little commercial traffic that even ardent canal fans admit that Tenn-Tom is "perhaps the last ever," and the overall system has been described as a "rip-off."

Infrastructure costs are hard to estimate; it's routine for projects to cost 4 to 5 times the estimates. Benefit calculations are a lot more subtle. Traffic is hard to estimate because transportation systems interact. So many highways competed with Tenn-Tom that switching to the canal simply wasn't worthwhile for most freight.

Uneconomic Infrastructure Fiascos

The consensus seems to be that Tenn-Tom wasted so much money that nobody will finance a canal ever again. Unfortunately, politicians are skilled at overcoming obstacles to spending money.

For example, many newspapers fumed against the Boston "Big Dig" which was estimated to cost $3.2 billion in 1986.[116] It actually cost at least $16 billion and the last lawsuit was settled in 2009.[117]

Denver voters approved a $1.7 billion airport in a 1989 referendum, but the cost mushroomed to $4.8 billion by the time the airport opened in 1995.[118]

The Washington DC Metro is being extended towards Dulles Airport but the project may not be completed all the way due to arguments over the route and environmental lawsuits. This is particularly galling since the state of Virginia gave the toll road from DC to Dulles to the airport authority so that the tolls could fund the metro. There's skepticism that the line will ever be built. "Believe it

---

[116] "Big Dig overrun is just plain big" *Boston Globe* July 14, 2002

[117] "With two final settlements, Big Dig litigation ends" *Boston Globe*, March 26, 2009

[118] Transportation data from Alan Altshuler and David Luberoff, *Megaprojects* (Washington: Brookings Institution Press, 2003)

when we see it" is the watchword. After all, the connection was planned 40 years ago and it could well take another 40 years.

What's more, this new project is unnecessary. A rail line ran from Washington DC out to the Dulles airport site ran for 100 years before the airport was ever built. The railroad brought gravel and asphalt in enormous quantities while the airport was under construction. Ten years later, it was abandoned and paved over for a bike path.

Could it be restored? Not without affecting many back yards. Instead of using the existing right-of-way, we're paying for new construction involving tunnels, elevated tracks, and rails down the center of a major highway where there are no residents to complain. A little foresight after Dulles Airport was built could have saved taxpayers untold billions and several decades.

The famous, or infamous, 8.5 mile Second Avenue Subway in New York City has been talked about even longer.

> Beloved, believed in, glimpsed fleetingly only to disappear again for decades, the Second Avenue subway has long seemed to be New York City's version of the Loch Ness monster. The plan has been on the drawing board since the year Babe Ruth hit his first home run for the Yankees—that is to say, since 1920, when it was envisioned as part of a massive subway expansion that brought us the IND, the trains that now run under Sixth and Eighth avenues. But the Second Avenue subway was derailed by the Great Depression, and despite a string of vigorous efforts, the plan just never got back on track.
>
> [In 1951] New Yorkers approved $500 million in government bonds for the project. Officials quietly spent most of the half-billion dollars on repairs. When news leaked that the money was gone and there was still no subway, a furor erupted. "It is

highly improbable that the Second Avenue subway will ever materialize," the Times lamented.[119]

If a public business raised money for a purpose described in the prospectus and spent the money on something else, the managers would go to jail. Nothing happened to the government employees who misused the people's money.

The article estimates the current cost of the 8.5 mile line at $17 billion, or $2 billion per mile. Despite the optimistic tone in the 2004 article, no construction activity had taken place as of 2010.

Subways cost less in China:

> Mr. Chan [Guangzhou subway construction project supervisor] said that it cost about $100 million a mile to build a subway line in Guangzhou, including land acquisition costs for ventilation shafts and station entrances.
>
> By contrast, New York City officials hope to build 1.7 miles of the long-delayed Second Avenue line in eight years at a cost of $3.9 billion, or $2.4 billion a mile. The city expects to use a single tunneling machine.[120] [The Guangzhou project uses 60 tunneling machines simultaneously.]

Bureaucracy is so complex that it's harder and harder to build anything on time and on budget unless the government gets out of the way. Increased costs reduce return on the investment. The extra overhead of regulation can turn a previously profitable infrastructure investment unprofitable or make a project that would have enormous benefits like the Second Avenue subway take too long for any one political administration to get anywhere.

---

[119] "The Line that Time Forgot" *New York Magazine*, March 29, 2004
[120] "Clash of Subways and Car Culture in Chinese Cities" *New York Times* March 26, 2009

Then there's the Angel's Flight, a 298 foot long railroad that carried office workers up Bunker Hill in Los Angeles. The railroad opened on the last day of 1901; those who couldn't afford the one-penny fare walked up 207 steps for free. The railroad shut down for repairs in the name of urban renewal on May 18, 1969.[121]

It reopened in February 1996, with the fare raised to a quarter. It took 27 years to rebuild a railroad shorter than a football field, or slightly more than 10 feet per year. Angel's Flight shut down after a Feb. 1, 2001 accident killed a passenger and injured another. On February 25, 2009, the *Los Angeles Times* reported that the renovated railway had been tested thoroughly but nobody knew when it would open. "It's impossible to give a date other than soon."[122] It briefly reopened in 2011 but today is once again indefinitely shut down.

Angel's Flight and the Second Avenue Subway are run by government agencies that spend tax money. There are no investors to push the projects forward. Does anyone care how long the project takes or how much it costs? Of course – the longer it takes, the longer government employees keep their jobs. The higher the cost, the more money politicians can direct to their friends. Who cares about taxpayers or people who might benefit from the project?

There's another problem with infrastructure funding – federal money builds but doesn't maintain. The I35W bridge across the Mississippi River in Minneapolis collapsed in August, 2007.[123] Uncle Sam bought the city a new bridge so they didn't have to pay to fix the old one. State and city governments gain by letting infrastructure fall to pieces.

---

[121] "Angel's Flight Bridges the City's History" *Los Angeles Times*, Feb. 2, 2001, p A-29 available online at http://articles.latimes.com/2001/feb/02/news/mn-20070

[122] "Angel's Flight takes a step towards reopening" *Los Angeles Times*, Feb. 25, 2009 http://latimesblogs.latimes.com/lanow/2009/02/mechanics-teste.html

[123] "Dozens missing as Minneapolis search efforts are halted," *New York Times*, August 2, 2007

Some Successes

The California earthquake of Jan 17, 1994 showed how much delay is introduced by "normal" procurement procedures. The quake damaged so many important highways in the Los Angeles area that the government suspended contracting policies during the emergency:

> The Department is committed to speeding turnaround times for funding approvals and implementing innovative contracting procedures, and providing other forms of regulatory relief designed to cut highway repair times. An innovative form of low-bid contracting...Using this method of contracting permits damaged facilities to be returned to use in record time. For example, the Gavin Canyon-Interstate 5 bridges are planned to be rebuilt in only 130 days, and the I-40 bridges in 140 days. The incentive clauses may induce the contractors to finish even earlier. Under standard contracting procedures, the reconstruction of bridges of these types would take many months longer.[124]

The results?

> ...the governor ordered the suspension of normal state contracting procedures... The damaged section of Interstate 10 was finished seventy-four days ahead of schedule, earning the contractor nearly $1.5 million in bonuses. Interstate 5 connecting Santa Clarita to the rest of Los Angeles County was

124 Statement of Rodney E. Slater, Federal Highway Administrator, before a Southern California Earthquake Hearing chaired by Senator Dianne Feinstein, April 4, 1994, http://testimony.ost.dot.gov/test/pasttest/94test/Slater1.pdf p 6

completed one month ahead of schedule on 17 May, garnering its contractor additional millions in bonuses. Although it cost the state more than $20 million in early completion bonuses, most major freeway sections were repaired in five months, allowing traffic to begin to return to "normal."[125]

Think about those "early completion" bonuses. The bureaucracy wrote the contracts assuming "normal" completion; contractors beat the schedule by many days. Contractors build unnecessary delays into the bid price. They know how to get around the delays when it's in their interest to get the job done quickly but they don't bother the rest of the time.

Suspending bureaucratic oversight sped the projects by "many months." The Department didn't explain why such effective streamlined procedures couldn't be used under normal circumstances.

The "emergency" bridges aren't less safe than normal ones. What benefits do these regulations offer in exchange for massive cost increases and delays? Nobody asks – politicians know there's no good answer, but they haven't the power to tell the bureaucrats to buzz off except under extreme circumstances. It takes an earthquake to bypass the bureaucracy.

This isn't just a California phenomenon; similar accelerated procedures have been used successfully on the East Coast.

> [Donald] Trump rebuilt the Wollman Skating Rink (currently managed by The Trump Organization) in Central Park, a project that was particularly special to him. The city had been trying for <u>seven years</u> to rebuild and restore the Rink, whereupon Trump interceded and did so in <u>three</u>

---

[125] Bolin, Robert, Stanford, Louis, *The Northridge Earthquake* (Routledge, 1998) pp100-101

<u>months</u> and at only 10% of the city's $20 million cost.[126] [emphasis added]

Ordinary Hawaiian citizens gave further evidence of government ineptitude when compared with private capabilities:

> LIHU'E, Kaua'i — When the state has no money to fix a road to a popular park on Kaua'i, local residents don't just sit on their hands. They bring in the heavy equipment and do it themselves.
>
> Volunteers are making major repairs to open an access road to West Kaua'i's premier state beach park, Polihale, which has been closed since December.
>
> The state said in February it didn't have money to fix the road, which was washed out by heavy rains late last year.
>
> So beginning March 23, a team of volunteers brought in a crane, steel bridge parts, welding equipment, a dump truck, excavators, a cement mixer and more to do the job — all at no charge. The volunteers are continuing the work this week and hope to have the road open by the end of the month.[127]

Common Elements

The successful projects had a common element – government got out of the way. Construction people will tell you that government inspectors from OSHA on down have the power to shut a project down for essentially any reason, or for no reason, and there's no

---

[126] Press release from Trump International Hotel Las Vegas, available online at http://www.trumplasvegashotel.com/_files/pdf/press_releases/TRUMP_HOT EL_COLLECTION_Donald_Trump_Bio.pdf p 2

[127] "Residents on Kauai work for free to fix road to Hawaii state park," *Honolulu Advertiser*, April 7, 2009

penalty for being wrong. This invites both delays and bribery. New York City had tried to repair the skating rink for seven years; Mr. Trump did it in three months at 10% of the city's cost estimate because the government got out of the way.

The paperwork needed to get a project going has multiplied amazingly. Environmental impact statements have pretty much killed large private-sector projects. Even projects with government approval can be delayed essentially forever.

> The plans for the Manchester [New Hampshire] Airport Access Road (MAAR) have been fought over passionately for 20 years. A major issue was the impact of the river bridge on eagles that nest along the river.
>
> Other issues have been the scale of new access provided for economic development.... A thousand acres (405ha) of land for industry has been opened up for development by the ramps – the largest in southern New Hampshire – pitting developers and tax-base enhancing local officials against enviros and other anti-development elements...
>
> The project got full permitting – the federal Record of Decision – in April 2003 but even then it took four years for construction contracts to be awarded.[128] [emphasis added]

Any project large or small attracts protests from people nearby who are opposed to any changes. In a recent meeting about a new cell tower near my house, someone who lived miles away protested, "It's in my view-shed, I should be compensated!"

Why should this person be heard at all? He hadn't paid for the land on which the tower was to be constructed and didn't offer to; he had no right to an eternally unaltered view. Who does? Yet similar protests and lawsuits routinely delay projects to the point

---

[128] *Toll Roads Newsletter*, August 2007,
http://www.tollroadsnews.com/node/3083

where their promoters give up and society has to do without the benefits.

In the past, politicians won reelection by accomplishing something. Now, they build their careers on opposing new projects, pandering to protesters, talking, studying, and hiring consultants at vast expense as opposed to getting anything built.

It's possible that no private organization will ever again be able to build anything of major significance in the United States. Although the private sector can afford small projects like Mr. Trump's skating rink, most major projects are funded by the government because only the government can afford the delays and other costs that are imposed by government regulations.

Not Politics, Opportunity!

Politics has always been involved in infrastructure projects. Since politics attracts thieves and bureaucratic sluggishness, the theft, regulatory obstructions, delays, and outright graft that so increase the costs of non-emergency infrastructure construction have always been with us. The *Economist* of Feb. 26, 2009 discussed the Erie Canal, which opened in 1825, and the Panama Canal that connected the Atlantic to the Pacific in 1914.

When the Erie Canal was proposed in 1807, Virginians opposed the idea of a construction project that would increase the commercial importance of New York City. Thomas Jefferson, Virginian that he was, dismissed the canal as "little short of madness."[129]

The Panama Canal received support from Presidents Theodore Roosevelt and William Taft who arranged for federal funding. The canal also needed diplomatic support and government muscle – what became Panama was part of Colombia and the Colombians weren't enthusiastic about "Yankee imperialism."

---

[129] *Economist* Feb. 26, 2009

The Americans arranged a revolution that declared the relevant part of Colombia to be independent and recognized the new country of Panama in record time. This brought Sen. Hayakawa of California to say, "Of course it's ours. We stole it, fair and square."[130] Without government political, diplomatic, and financial support, the Panama Canal couldn't have been built and World War II might have ended differently.

Books such as *The Railroad and the Space Program*[131] and *The Decision to Go to the Moon*[132] show that the United States government has always been deeply involved in promoting, permitting, and funding infrastructure projects. This is good as long as the project is useful and the benefits outweigh the actual costs as opposed to the estimated costs. Problems arise when they don't.

It's hard to compare the graft and waste of the transcontinental railroad with waste during Boston's Big Dig, but it's clear that honesty was not a major characteristic of the politicians or contractors involved in either case. The earlier projects were so successful in terms of economic return to society, however, that corruption didn't affect the big picture. When the project returns so many times its cost, padding the bills by even a factor of ten doesn't negate the return on the investment.

Although the space program didn't yield direct profit, the technologies developed to achieve "Man on the moon by the end of the decade" increased computer use and boosted activity in other sectors of the economy. Since every dollar spent you or I spend on computers becomes income to someone else, governments at all levels gained greatly from these investments via sales and income taxes.

The Tenn-Tom canal was funded in precisely the same way as the Erie and Panama Canals, that is, after much political infighting over funding, control, and allocation of construction contracts with

---

[130] "Time Magazine," August 22, 1977
[131] *The Railroad and the Space Program* (Cambridge, Mass: MIT Press, 1965)
[132] *The Decision to Go to the Moon* (Cambridge, Mass: MIT Press, 1970)

the odd kick-back here and there. The Erie made vast profits for society; Tenn-Tom doesn't even cover its own maintenance. Why?

Did the Tenn-Tom politicians steal more than the politicians involved in the Erie project? Were the Tenn-Tom contractors more crooked? No, the difference is that the Erie and Panama Canals opened up untapped markets. The Erie Canal reduced transportation costs by 75% because it competed with unpaved roads. The Panama Canal cut shipping distance from New York to San Francisco in half and avoided dangerous storms around the southern tip of South America. Neither canal had any competition, but by the time Tenn-Tom came along, there were so many alternate transportation modes available that there was no way it could make a profit given its overall cost.

There appear to be few if any remaining areas where government-sponsored infrastructure projects can show vast enough benefit to outweigh bureaucratically bloated costs. The construction industry and bureaucrats don't want to give up their incomes, of course, so we fund projects such as the Tenn-Tom canal and the Big Dig which drain society.

Instead of benefiting the economy as in times past, government spending on infrastructure now consumes resources without yielding comparable benefits. Infrastructure investments could be beneficial; but political corruption and sluggishness add so much overhead that they aren't. As government grows faster than the economy can grow to support it, as regulations proliferate and make it more difficult to generate enough economic activity to support our growing population, we're seeing our standard of living decline.

Infrastructure projects generally involve government, so it's natural that bureaucratic waste would increase the cost of roads, airports, and other projects that should benefit society. Non-government actors can also increase the costs of other goods and services beyond what society can afford. The next chapters will discuss the benefits and economic perils of manufacturing.

6 – Who Eats the Pie?

The Confucian cycle of starting a dynasty, prosperity, stagnation, and collapse could take as long as 300 years. The same forces of human nature drive businesses, but businesses couldn't get big enough to require internal bureaucracies until the industrial revolution made mass production possible. The business cycle of growth, stagnation, and decline goes much faster than the dynastic cycle; "shirt sleeves to shirt sleeves in three generations," as the saying goes.

Since the industrial revolution, manufacturers have coped with changing technology, markets, customer tastes, new raw materials, training workers to carry out new processes, management fads, wars, unpredictable laws, and a host of other variables. One problem stayed the same – how do we share the wealth produced in factories?

When a factory produces iron using iron ore and coal, for example, how should we divide the pie among those who own the land, who dig coal and iron out of the ground, who provide machinery for the factory and who work in the factory? What about those built the factory, manage it, or sell its products? When iron is used in pots and pans, how do we divide the profits between factory owners and workers? What about the checkout register girl and the bureaucrats who collect taxes from everybody.

These issues are so contentious that governments get involved. A government's attitude towards industry is called "industrial policy."[133] This includes rules about employment, safety, factory operation, hiring, firing, competition, marketing, billing, payment, contracts, and many other matters.

---

[133] Swann, Dennis *Competition and industrial policy in the European Community*, (Taylor & Francis, 1983) p 3

Classical China had little need for industrial policy because China refused to industrialize. This was partly because Confucius taught that merchants and people who worked with their hands were inferior to scholars and bureaucrats. Businessmen were useful, but no man of good breeding would take them seriously.

The Chinese had sophisticated bronze casting factories early in their history and their pottery was well known from ancient times, but they never developed mass production. The Chinese could handle the complexities of large enterprises – the Chinese bureaucracy was the largest organization on earth for centuries.

Innovations such as the automobile, the cell phone, and electricity brought profound social change. Change was anathema to the scholars and rulers in the Chinese rulers and scholars. If you're on top, any change is for the worse – there's nowhere for you to go but down – so it makes sense to suppress change if at all possible.

Change is constant in a society where people are free to innovate. A market-based economy is pitiless in wiping out businesses that don't keep up. Very few products create entirely new markets without displacing something else. Pocket calculators made mechanical calculators, slide rules, and abacuses useless. PCs forced IBM to change its core business from leasing mainframes to consulting. Cell phone users are giving up land lines. When was the last time you used a pay phone or a phone book?

Joseph Schumpeter invented the concept of "creative destruction"[134] to describe the process by which new businesses and products replace older ones. Customers who buy portable transistor radios instead of plug-in tube radios like creative destruction, but RCA's stockholders and employees who profited from the tube radio business until Sony replaced them, were unhappy as jobs and pensions vanished.

---

134 McCraw, Thomas K., *Prophet of Innovation: Joseph Schumpeter and Creative Destruction* (Belknap Press of Harvard University Press, 2007) "Creative destruction," he said, "is the driving force of capitalism." Offering products that are more wonderful than money helps, of course.

Failing business owners or workers with political influence often ask for government help, urging politicians to ban competitors or give subsidies as with Amtrak. Paying politicians to write rules to kneecap your competitors leads to costly inefficiencies, but it's become so common that the term "crony capitalism" was coined to describe it.

Factories and Energy Consumption

High-volume manufacturing consumes enormous amounts of energy. The more energy each person consumes, the more prosperous the society.

Classical China more or less ignored vast coal resources. People who lived near coal seams used coal for cooking, but most potters, bronze casters, and other manufacturers used charcoal made by burning trees. Without industrial energy sources, power came from muscle. Human muscles did the work because China had few animals.

Muscle-powered agriculture made life "nasty, brutish, and short"[135] for farmers at the bottom of society. Madame Chiang Kai-Shek, wife of the Chinese general who lost a civil war against Communist Party Chairman Mao Tse-Tung, graduated from Wellesley College in 1917. She addressed the student body in 1943.

Madame Chiang illustrated the benefits of American manufacturing by telling about her uncle. He was a man with many interests but he spent his life pumping pedals to lift water a few feet to a rice paddy. Pumping his life away wasted his intelligence and creativity. A mechanical pump running for a few hours, she said, could replace his entire working life, but the village had no pump, gasoline, or electricity. Anything that couldn't be made in the village was unattainable and survival required a great deal of hard labor.

That's the way it was for almost everyone in the world until the Industrial Revolution freed millions from subsistence farming.

---

[135] Hobbes, Thomas, *Leviathan,* wrote "solitary, poor, nasty, brutish, and short."

Imagine what it was like to be bound to the land, working from dawn to dusk every day of the year with no electric lights.

The Chinese muscle-powered way of life was sustainable. Society was solar-powered: the sun made trees and crops grow. If the Chinese maintained the dikes that kept water flowing to their fields, poured all the night soil back onto the fields, and cut trees no faster than they grew, life could go on indefinitely. Everything was recycled in an endless pattern for five thousand years. This sense of life's unchanging nature contributed to their reluctance to innovate.

Society is no longer sustainable now that the Chinese use coal. There is a lot of coal, but it will be gone someday. Unless a new energy source comes along before the coal runs out, civilization will collapse back to muscle-powered agriculture.

Recent industrial growth has contributed greatly to the Chinese quality of life. People lived longer as new energy sources meant they didn't have to work as hard. Average world life expectancy was about 30 years in 1900 and people lived to age 50 in developed countries. 110 years later, life expectancies have risen to 67 years worldwide and 78 years in developed countries.[136]

The Spread of Knowledge

Industrialization requires far more knowledge than agriculture does. Farm kids learned enough from family and friends to start farming in their teens. Industry requires a great deal of specialized knowledge among maintenance staff and process designers. Low-level assembly line tasks, in contrast, require less knowledge than farming.

Keeping factories running requires skills in metallurgy, power generation and transmission, machine design and repair, and many others. Oral tradition and apprenticeship are enough for farming and handicrafts but can't convey the amount of knowledge needed

---

[136] "A Slow-Burning Fuse," *Economist,* June 27, 2009 p 3

for industry. Maintaining factories requires literacy and the ability to print books and training materials at low cost.

Johannes Gutenberg developed a movable-type printing press around 1450. Before Gutenberg, documents were hand-drawn and hand-illuminated. Movable type made it easier to generate body text, but initial capitals continued to be hand-drawn.

Gutenberg laid the foundation for the Industrial Revolution by making it possible to spread information at lower cost. Books were still expensive because a Gutenberg Bible used the skin of 50 to 75 sheep.[137] It was available only to the rich whereas hand-drawn Bibles had been limited to the super-rich. Although Gutenberg made a breakthrough that would eventually make books widely available, there remained a chicken-and-egg problem.

Cheaper books needed cheaper paper. There was no reason to develop cheaper paper until there were enough literate people to create a demand for books, but there was no reason to learn to read until books were widely available at a price people could pay.

Once cheaper paper became available, more books were available so more people found it worthwhile to learn to read. This virtuous cycle took so long that the industrial revolution had to wait centuries after Gutenberg.

This didn't stop movable type technology from spreading because it was so much faster than hand-lettering. Printing businesses started in Mexico City in 1539 and in Cambridge, Massachusetts, in 1638.[138] This laid the foundation for spreading enough knowledge to achieve critical mass for rapid technical progress.

Isaac Adams patented a steam-powered printing press in 1836. This became the standard press for the rest of the century and further reduced the cost of books.[139] The steam press couldn't

---

[137] Hassan, Robert, Thomas, Julian, *The New Media Theory Reader*, (McGraw – Hill International, 2006) p 13

[138] Ibid., p 14

[139] Marolda, Anthony J., *The Inventor and the Inventor's Son: The Two Isaac Adams* (Procyon Press, 2007)

become common until enough knowledge had been accumulated to make it possible to maintain and operate a steam engine in every print shop.

The Chinese abandoned movable type printing centuries before Gutenberg because it couldn't handle the details of their hand-drawn documents.[140] Writing Chinese is as much an artistic endeavor as it is communication. Some characters vary subtly based on adjacent characters, for example. The Chinese used wood blocks to print entire pages, but never used individual letters as Gutenberg had.[141] Movable type looked good enough for Europe, but not for China.

Manufacturing and the Quality of Life

Manufacturing societies have far more material possessions than pre-industrial societies. No nation can consume more goods than are manufactured in the country, plus what's imported, minus what's exported, regardless of government welfare policy. Goods that aren't produced simply can't be consumed.

Satisfying American-style consumer demand requires high-volume manufacturing and houses with enough closet space to store it all. Factories need high-density energy sources. Wood doesn't burn hot enough for most industrial purposes and the supply is limited by tree growth. Windmills and water wheels have been used

---

[140] There's speculation why the Chinese didn't use a phonetic alphabet. Mere peasants could have learned to read which would make scholars less elite. The second problem was that when the barbarians took over, they could have learned to read. The new Emperor would demand "Show me the files," but he couldn't read them. He'd command, "Teach me to read" and give up after learning 30 or 40 out of 50,000 characters. The mandarins would say, "We'll teach your sons to read, sir!" By the time barbarian princes learned to read, they'd be Chinese in outlook. Obfuscation is the favorite tool of bureaucrats when faced with difficult masters; there are no obfuscators as skilled as those who invented the most difficult written language on the face of the earth.

[141] Hassan, Robert, Thomas, Julian, *The New Media Theory Reader*, (McGraw – Hill International, 2006) p 13

since ancient times but don't provide enough energy for large-scale manufacturing.

The Industrial Revolution came slowly. Rev. William Lee invented a knitting machine in 1589. Queen Elizabeth I refused to grant him a patent because she didn't want knitters to lose their jobs, so his invention had no impact on society.[142]

Abraham Darby learned to substitute coke for wood when smelting iron ore in 1709[143], but high-volume manufacturing couldn't really get going until 1712 when Thomas Newcomen built the first commercially-successful steam engine.[144]

Coal-powered steam was the first practical power source other than wind, wood, water, or muscle. The steam engine could pump water out of deep coal mines which made more coal available at a lower price. By this time, paper had become cheap enough to spread knowledge of the new manufacturing techniques engineers and inventors were developing. Cheaper energy and cheaper books helped make the Industrial Revolution possible.

Coal is mined faster than it forms in the ground, of course, so the economy immediately became unsustainable over the long term. Modern environmentalists view this as a reason why the Industrial Revolution was a Bad Idea; Madam Chiang's uncle who pumped his life away and the generations of women who spun wool into thread and knitted all their clothes would beg to differ.

Sir Richard Arkwright used waterpower for weaving cloth in 1769.[145] The steam engine later made it possible to put factories

---

142 Walton, Perry, *The Story of Textiles*, (J.S. Laurence, 1912) p 93 He was inspired to invent the machine because he was courting a young lady who paid more attention to her knitting than to him. He wanted to make knitting unnecessary. Queen Elizabeth's concern for knitters' jobs illustrates the fact that successful governments worry about the impact of innovation on their citizenry. After all, unemployed people consume tax revenue.

143 Evans, Charles, Rydén, Göran, *The industrial revolution in iron: the impact of British coal technology in nineteenth – century Europe* (Ashgate Publishing, Ltd., 2005) p 19

144 Raymond, Robert, *Out of the fiery furnace*, (Penn State Press, 1986) p 158

145 Beggs, Mary, and Humphreys, Hugh, *The Industrial Revolution*, (Taylor & Francis, 2006) p 19

where waterpower wasn't available. Powered weaving spread so slowly that traditional artisans didn't start smashing the machines that were replacing their traditional ways of earning a living until 1811. By that time, industrial wealth had spread so much that the English were never going back.

Robert Trevithick demonstrated a steam locomotive in 1804.[146] His technology was used in George Stephenson's *Rocket* which made its first public run on the Liverpool and Manchester Railway in 1830. On this inaugural trip, the *Rocket* killed William Huskisson, Liverpool's Member of Parliament. He was looking the other way when the train blindsided him, proving Confucius' point that technological change could cause problems for the ruling elite.

Manufacturing Built America

Americans watched developments in England and tried to imitate them. Robert Fulton ran a steamboat on the Hudson River in America in 1807.[147] New England textile mills started high-volume production with machinery built from drawings that had been smuggled out of England. Protecting commercial secrets can be as worthwhile as protecting national defense secrets.

The Amoskeag Company of Manchester, New Hampshire started a mill in 1838. Sales grew until the firm had 20,000 spindles and 600 looms in 1850.[148] Amoskeag Mills peaked at more than 17,000 employees[149] who collectively produced a mile of cloth per minute.

American industry was built on gender discrimination. Women were hired first because they were better at tending spinning and weaving machines than men were.[150]

[146] Howe, Michael, *Genius Explained*, (Cambridge University Press, 2001) p 73
[147] Dickinson, Henry, *Robert Fulton, engineer and artist*, (John Lake, 1913) p 216
[148] Browne, George Waldo, *The Amoskeag Manufacturing Co. of Manchester, New Hampshire: A History*, (Amoskeag Manufacturing Company, 1915) p 86
[149] Hareven, Tamara K. , Langenbach, Randolph, *Amoskeag* (UPNE, 1995) p 10
[150] Ibid., p 117

For the first time in history, women could support themselves and didn't need men to feed them.[151] Many were appalled at the thought of women earning their own money because women who supported themselves would want to run other aspects of their lives. Although it would be more than 100 years before situations like "Sex and the City" or "Charlie's Angels" were even theoretically possible, the Industrial Revolution eventually allowed women's emancipation.

Cloth prices dropped as production multiplied. Customers could afford more clothes. Mills grew with increased demand. This brought economies of scale and forced the company to recruit workers from as far away as Montreal and the farms of Europe.

Amoskeag's profits peaked during World War I but declined after the war.[152] Lower-cost southern competitors gained market share because they had newer machinery and were located closer to raw materials. The resulting overcapacity cut prices for all textile mills.   Amoskeag repeatedly cut production, wages, and employment, bringing conflict between management and workers.

On Feb 2, 1922, Amoskeag management made a unilateral announcement of reduced wages and increased the workweek from 48 hours to 54. Workers went on strike but the company outlasted them and most of the mills were running again by November.[153] The strike destroyed workers' trust in the firm as surely as corruption destroys citizens' faith in government. This made it harder to run the mills.

During the decade after the strike, the firm started a company union to try to control the labor force and keep out the United Textile Workers Union. Increased productivity lowered the overall cost of living by 20% but wages declined 40%. Workers abolished the company union, recognized the UTWU, and went on strike in

---

[151] Hareven, Tamara K. , Langenbach, Randolph, *Amoskeag* (UPNE, 1995) p 118
[152] Hareven, Tamara K., *Families, history, and social change: life – course and cross – cultural perspectives* (Westview Press, 2000) p 35
[153] Hareven, Tamara K, Langenbach, Randolph, *Amoskeag* (UPNE, 1995) p 297

1933. The governor called out the state militia when the strike became violent.

Management couldn't lower wages after the strike, so they sped up the machinery to lower costs to match their competitors. Sit-downs and local stoppages continued. In 1934, the mill workers joined a national strike. Although the strike was called off after a few weeks,[154] Amoskeag mills closed permanently in 1935 leaving its 17,000 workers unemployed.[155]

Amoskeag could've kept going if workers hadn't resisted lower wages so vigorously. Unlike bureaucrats who use government power to force taxpayers to fund their activities, the mills couldn't keep operating when costs became too high.

Many employees had used family connections and knowledge of job openings to get their relatives jobs in the mills; entire families became unemployed at once. Parents had encouraged children to lie about their ages, drop out of school, and work in the mills. They were shocked to find that their uneducated children were unprepared for other employment.

Modern unions try to use political connections to ask government to ban competitors or give money to failing businesses directly. Keeping businesses open to "protect jobs" may seem charitable in the short term but the long-term cost of such market meddling is borne by society as a whole.

The Business Cycle and Loss of Virtue

Amoskeag had 6 managers throughout its history. These managers made all local decisions while reporting to the directors in Boston.

---

154 Hareven, Tamara K, Langenbach, Randolph, *Amoskeag* (UPNE, 1995) pp 25 – 26
155 Steinbicker, Earl *Daytrips New England*: (Hastingshouse/Daytrips Publ., 2001) p 271

The last three managers came from the Straw family.[156] Ezekiel Straw became manager in 1856 and started a pattern of corporate care for workers that his son Herman maintained.

Confucian virtue applies within any group. Taking care of the employees built the company into an extended family whose workers were intensely loyal and took great pride in high-quality work. Happy, hard-working employees took care of customers, customers took care of the company, and the company could afford to take care of the workers.

The third Straw, William, couldn't maintain worker loyalty as the company declined. To be fair, it's hard to maintain loyalty while cutting pay and speeding production, even though these measures were needed to save jobs.[157]

Workers who had known the long-term, stable relationship with previous generations of Straws didn't believe that the century-old company could go bankrupt, but Amoskeag Mills couldn't cope with strikes while selling against lower-cost competitors. The Depression finally put this once-mighty industrial enterprise out of business

Imperial China avoided the fluctuations and uncertainties of the capitalistic business cycle by choosing not to industrialize. There were famines, to be sure, but the economy was simple enough to avoid economic disasters like the Great Depression that finished off Amoskeag Mills.

Lack of industrial opportunity doomed the vast majority of Chinese to work themselves to death in muscle-powered agriculture instead of taking less demanding jobs in "sweatshops." China's technologically inferior army was no match for the European powers. In addition, federal, state, and local governments benefitted from the century of taxes paid by Amoskeag; the Chinese government lost the opportunity to tax such businesses because there weren't any.

---

[156] Steinbicker, Earl *Daytrips New England*: (Hastingshouse/Daytrips Publ., 2001) p 16

[157] Retreat is the most difficult form of warfare – old military saying

The Power of Communication

Corporate loyalty was so strong that even after the collapse, many people still took pride in having worked "at Amoskeag." Virtuous leaders maintain good communications at all times so that employees will listen during bad times. If Amoskeag management had been more open, workers might have accepted cuts and helped figure out new products. At least the firm could have closed down more smoothly than throwing entire neighborhoods out of work at once.

Sensible workers understand the value of employer survival. For example, rotary-engine Mazda sports cars enjoyed brisk sales until the gasoline crisis of the early 1970's. Sales essentially stopped because their zippy rotary engine had low gas mileage.

Workers complained that their bosses had put their incomes a risk. Management apologized and asked if they should resign. The workers said "No." They suggested that everybody take big pay cuts and work like beavers to get a new model out. The banks offered to carry the company because everybody promised to share the pain. Mazda survived because workers understood the situation well enough to put short-term interests aside during the crisis.

Mazda had an additional advantage - their union represented only Mazda workers so the union wanted Mazda to survive. United Textile Workers Union members worked for many different businesses. UTWU leaders didn't particularly care whether Amoskeag employees kept their jobs because they had organized Amoskeag's competitors. If Amoskeag went under, their markets would go to other businesses who would hire more people. These new employees would pay dues to the UTWU. The UTWU had no skin in the game whereas the Mazda union would go under along with Mazda.

Mazda workers knew what they had to do to save the firm because Mazda had told them more about the business than most American firms do. The employees had confidence in their long-term survival and were willing to suffer in the short term.

I've watched American auto workers watching company TV network during breaks. They'd mutter about inadequate pay whenever management bragged about sales. American management rarely explains where the revenue goes – raw materials, taxes, rent, wages and such – so employees wonder why they can't have more.

I never understood why management didn't talk about the taxes they paid or display a pie chart showing how wages dwarfed profits. If employees knew the issues their bosses faced in splitting the pie, they might be more content with their share. If other taxpayers and politicians realized just how much businesses and their employees pay into society, they might appreciate businesses more.

Secrecy may work when profits are high, but trust takes years to build. Cuts needed to survive a downturn may lead to open warfare as at Amoskeag unless virtuous leaders explain what's going on years in advance. When followers understand a crisis, they usually know what to do about it without being told. This may save the firm during bad times.

The next chapter shows how the Detroit automobile manufacturers failed to learn from the Amoskeag experience. They went through the same cycle of high profits, struggle against lower-cost competitors, labor strife, and finally bankruptcy.

7 – Automobiles and the Middle Class

Cloth is a relatively simple product. Although there are many different fibers and weaving patterns, manufacturing cloth involves simpler processes than manufacturing products such as steam engines or automobiles. The Chinese didn't develop high-speed spinning and weaving equipment like the Amoskeag mill machinery, but they set up high-volume manufacturing of greater complexity when they built a fleet of ships to explore the Pacific and Indian Oceans.

From 1405 to 1433, Emperor Zhu Di sent seven expeditions of Chinese "Dragon Ships" to explore the "four corners" of the world. Fleets had up to 300 ships as long as 400 feet. Some were as wide as 160 feet. These floating cities were crewed by up to 28,000 men.

Under Admiral Zheng He, the Chinese navy explored the China Sea, the Indian Ocean, traveled as far as Africa, and may have discovered Australia. Indian and Arab nations kept records, so this fleet is well documented outside of the Chinese records.[158]

In 1414, Admiral Zheng brought the Emperor a giraffe which had been given by the King of Bengal. The Emperor's staff decided

---

[158] Summarized from Levathes, Louise, *When China ruled the seas: the treasure fleet of the Dragon Throne, 1405-1433* (Oxford University Press US, 1996) The book *1421, the year China Discovered America* gives evidence that the Chinese had a short-lived colony in America. Mirriam-Webster defines the word "honcho," meaning boss, as derived from the Japanese word for squad leader or war party leader and says it originated around 1955. If its use is in fact older, it could have come from the Chinese because the characters and sounds are the same. Most of the records were destroyed when the Emperor decided not to pursue further exploration.

that the giraffe was a good omen; the Emperor said that it was a reward for his virtue and the virtue of his father.[159]

Even though Admiral Zheng established diplomatic relations with foreign countries and brought back strange and interesting artifacts, his voyages were controversial. Opponents complained that the expeditions "wasted tens of myriads of money and grain, and moreover the people who met their deaths on these expeditions may be counted in the myriads. Although he returned with wondrous and precious things, what benefit was it to the state?"[160]

China could have ruled the known world, but turned inward when the next Emperor ascended the throne. Within a hundred years, it became a crime to go to sea in a multi-masted ship. When urged to continue trade, the Emperor asked, "Why should we do that? Everything we want is right here."

The organization and skills needed to construct 300 of the largest wooden ships ever built goes beyond what was needed to organize 17,000 textile workers at Amoskeag mills. Manufacturing 300 ships and all the cordage, sails, supplies, and other elements needed to put to sea required assembly-line techniques and interchangeable parts.

There were no intellectual obstacles to adopting mass production and building a vast navy-based empire as the British did; the Chinese simply chose not to.[161] Turning inward after enjoying the benefits of international trade for several decades is as mysterious as America abandoning its exploration of the moon after several successful round trips, perhaps for some of the same reasons.

The assembly-line techniques the Chinese used to make so many ships involved specialized crews who moved from ship to ship rather than having the ships move along an assembly line. We don't

---

[159] "Giraffes in a coal mine," *Wilson Quarterly*, Spring 2007, p 76
[160] Ibid.
[161] Steam engines weren't available during the peak years of British naval power; Chinese ships were the equal of anything the British had, with the exception of lacking cannon because the Chinese had chosen not to pursue gunpowder.

have all the details how they mass-produced the 8,000 terra-cotta soldiers in the army left to guard the grave of Emperor Shih Huang-ti around 222 BC[162] but we know that mass production techniques were used:

> Qin Shi Huangdi decreed a mass-production approach; artisans turned out figures almost like cars on an assembly line. Clay, unlike bronze, lends itself to quick and cheap fabrication. Workers built bodies, then customized them with heads, hats, shoes, mustaches, ears and so on, made in small molds.[163]

The Chinese had the intellectual ability to engage in mass production at least 1,900 years before Sears, Roebuck & Co. pioneered the manufacturing processes which would eventually be used in the automobile business. When Sears' Chicago mail-order plant opened in 1903, workers stayed where they were and work came to them instead of workers moving from place to place.

Five years before Henry Ford's Model T line, this was the first modern mass-production plant, complete with the breakdown of all work into simple repetitive operations, an assembly line, conveyor belts, standard interchangeable parts and, above all, planned plant-wide scheduling.[164] Admiral Zheng would have understood.

The Ford Motor Company was Henry Ford's third attempt at manufacturing autos; the Model T was his 9th model.[165] 5,986 were sold for $850 in 1908. By 1916, the price had dropped to $360 and 585,388 were produced.[166] So many people admired the way the

[162] Durant, William. *Our Oriental Heritage*, (New York, Simon and Schuster, 1954) p. 636
[163] "Terra Cotta Soldiers on the March," *Smithsonian* magazine, July 2009
[164] Drucker, Peter Ferdinand, *Management: Tasks, Responsibilities, Practices*, (Transaction Publishers, 2007) p 53
[165] Hounshell, David A., *From the American System to Mass Production*, (JHU Press, 1985) p 218
[166] Ibid, p 224

Model T was made that the ideas behind volume production were named the "Ford System" even though Ford came after Sears.

As at Amoskeag mills, working for Ford was better than toiling in the fields. Ford's 1914 moving assembly line in the Highland Park was so productive that he could offer the unprecedented wage of $5 per day. Ford could pay workers more because Ford factories were more productive than competitors'. In 1914, Ford employed 13,000 people and produced 260,000 Model T's; the rest of the industry employed 66,000 people and produced 287,000 cars.[167] By rearranging manufacturing processes to minimize labor needed to produce a car, Ford could pay fewer workers higher wages.

Throughout Model T production, Ford divided the benefits of increased efficiency between three parties: customers paid lower prices, workers were paid more, and Ford's net worth grew as profits increased. A worker earning $5 per day could pay the list price of a Model-T in fewer than 80 days of work. A factory line worker could become a car owner, a privilege which had been reserved for the wealthy.

This favorable ratio between the price and pay allowed factory workers to buy the cars they made. In 2009, in contrast, a Toyota Yaris sold for roughly $13,000 while workers working in factories which produce automobile components get paid between $20,000 and $40,000 per year. Ignoring such extras as sales tax, registration and insurance, a worker earning $20,000 would have to work more than six months to pay for a car, even if he got an employee discount.

Employment grew for decades. Plant engineers strove to increase productivity. Each worker produced more cars every year. Increasing productivity reduced the amount of work per car but also lowered prices. For many years, sales grew fast enough to create jobs faster than productivity growth reduced the need for workers.

---

[167] Pelfrey, William, *Billy, Alfred, and General Motors: the story of two unique men, a legendary company, and a remarkable time in American history* (AMACOM Div American Mgmt Assn, 2006) p 179

Many jobs were automated out of existence when sales no longer grew fast enough to maintain employment. When sales leveled off, productivity increases reduced the number of workers. UAW membership peaked at 1.53 million in 1979 but has fallen to 376,000[168].

The Creation of the Middle Class

Car sales exploded after WW II. Factories switched to civilian goods for which there was great demand. Workers and soldiers had saved most of their pay because with the factories churning out war material, there hadn't been much to buy.

The war destroyed European and Japanese factories, roads, telephones, and other infrastructure which they had to rebuild. American manufacturers had intact factories selling into pent-up demand all over the world. For years, sales were limited by manufacturing capability; cars, telephones, and everything else sold as fast as factories could be opened.

High sales supported high wages and created a middle class. Manufacturing was broken down into simple steps, so high-school graduates could gain middle class status by working in the plants.

Clouds on the Horizon

All was not well on the labor front. Before and during WW II, John L. Lewis organized American coal miners into the United Mine Workers union. He defied the law against strikes during the war and took a half-million miners out in 1943. He wanted his union to

---

[168] "UAW Moves More Softly on Foreign Auto Plants," *Wall Street Journal*, Dec. 9, 2011

operate welfare systems paid for by the companies;[169] the companies refused. After six weeks, the President seized the mines and sent his Secretary of the Interior to work out a deal.

In the end, companies paid so much per ton of union-mined coal to fund medical care and retirement benefits. The union appointed two out of the three trustees. This gave them control of the money which cemented their power over union members.

President Truman's plans for a national health care system had been defeated in 1948, but he still dreamed of providing health care for Americans any way he could. If businesses would get involved, Truman would be happy to see the issue decided by collective bargaining rather than through the political process.[170]

In Detroit, Walter Reuther was inspired by Lewis' example and started organizing the United Auto Workers in the mid-1930's. He led workers in bloody battles with Ford and GM and survived two assassination attempts that crippled his right arm.

Reuther believed that only government had the resources to provide universal health care and pensions for all. Reuther overestimated government's ability to provide health care and pensions because he didn't anticipate the 20-year increase in lifespan that was getting underway. To be fair, nobody else realized that pensioners would collect for 30 years instead of five.

Reuther sincerely believed that company-provided benefits were second best because only unionized workers would benefit. He was skeptical of the mineworkers' agreement that gave the union responsibility for health care. He wanted government to pay medical costs.

---

[169] In wanting the union to take responsibility for health care and pensions, Mr. Lewis followed the thinking of Samuel Gompers who led the American Federation of Labor. Mr. Gompers feared that if government provided health care and other benefits, workers would be less loyal to unions. Miller, Matt, *The Tyranny of Dead Ideas: Letting Go of the Old Ways of Thinking to Unleash a New Prosperity* (Macmillan, 2009) p 67

[170] Miller, Matt, *The Tyranny of Dead Ideas: Letting Go of the Old Ways of Thinking to Unleash a New Prosperity* (Macmillan, 2009) pp 72-74

After the Republicans took control of Congress in 1946, Reuther had to abandon his battle for universal health care and decided to make the companies pay. The "Treaty of Detroit," the popular name for the 1950 UAW contract, gave a 20% pay increase, a pension of $125 per month, and hospital and medical benefits. Reuther couldn't persuade the companies to let the union control the funds.

Reuther had hoped that the companies would decide that the costs were not sustainable and would push for government-paid benefits, but with overseas competitors bombed flat, the auto makers were able to pass the costs on by increasing prices.[171] The UAW also fought for retirement pensions as well as wage increases.

Between the "Treaty of Detroit" and wartime restrictions on wage increases which encouraged employers to give benefits instead, we wound up with today's employer-centered system of health insurance. People with insurance don't pay medical bills and have no reason to worry about cost. Having customers who don't care about cost distorts the health market and lets providers run up expenses, but nobody realized this would happen.

The union had a monopoly over the supply of labor for car makers because their contracts required that the union be recognized in all new facilities. This let them establish "pattern bargaining." They'd select the weakest of GM, Chrysler, or Ford, threaten a strike, win increased pay and benefits, and enforce the same terms on the other two. This transferred wealth from stockholders to the union and workers. Between 1950 and 1990, car prices went up four times while the monthly pension promised to retired auto workers went up eight times. Car buyers paid for most of this because the Big Three had essentially no competition.

It's hard to remember times with no foreign-made cars on American roads but when I entered MIT in the fall of 1963, there were no Japanese cars in America. There were so few cars on Japanese roads that my walking skills hadn't been tuned to avoiding

---

[171] Miller, Matt, *The Tyranny of Dead Ideas: Letting Go of the Old Ways of Thinking to Unleash a New Prosperity* (Macmillan, 2009) pp 75-78

cars. Having moved from a bicycle-oriented society to an automotive culture in one flight, I was hit by cars three times my first year.

Fortunately for me, traffic in front of MIT is congested and these were slow collisions. I walked away, paid Charlie the Tech Tailor to patch my clothes, and learned to dodge cars. The automobile separates pedestrians into two categories – the quick and the dead.

As I learned to dodge traffic, foreign manufacturers learned to sell cars in America.

The End of the Glory Years

The world didn't stand still for the Big Three, of course. The Europeans, Japanese, and Koreans built factories and started selling cars in the US.

GM lost market share which reduced cash flow and cut the number of active workers. Union negotiations allowed workers to retire at younger ages while people lived longer and longer. Instead of a worker retiring at 65 and collecting pensions for 10 years as expected in the 1950s and 60s, workers retired at 55 and collected for 30 years. Having each worker collect a higher pension for three times as many years as planned threw cost estimates off.

As Starbucks spends more on health care than on coffee,[172] GM spends more on health care than on steel. Fortunately for the UAW, the union has always had a friend in the White House who can print money. The United States government has bought far enough into GM that pensions will become everyone's problem, not just a problem for the annihilated GM stockholders.

The solution proposed by the union, Democratic politicians, and many suffering corporate bosses is for government to take over health care and pension costs entirely on the grounds that only the government can afford the astronomic costs. This argument is half-

---

[172] Miller, Matt, *The Tyranny of Dead Ideas: Letting Go of the Old Ways of Thinking to Unleash a New Prosperity* (Macmillan, 2009) p 78

right – private enterprise can't afford pensions or health care – but government can't either. People are living too long for any pension system to survive, and the longer they live, the more health care they need. Unless fundamental changes are made in our pension and health care systems, society will collapse from those costs alone.

Confucius predicted that society would collapse when government employees siphoned off too many resources. He didn't anticipate ordinary citizens getting money from the government, but he'd have recognized that there's no limit to citizens' greed. Once government got into the welfare business, demand for benefits became unlimited just as bureaucratic greed is unlimited.

Not even the world's most profitable business could afford union-driven levels of pay, health care, pensions, and early retirement. Management and the UAW forgot about keeping automobile prices low to benefit customers. They took too much out of the business to benefit themselves. Lack of virtue destroyed the auto firms.

We hope that this mechanism doesn't take down the entire country, but there's not much reason to be optimistic. Few groups back off voluntarily once they've found a source of income that goes on long enough for them to forget about the earlier, leaner times. It appears that prosperity is the enemy of virtue.

8 – Labor Unions and International Trade

Except for the brief period when the ships of the "Dragon Fleet" ruled the Indian Ocean as far as Africa, classical Chinese society had no international trade to manage so their businesses didn't have to worry about foreign competition. Ignoring outside influences made life more serene for Chinese scholars and bureaucrats.[173] American businesses and unions are not so fortunate.

From right after WW II until the mid 1980's, the American automobile industry was the largest in the world and the United Auto Workers union was the only source of labor. These two monopolies led to union success at winning wage increases, health care, and pensions. Being the only source of labor was so valuable that the UAW routinely threatened violence against factories or against anyone who'd do "their" work for less money, just as the textile workers' strike became violent at Amoskeag.

Maintaining union power required that unionized businesses be the only firms that could supply automobiles to American consumers. If automobile companies could have hired workers from some other source or customers could have bought cars from other companies, unions would not have been able to collect such generous pay.

American manufacturers enjoyed a golden age because foreign competitors were rebuilding factories destroyed by WW II. The "Big Three" car companies could pay the union pretty much whatever it

---

[173]   Their serene isolation came to an end when the European powers discovered the Chinese market. They saw that the Chinese lacked guns and artillery and were powerless to stop them from doing whatever they desired to do in China.

demanded and raise prices as needed to make a profit. As overseas businesses repaired the damage and sent engineers to the US to learn the latest production methods, however, competition appeared.

Unions hate competition as much as businesses and bureaucrats do. Time after time, unions and management lobbied the government to bar foreign competitors from American markets instead of changing their uncompetitive ways.

President Carter tried to protect TV manufacturers such as Zenith and RCA from Japanese competition. This didn't work because the Japanese soon lost the TV market to lower-cost Korean competitors.

American car buyers wanted Japanese cars more than they wanted UAW-made cars back in the 1970's. The UAW and the Big Three lobbied President Reagan to "persuade" the Japanese to restrict automobile imports for a few years. Car buyers resented being told they couldn't have Japanese cars and sometimes paid more than the sticker price. Such high demand increased Japanese profits and strengthened their dealer networks. Eventually, the import restrictions were removed.

It's now too late to keep out foreign autos by trade agreements, but expecting that President Reagan's import restrictions might come back at any time, the Japanese built assembly plants in Southern states which had "right to work" laws. The Japanese took care to maintain good relations with their employees, flying line workers from Japan to teach Americans the proper corporate spirit.

Despite the problems in the United States, GM built a successful business selling small, fuel-efficient cars in China. Foreign manufacturers were able to cover the costs of building American plants because their non-union plants are so much more efficient. GM wanted to increase profits by importing Chinese cars to the US instead of setting up an American plant staffed by high-cost UAW members. Michigan Congressman Gary Peters, (D-Bloomfield Township), who owes his office to UAW support, urged GM to drop this plan:

"They can build those vehicles in the United States. They can build small vehicles (here)," Peters said, noting that Ford Motor Co. and the Chrysler LLC-Fiat SpA alliance plan to build small cars in the United States.

"The priority has to be to keep domestic American jobs. The reason the taxpayers have made substantial investments in these companies ... is to keep American workers working in American plants."[174]

With all due respect to the Congressman, history shows that American car buyers won't pay higher prices for cars just to keep UAW members employed. If they were willing to do that, GM wouldn't have gotten into financial trouble in the first place, which eventually resulting in having to be bailed out of bankruptcy by the US government at a cost of $50 billion,[175]

Those who ignore the lessons of history are compelled to repeat them.[176] High labor costs drove GM bankrupt, and the Congressman seems determined to keep their costs high. American taxpayers weren't happy to have the government give so much money to GM and Chrysler, even on the pretext of preserving American jobs; it's not clear that this bailout could happen again.

Like Amoskeag Mills, the Big Three lost market share to lower-cost Southern competitors. Unless GM, Ford, and Chrysler can escape their uncompetitive cost structure, their ultimate fate will be the same no matter how much taxpayer money they receive.

---

[174] *Detroit News*, May 14, 2009 available at
http://www.detnews.com/article/20090514/AUTO01/905140483/1148/auto01/Michigan+congressman+calls+on+GM+to+reverse+Chinese-made+import+decision

[175] "GM Tries 'No-Haggle' Prices," *Wall Street Journal*, July 11, 2012, p B2

[176] Santayana, George

Benefits of Manufacturing

No society can consume more goods than are available. Similarly, any business that pays its workers more than the value they produce goes out of business. Manufacturing jobs pay more than most jobs. This is possible because modern factories are highly productive due to a combination of automation and careful product design.

Politicians worry about the loss of manufacturing jobs because voters earning middle-class wages are happy constituents. Commentators blame other countries for "unfair trade practices" because the American economy doesn't have nearly as many high-paying manufacturing jobs as in earlier decades. Pundits claim that other countries sell products in the US at a loss.

How can competitors make money by selling products for less than they cost? Simple, conspiracy theorists insist: they'll drive US manufacturers out of business, then raise prices to earn back their losses. *Manufacturing and Technology News* expressed this view:

> The United States economy will soon be facing a more severe crisis due to the Obama administration's spending splurge that is harming America's long-term prosperity. Obama's policies are focused on fixing a cyclical housing market downturn, and they do nothing to restore the U.S. manufacturing base, the true source of wealth. ... The only way to fix the economy is to restore the U.S. manufacturing base, and that can only happen by dealing with unfair trade issues. Rising unemployment coupled with losses of stock market and real estate wealth means the country cannot rely on consumer spending to drive economic growth. Incomes only rise with restoration of manufacturing and increased productivity, Navarro [professor at the Merage School of Business at the University of California-Irvine] notes. Manufacturing jobs pay

more and have a higher job multiplier. Only by leveling the trading playing field will U. S. companies begin reinvesting in production and thereby drive productivity and growth.[177]

The magazine feels that if only the Chinese would stop selling us manufactured goods at such low costs, we'd be able to prosper again as manufacturing made up for the drop in consumer spending; but it isn't nearly that simple. Unions have pushed up labor costs, partly by demanding pay increases and partly by negotiating work rules that hinder efficient factory operations.

Union members ask for whatever they can get and try to minimize the work they have to do just as you and I would. This leads to difficulties in auto plants. An engine plant costs between $300 and $800 million depending on the number of models produced, and the cost of the inventory may equal the cost of the plant.[178] Such plants are designed to make four engines at $2,500 each per minute. The plant produces $10,000 worth of products per minute or $166 per second, but only if every worker does his job perfectly four times per minute all day, every day.

If a worker slows the line for 5 seconds, those 5 seconds are gone forever. The plant has lost $833 worth of output. Management strives to get every second of productive time any way they can.

Sometimes a station breaks down and engines can't get past it. Parts accumulate upstream and downstream stations empty out. When a worker's station is empty and he has nothing to do, he can't leave. He can't see very far up the line, so he has no idea when to expect the next part. If he's not at his station when it arrives, unpleasantness comes, wrapped in industrial-grade adult language.

---

[177] "Govt. Stimulus Masks Long-Term Economic Decline And Leads To Loss Of U.S. Sovereignty" *Manufacturing and Technology News*, Volume 16, No. 7 April 3, 2009 available at
http://www.manufacturingnews.com/news/09/0430/navarro.html

[178] Whitney, Daniel, Peschart, Guillermo, Artzner, Denis, "Cost Performance of Automobile Engine Plants," (Massachusetts Institute of Technology, 1997) p 9

Years ago, I worked on a project installing a display at each station that showed what engine types were flowing down the line. If the engine in front of you needs a red oil pan and you only have blue pans, everything waits until you get a red pan. The display now warns you that the red part is coming, so you can order it in advance.

Our system didn't suggest what to do; it gave the plant people a detailed, real-time view of what was happening on the entire line. Everyone had an opportunity to see problems coming and fix them. It cost $10 million and gave the plant an extra $90 million in profit the first year. Our system paid for itself in just over a month. Over the next year or two, it helped increase throughput by about 20% which is huge in a billion-dollar facility.

Winning Hearts and Minds

Union workers are paid hourly with a higher rate for overtime beyond 8 hours per day. UAW members like overtime so they normally don't want the plant to run efficiently. Union members often suspect vendors of plotting with management to cut their pay by increasing throughput. The union not only accepted our system, they gave us an award for improving the quality of plant floor life. Why?

You wouldn't like being chained to your station until the next break, particularly when you'd like to go to the bathroom and you're stuck 5 or 10 minutes with nothing to do. Our system showed what was coming down the line.

When an operator saw an inch of black upstream of his station, he knew that nothing would arrive for 5 minutes and he could go. A two-inch gap let him step outside for a smoke. As long as he got back before the next part arrived – and thanks to our system, he knew he could – he'd get a break that cost nobody anything and made him happier. He wasn't "goofing off" because there was nothing he could do until parts arrived at his station.

The century of bad blood between management and union means that opportunities to help both sides are rare. Increasing productivity means fewer jobs and less overtime; most changes that benefit workers increase costs.

Two Automobile Industries

America has two automobile industries – one bound by a union which monopolizes the labor supply and another based on more virtuous non-union factories. Unionized plants keep prices high so that non-union firms can earn higher profits. Unionized firms are so uncompetitive that billions of dollars of taxpayer's money were needed to keep them in business,[179] whereas non-union plants are surviving the recession without government help.

We've seen this situation before. Since the 1920's, American railroads had been arguing that federal regulations made it impossible for them to compete with trucks and that they would eventually be driven out of business. The collapse came in the late 1960's when the government took over Penn Central, the remains of the once-great New York Central and Pennsylvania railroads.

The Carter administration faced a $300 billion bill for bailing them out. President Carter saw that it would be better to change the law so railroads could be profitable than to subsidize them forever.

> In his message to Congress, Mr. Carter warned of a "catastrophic series of bankruptcies" and "massive federal expenditure" unless deregulation could "overhaul our nation's rail system, leading to higher labor productivity and more efficient use of plant and equipment."[180]

---

[179] "A dogfight no one can win," *Economist*, August 13, 2009, reports "General Motors alone has been propped up to the tune of $55 billion."

[180] "If Obama had Carter's Courage," *Wall Street Journal*, June 3, 2009

Changing longstanding rules is never easy. Unions think "higher labor productivity" is a plot to make them work harder; companies think the unions are trying to bankrupt them. President Carter twisted arms. The 1980 Staggers Act ended a century of federal regulation and railroads became profitable.

Unionized automobile companies are in a similarly impossible position – they can't remain viable when they're required to make fuel-efficient cars that are smaller than customers want and deal with a monopoly labor supplier while competing with foreign manufacturers whose vehicles already meet most mileage requirements.

Unionized plants make a profit on large cars because labor makes up a smaller percentage of overall cost, but unionized plants can't compete on small cars unless unions make major concessions.

The Carter administration deregulated freight, but didn't help passenger trains – taxpayers have preserved union jobs by pouring billions of dollars into subsidizing Amtrak passenger services which run "empty trains for no one."[181] Unless unionized automakers can find "higher labor productivity and more efficient use of plant and equipment" as President Carter put it, we'll be subsidizing unionized automobile plants forever.

Manufacturing Lives On

Despite decades of job losses, reports of the death of American manufacturing are much exaggerated. Manufacturing still accounts for a significant share of American GNP. *Forbes* reports that 12 million Americans work in manufacturing and produce $1.6 trillion. This is one-fifth of world manufacturing, more than any other

---

[181] "Senator Holds Up Bill on Train Safety Device," *Wall Street Journal,* Sept 26, 2008, reports that Amtrak's subsidy is $14 billion over a five-year period.

nation. American manufacturing isn't vanishing, but jobs are – factory employment peaked at 19.5 million jobs in 1979.[182]

Unions and industrial policy agencies such as OSHA and the EPA have pushed the cost of factory workers so high that manufacturers invest huge sums to eliminate jobs. The more a job pays, the more a business invests to eliminate it.

UAW members cost the automakers $70 per hour[183] and an engine plant costs $800 million or more. Management must maximize production to justify the investment and tries to run such expensive facilities at least two shifts per day.

Installing an oil pan or fuel rail manually costs the plant $70 per hour, or $154,000 per year per shift assuming no overtime. Staffing that workstation for two shifts costs $308,000 per year. A machine costing $308,000 to replace one job pays back its cost in a year. If investors can accept a two-year payback, a factory can pay $600,000 for a machine to replace one job. In addition, the machine can run for three shifts instead of just two.

With such powerful incentives to automate, is it any surprise that UAW membership, which peaked near 1.5 million members in 1979, fell to less than half a million in 2008? This is the first time membership has been below 500,000 since 1941.[184] UAW members are simply too expensive – no customer is willing to pay $70 per hour to have nuts tightened as his car comes down the assembly line.

Economically speaking, American manufacturing is in good health. Increased automation means that manufacturing jobs are dying thanks to unions and government efforts to increase costs. Some manufacturing companies compete with highly automated plants that create few jobs. As a nation, we're better off than if we

---

[182] A special report, "Made in America," *Forbes Magazine*, May 28, 2009 http://www.forbes.com/2009/05/28/american-manufacturing-factories-business-makers_land.html

[183] Sherk, James, "UAW Workers Actually Cost the Big Three Automakers $70 an Hour" Web memo #2126, Heritage Foundation, December 8, 2008, available online at http://www.heritage.org/research/economy/wm2162.cfm

[184] "UAW membership lowest since World War Two," *Reuters*, March 28, 2008

had no manufacturing at all; but it's a shame that so many good, solid, middle-class jobs have vanished because workers cost so much.

The Light Dawns

For the last half of the 20th century, American manufacturers produced incandescent light bulbs on high-speed machines with essentially no labor. Although well accepted, these bulbs turn only about 10% of the energy they use into light; the rest turns to heat.[185] Heat loss isn't so bad during the heating season, but costs a lot when the heat has to be removed by air conditioning.

Compact fluorescent bulbs produce four times as much light per unit of power and they last longer. If a compact bulb lasts as long as it should, it saves about $30 worth of energy over a 10-year period.[186] The International Energy Agency estimated that replacing incandescent bulbs with compact fluorescents would reduce worldwide electricity demand by 18%.

Despite these advantages, compact fluorescent bulbs didn't sell because of slight savings, high cost, unacceptable light color, turn-on delays, and a high failure rate. Bowing to environmental concerns, Congress passed a law phasing out incandescent bulbs by 2012.[187]

There are problems. The new bulbs contain mercury, which is a poison. Used light bulbs have become hazardous waste. What fruitcake expects Americans to use hazmat technology and wear moon suits to clean up broken bulbs?

The new bulbs have such complex shapes that they can't yet be made on high-volume machines. American labor costs far too much when hazardous materials are involved. Most compact bulbs are

---

[185] Dauvergne, Peter, *The Shadows of Consumption: Consequences for the Global Environment* (MIT Press, 2008), p 229
[186] "FAQ: The End of the Light Bulb as We Know It", *US News*, December 2007
[187] Ibid.

made in China where workers are cheaper and environmental regulations are not as strict. *TimesOnline* reports:

> When British consumers are compelled to buy energy-efficient lightbulbs from 2012, they will save up to 5m tons of carbon dioxide a year from being pumped into the atmosphere. In China, however, a heavy environmental price is being paid for the production of "green" lightbulbs in cost-cutting factories.
>
> Large numbers of Chinese workers have been poisoned by mercury, which forms part of the compact fluorescent lightbulbs. A surge in foreign demand, set off by a European Union directive making these bulbs compulsory within three years, has also led to the reopening of mercury mines that have ruined the environment.[188]

The European switch to fluorescent bulbs which was supposed to reduce electricity use and preserve the environment in Europe poisoned "large numbers of Chinese workers." The Chinese know about mercury poisoning:

> In China, people have been aware of the element's toxic properties for more than 2,000 years because legend has it that the first emperor, Qin, died in 210BC after eating a pill of mercury and jade he thought would grant him eternal life.

Environmentalist light-bulb mandates have created thousands of "green" jobs on the other side of the world but the jobs are not nearly as green as advertised to the new workers.

Ironically, zapping filaments with a laser shone through the glass after the bulb is sealed makes old-style incandescent lights

---

[188] "'Green' lightbulbs poison workers," *TimesOnline* from the *Sunday Times*, May 3, 2009

produce twice as much light.[189] Now that government has bent the market with regulations and the plants have closed, however, introducing a new version of the old technology would be difficult. We shouldn't expect environmentalists, who created the problem, to care about mercury-poisoned foreigners any more than we hear of American feminists caring about oppressed Muslim women overseas.

The Tradeoffs

Unions and management fought a low-grade civil war in the 1930's. Workers won the right to organize, but union numbers are lower today than they were then.

The problem is, unionization works only in labor-intensive industrial environments or in government employment where cost is unimportant. It would do a farmer no good to strike – his farm would produce no food and he'd starve. Skilled professionals can usually command whatever price they please. They are hired and fired individually so unionization is no use to them.

Work stoppages can cripple large, labor-intensive industries that have tremendous fixed investments and costs. Even when workers can be replaced, striking workers threaten violence to keep "scabs" from taking "their" jobs for less money.

The threat of strikes pushed wages up until unionized firms either went out of business or moved offshore. Most surviving American manufacturers are either non-union or are so highly automated that they operate with essentially no employees.

So far, Boeing Aircraft is an exception. Aircraft are the most complex and expensive mass-produced machines ever built so it's difficult for new competitors to enter the business. Boeing is

---

[189] "Regular Light Bulbs Made Super-Efficient with Ultra-Fast Laser," physicsorg.com, May 29, 2009, to be published in an upcoming issue of *Physical Review Letters*

profitable despite a 57-day machinists' union strike in 2008 that cost $2 billion in profit.[190]

This won't last, however. The Chinese space program has put astronauts in orbit. Boeing's profitability will drop when the Chinese decide to make passenger aircraft. Pay and benefits at Boeing will go down, either gently to keep Boeing alive or all at once as the company folds. We can't afford American-style wages, benefits, and regulations in the face of global competition.

Just because a company like GM is doomed doesn't mean that the entire industry has to die. American auto manufacturing is healthy in nonunion southern factories under foreign flags. American light-bulb manufacturing was in great shape until a Congressional mandate exiled it to China.

American manufacturing plants would be more profitable and more likely to stay if unions relaxed their demands and bureaucrats relaxed their regulations,. Most businesses and most American executives would rather operate in the United States than the backwoods of China. Most businesses would rather pay tax to the American government than to the Chinese government, if it were economically feasible for them to do so. The same union leaders and politicians who created the problem blame the companies for outsourcing.

The bottom line is that unions can destroy as much economic value as bureaucrats. Instead of letting GM and Chrysler go bankrupt so that another firm could have operated the worthwhile plants more efficiently, the UAW used political influence to force the government to spend taxpayer dollars to keep the overpaid status quo.

GM received $15.4 billion in government loans by May, 2009, and had about 60,000 UAW workers.[191] GM shed 20,000 workers. Protecting 40,000 union jobs cost $3,850,000 in government loans

---

[190] "Boeing Strike Ends; Machinists Back on the Job Sunday," *the Seattle Times*, Nov 1, 2008
[191] "GM – UAW Reach Crucial Cost-Cutting Pact," *Wall Street Journal*, May 22, 2009, p B1

per job. GM will probably need billions more.[192] Private businesses create jobs for a lot less than that, but such jobs wouldn't generate UAW dues or campaign contributions.

The country doesn't need GM or Chrysler. Foreign-owned factories can make more than enough cars to satisfy American demand. Putting money into keeping Detroit plants going will lead to overcapacity and we'll waste even more money.

It's better for society to let dying businesses die, but no group lets its rice bowl disappear without a fight, no matter what the cost to society. The next chapter explains how union attitudes helped put many once-profitable businesses out of business. This often preserved union power in the remaining businesses, but ended up destroying jobs and reducing government revenue over time.

---

[192] "A dogfight no one can win," *Economist*, August 13, 2009, reports "General Motors alone has been propped up to the tune of $55 billion."

9 – Labor Unions Sow Disunity

Every family, business, and nation must mount a unified response to major threats. Families experience medical emergencies and loss of work. Competitors offering better products or lower prices threaten businesses. Nations suffer natural disasters and foreign invasion. Internal unity is required for dealing with major problems. Effort lost in internal argument makes it hard to deal with problems.

Historians spoke of China as a "rope of sand" because most citizens were more loyal to their families and towns than to the Emperor or the nation. The Emperor had to make sure that the bureaucracy acted virtuously because selfish bureaucrats destroyed whatever loyalty citizens might otherwise have shown toward the central government. Disgust with government made it hard to mobilize to resist invasion or to clean up after a flood.

Citizens tended to be loyal to the Emperor when his officers served them. People got upset at local leaders and didn't care what happened to the nation during periods of corruption.

Most citizens could ignore invasions. The Mongol hordes would storm the capital, decapitate the Emperor, and kill a few officials. That wouldn't affect citizens much further than a few days' ride from the capital because they didn't care who took their taxes.

A new dynasty didn't affect most Chinese, but company down-sizing or bankruptcy affects entire households. Amoskeag labor unions worked to transfer worker's loyalty from the firm to the union because the union wanted workers to pay dues. Having lost workers' loyalty, Amoskeag couldn't rally the troops against competitors.

Labor unions claim to serve workers well enough to earn the dues members pay, but like government bureaucrats, most union leaders end up being concerned with their personal welfare instead of serving their members.[193]

Companies with many employees need internal bureaucracies. Contending with labor unions makes a business more bureaucratic. This limits the company's ability to respond quickly to new opportunities or competitors. Most businesses fail instead of adapting when faced with new competition.

Union Attitudes, Up Close and Personal

I've worked in computer system development since 1964, developing and installing systems in unionized organizations such as Ford, Chrysler, and the New York Times. Samuel Gompers' worry that workers would be less loyal to the union if government provided benefits seems reasonable – successful unions make sure that members' loyalty lie with the union and not with the employer. The UAW named its headquarters "Solidarity House" to remind workers to stand together against those evil, bloodsucking employers who provide jobs, paychecks, and benefits.

I learned about union loyalties first-hand at the *New York Times* in 1971-1975. Newspapers had used Linotype machines for 100 years. Each key press caused an individual letter mold to drop into place. When a row was finished, the machine piped molten lead against the molds and cast a "line of type," hence "Linotype." Lines of type were clamped one atop the other in frames to make pages.

The *Times* had three important departments: Editorial, Pre-press, and the Press Room. Editorial typed articles on paper, rolled them into "stories," and sent them to Pre-Press via a pneumatic

---

[193] "Union's Rich Assets Recall the Glory Days," *Wall Street Journal*, May 21, 2009, p B1 reports that the UAW has $700 million in US treasuries, $321 million in other investments, and $100 million in fixed assets including a $3 million townhouse in Washington DC and a $33 million lakeside retreat and conference center. This resort lost $23 million over the past 5 years; the union borrowed to keep it afloat.

tube. Linotype operators unrolled the stories, set them in type, and tubed galley proofs back to Editorial for correction.

Union workers locked corrected stories into frames that printed one newspaper page. A dumbwaiter carried frames of type to the pressroom. The pressroom printed 12 million copies of the *Times* in a few hours. A conveyor through a hole in the wall took them to the trucks and they were gone.

Those three interfaces – the pneumatic tube, the dumbwaiter, and the hole in the wall – defined the *Times'* organizational structure as it had been for a century.

Linotype Operation

When I first saw a Linotype, I was surprised that it worked at all. Each key controlled a tube that held a stack of little metal molds for individual letters. There was a separate stack for a, another for A, and so on for all the 90 letters and symbols the *Times* could print.

When the operator pressed a key, the tube opened and one letter mold slid down into the accumulating line of type. When the operator finished the line by hitting the Enter key, a clamp pressed the accumulated molds tightly together. A valve opened and hot lead flowed against the molds. This cast a line of type, which, after cooling for a few seconds, was stacked in an output tray.

The clamp released, and an arm swung the molds back to the top of the machine to be sorted and put back in the tubes. Although the machines had a great many moving parts, 100 years of refinement had made them reliable.

Refinement couldn't make them fast, however. It took time for each letter to fall from the tube into the accumulator. Operators were able to set 4,000 to 10,000 characters per hour. A good typist can type 100 five-character words per minute, or 30,000 characters per hour. Computerization would eliminate 2/3 of the typesetters.

Linotype operators had to join the International Typographer's Union that imposed costly practices such as the "bogus" rule. When an advertiser typeset an advertisement to ensure accuracy, the paper used the material provided by the customer. After the press run, however, the union set up a duplicate ad, ran proof copies, corrected errors, and finally melted down the "bogus" advertisement without using it. This was classic union "make-work" and "featherbedding."

The extra work meant that the *Times* needed more union employees who paid dues. The fact that unneeded costs and low productivity put the paper's survival at risk didn't seem to register with the members. The *Times* had existed for a century. Most workers had inherited their jobs from their fathers and grandfathers before them; how could they end up out of work?

The *Times* was losing money and was about to go out of business like the *Herald Tribune* and other New York papers. The publisher hired a VP from the *LA Times* to build a computer system to replace the linotypes. The new VP was steeped in *LA Times* lore concerning the union-sponsored bombing of a *LA Times* building on Oct. 1, 1910, which had killed 21 people.[194] Management seemed to feel that his understanding of this tradition would help him remember where his loyalties lay.

Nobody at the *Times* knew how to set type with a computer. The VP went to MIT for some pixie dust and hired a friend and me. We wrote network and editing software that took wire-service copy and other electronic input, let editors make changes in a rudimentary word processor, and created film from which printing plates were made. Entering data three times faster and handling film cost far less than setting type from lead slugs.

As our work progressed, the typesetters tried to stop us. I couldn't understand this – the *Times* had conceded that no employees would be fired; they'd simply not be replaced as they retired. I could understand union opposition to having its power

---

[194] The memory of the bombing is still fresh. The *LA Times* published an Oct 1., 2008, editorial reminding people that two union members had been convicted in the bombing and that the same group had committed more than 100 bombings at non-union sites around the country. The detective who gathered evidence to convict them became the head of what evolved into the FBI. He was followed by J. Edgar Hoover.

and income reduced by having the number of workers reduced, but why would union members insist on maintaining work practices which had thrown so many of their counterparts out of work?

A senior *Times* employee explained that typesetting jobs had always passed from father to son. If the publisher could pass the paper to his son, why couldn't the workers expect to pass their jobs to their sons? They were as reluctant to tell their sons they'd made false promises as the Amoskeag workers had been. Concern for financial security is a multi-generation issue.

Unions were also fighting each other. One day, I got a call as I was preparing the next software version. "You know that first screen menu? Where users decide what to do?" I said "Yes." "We need another menu entry. Just put the new one at the bottom and give it the next number." I could do that, but I needed to know what the new menu entry should do. "Have it do exactly the same as #3. We don't need a new function; we need a 2nd menu entry which goes to function #3. Don't ask, we'll tell you later."

I found out that classified ad and news typesetters used identical equipment but belonged to different unions. They originally used the same menu button to get to the editor and edited different files.

One of the unions complained that the other union planned to grab dues money by poaching their members. The offended union insisted that each union have a separate button. They watched each other closely to make sure that no union member used the wrong button even though they both opened the same program.

Vaporware

One day the VP announced a demo and asked for a run-through. We obliged and asked what time we should be ready to do the demo. He didn't want us near the computer room; he planned to do the demo himself. After another run-through, we took off.

A week or so later, he told us he'd done a demo for Bertram Powers, the head of the International Typographer's Union. "As you see, Mr. Powers," the VP said, "we can print the *Times* with 20 secretaries. We don't need your men. We will publish this paper profitably or not at all. If your men walk out at the end of their contract, I swear to you, they will never walk back in again." Mr. Powers agreed to "unlimited automation," and the only remaining issue was how much the *Times* would pay linotype operators who retired early.

It wasn't all smooth sailing, of course. When the VP told us the union had accepted computers and told us to get the paper out, we said, "But sir, that was just a demo. You set two columns; the paper's a lot bigger. We're not ready to put out the entire *Times*."

This was before the term "vaporware" was coined to describe software that existed in demo form only. The VP didn't understand software much better than Mr. Powers had. I suspect it was easy for him to threaten the union with oblivion because he believed that the software was ready. He was somewhat displeased when we told him he'd been bluffing.

"How will you like it if you read in the paper that you guys made the *Times* miss an edition?" he thundered at his MIT minions.

"But sir," we pointed out, "if the system doesn't work, there won't be a *Times*. You won't be able to criticize us in print." Although what we'd said was true, we realized that we'd poured oil on troubled flames. The problem was that he'd agreed to let the redundant typographers retire too fast. The new contract required that anyone he hired to fill gaps caused by the computer system being late would have a job for life.

The rest of the project was a race between early retirement and software development. The VP had hired every programmer who understood typesetting. Nothing he could do could make us work faster; he stalked the halls lashing his tail and baying at the moon.

We made it, barely. We ran the first computerized pages on August 18, 1975. As workers retired, the *Times* eliminated 100 employees on each of 3 shifts, 7 days per week and became profitable.

Astonishing discoveries ensued. The *Times* had had problems with employee theft. Unionized order entry clerks pulled invoices out of piles of computer cards and the advertiser paid the employee half the amount on the card. The employees who had opposed automation the most strenuously had suspected that the computers would show how much money should come in and would make it harder for them to steal. The advertising department endured heated conversations for the next few months, but the result was an unexpected improvement in newspaper finances.

We're told that corporations have institutional memory, but I wonder. In 1993, the *Times* paid $1.1 billion for the *Boston Globe* whose union contract had lifetime employment provisions for a number of workers as the *Times* itself had once had. The *Globe* was profitable throughout that decade, but as advertising revenue fell, it, too, began losing money.

The *Times* threatened to close the *Globe* unless the unions saved at least $20 million per year by a 5% pay cut and ending lifetime employment provisions. Without concessions, management said, the *Globe* might lose $85 million in 2009.[195] The *Times* seemed to have forgotten its battle with the ITU a quarter-century earlier even though the publisher, "Punch" Sulzberger, was the same leader who'd hired the VP who bluffed Mr. Powers.

Unions Battling TV Imports

Private sector unionization requires that the union be the only supplier of labor and that businesses be at least quasi-monopolies. Competitors make it hard to meet the union's demands, and if the union can't extract more money, why pay union dues?

No one gives up a monopoly without a fight. When serious foreign competition threatens, the first resort for unions and management was to ask for import restrictions. Neither wanted to work harder or smarter, and management didn't want to fight their unions and their competitors at the same time.

TV manufacturers were the first to feel competition after the post-World War II recovery because it was easier for newly

---

[195] *New York Times* editorial, April 3, 2009

industrializing countries to make TVs than to make automobiles. A friend who worked for the Japanese government was stationed in New York while I worked for the *Times.* After he finished negotiating the agreement to limit Japanese TV sales in the US, we discussed Japanese imports versus union wages over dinner.

"I don't understand," he told me. "Mr. Strauss, President Carter's chief negotiator, was on TV last night and said that this agreement would not increase cost to American consumers. That makes no sense. Zenith can't compete with Japanese manufacturers. Mr. Strauss' position was that if we don't sell TVs here, the price will go up and Zenith can stay in business. How can he say our agreement won't affect the prices that Americans pay for TVs?"

My friend knew that American politicians lie like Japanese politicians, but he was surprised that Mr. Strauss believed that he could get away with that particular lie.

My friend went on, "Mr. Strauss is a smart man," he said, "but he doesn't know anything about the TV business. Zenith told him they couldn't compete with our manufacturers, but nobody told him that our guys are losing to Koreans who work cheaper than Japanese. Limiting the number we can sell means we can't gain market share by cutting prices. We'll sell higher-priced TVs with better profit margins. We'll move up-market, hold off the Koreans as long as we can, and cash out the TV business. Zenith won't last long anyway."

I reminded him that our Government people never met a payroll and didn't know much about any business. President Carter ran a peanut farm that was heavily subsidized by the government; he knew no more about the TV business than the Japanese prime minister, who'd come up through rice farming, did. My friend shuddered at the idea of the prime minister, whom he knew, getting involved in trade talks, and we turned to other topics.

Limits on Automobile Imports

I was in Japan one President and a few years later, and got an urgent invitation to lunch. His guys wanted me to help write a telegram to

Bill Brock, President Reagan's political fixer. Having won the TV negotiations, my friend was setting up restrictions on selling Japanese cars in America. This involved a lot more money and many more jobs than the TV talks had, and more cut-throat politics.

He told me what he needed. "Mr. Brock sent a telegram. My rivals in the ministry released a distorted translation to the Japanese press that makes it look like I'm selling out our car companies. Without clarification from Mr. Brock, I'll be in trouble."

"Can't you release your own translation?"

"That would look self-serving. Most Japanese don't understand some of the English words Mr. Brock used in his telegram to me. My rival's translation will seem more plausible and they won't believe mine. That's why I need you to help me write a telegram to Mr. Brock asking for clarification."

"Can't you phone him?" "There would be a record of the call being made but no recording. People would see the call as my getting caught and trying to wiggle out by asking him to cover for me."

So we wrote a telegram. "Does Mr. Brock know you're in trouble?" I asked. "Yes, he does. His translators didn't get everything, but he's a brilliant politician. The papers said where they got the translation; he'll know it wasn't from me. His guys will translate the Japanese news back into English. It won't come out the way he sent the telegram to me, so he'll understand when I ask for clarification."

"If I write the telegram, he'll know it came from an American. Is that OK?" "That will help. When he gets a message from me that I didn't write, he knows it's very important, so he pays attention."

The first step was to write the telegram we wanted Mr. Brock to send us. We knew that he knew that the problem involved translation and if we could feed him the right words, he'd send them back.

This was fascinating. When I suggested a word, the first question was how most Japanese would translate it. Then they had to decide whether Mr. Brock could use the word; after all, Mr. Brock had to worry about how his telegram might play in the American press after the Americans translated it back to English from the Japanese translation. It took a while, but we finally had the unambiguous reply we wanted.

We then wrote a much longer telegram that fed the reply to Mr. Brock without being too obvious. Our request for clarification would be made public, and it, too, would be translated into Japanese. I typed he telegram and we went to lunch.

"It's amazing," he told me. "Mr. Brock is a good politician, but he knows less about automobiles than Mr. Strauss knew about TV. He hasn't read Mr. Strauss' notes. I'm getting everything Mr. Strauss gave me because of precedent and I'm getting things Mr. Strauss wouldn't give me because, as I point out, TVs are different from cars. This is looking like such a good deal for our side that our car companies think it's some sort of subtle American plot."

"I wouldn't worry about that," I said, "Mr. Reagan was an actor and then a governor. He was a good spokesman for GE, but he doesn't understand business. He just wants the UAW off his back; that's why he got a political fixer instead of a businessman to handle it. I don't think it's a plot. I'd sign if it looks good to you."

When I got back home, he called. The reply Mr. Brock sent was exactly what we'd written except for a comma and a preposition.

The rest is history – the agreement told the Japanese exactly how many cars they could sell in the US each year. Knowing exactly how many to make a year in advance is a manufacturer's dream. The Japanese loaded their cars with options, cut costs, moved up-market, made a lot of money, and strengthened their dealer networks. When the agreement timed out, the Japanese were ready to renew but GM wanted it ended. Who won that one?

This illustrates a problem our government faces when dealing with other countries. We sent different groups of people to the trade negotiations; the Japanese sent the same team each time. Experts in negotiation teach that if you're conducting negotiations over the long term, individual memory of what went before is helpful. If you keep sending different people and the other side sends the same people, all else being equal, you're going to lose.

Automobile Unions

Union costs have been a matter of national discussion for some time. While President Bush II was considering whether to help GM and Chrysler, news reports stated that UAW workers cost twice what Toyota and Honda pay their non-unionized staff in the South if you include pension and health costs. This is an insurmountable burden for the Big Three, but unions present another problem that might be even worse than direct costs.

A systems integrator I worked for supplied computer systems to factories and sent me to Detroit to give a training class. It was scheduled weeks in advance, but the conference room wasn't set up as had been promised. Quick like bunnies, we rearranged the tables and were ready to teach.

A supervisor came by, and in shocked horror, demanded that we put the tables back. He explained that the UAW had jurisdiction over moving furniture. A grievance and work stoppage would follow if the union learned that non-union people had moved tables. The union set the room up two hours late. When I asked the supervisor how he expected to compete, he had no answer.

It gets worse. Our class explained how to use a vision system we'd developed. One of our cameras went missing during installation. We overheard a plant electrician griping to high heaven that our (adult language deleted) camera had blown out his home VCR; there was talk of his asking us to buy him a new one.

We never got our camera back – plant management discouraged us from pursuing the matter. To summarize, a union employee stole our electronic equipment, broke it, felt confident enough to brag about the matter, wanted to ask us to buy him a new VCR, and in the end we had to let it drop. Now we understood why $5 kitchen stools were chained in place – by the time we upgraded our chain so that our chair wouldn't "grow legs," the chain cost more than the chair.

If you think this is an exaggeration, consider the Coffee Pot War[196] at Ford's Sharonville, Ohio transmission plant, a two-million square foot industrial edifice with a parking lot built for 6,000 cars.[197] A supervisor named Robert Dewar told the story after working at Sharonville from 1974 until 1979, defying the predictions of a line worker who said he'd be driven out within three weeks.[198]

In Mr. Dewar's time, Sharonville was a union-management battleground. At one point, management took the only worker-owned coffee pot, supposedly to reduce the amount of time spent on break and increase productivity by keeping people at their workstations. Machines stopped running properly, however, and output dropped instead of rising. A tool needed to adjust many machines went missing; this brought production to a standstill.

The Coffee Pot War raged for days. Ford assembly plants in four states nearly shut down for lack of transmissions. In desperation, management gave back the coffee pot. The missing tool showed up and production returned to normal.[199]

I worked at Sharonville years after the Coffee Pot Wars. The atmosphere had changed because sales dropped so much during the gas crisis that workers and managers had spent years on layoff.

They'd learned that they had to cooperate to keep their jobs. Worker-owned coffee pots were now OK. These free enterprise pots gave better, cheaper coffee than the vending machines. You paid for coffee on the honor system.

Although union members were aware of their rights, they understood that they'd be laid off again if customers stopped buying cars. Management had gotten across the point that the goal wasn't shipping tons of transmissions; the goal was shipping tons of *good*

---

[196] Dewar, Robert, *A Savage Factory: An Eyewitness Account of the Auto Industry's Self-Destruction*, (AuthorHouse, 2009) p 85
[197] Ibid., p 1
[198] Ibid., p 12-14
[199] The Big Three were the most profitable businesses the world had ever known. It took close cooperation between management and labor to destroy them – neither party could have done it alone.

transmissions. Workers welcomed our vision systems because they made it easier to catch problems. Nobody at Sharonville stole our cameras, but we still had to chain our chair.

Sharonville workers now understood the relationship between customers and cash flow, between production and payroll. The Batavia plant some miles down the road was closing slowly and senior workers there had the right to bump more junior Sharonville workers. Batavia workers had the same attitude toward management that Sharonville had had in the days of Dewar's Coffee Pot Wars. Transferring veterans often had trouble adapting to the more cooperative Sharonville attitude. I was told that Sharonville people occasionally intercepted older transplants in the parking lot to "explain" the necessity of cooperating with management to ship good product. The Sharonville workers did not want to be laid off again.

Not all issues could be resolved, however. Big companies like Ford make direct medical payments, grabbing any profit the insurance company would make. Sitting at workstations all day doing the same task doesn't give much exercise and many plant employees were overweight. Obesity leads to expensive diseases. Sickness increases both medical bills and absenteeism. Most auto plants have high-end exercise facilities that their workers hardly use.

It's hard to get desk and plant-floor potatoes to use health clubs. The Sharonville plant hired a young woman named Lynn to try to get exercise-hating people to exercise.

I found her in the cafeteria putting up posters for a new exercise-related contest she'd dreamed up. "Is that contest going to work any better than the last two?" I asked her.

Lynn shook her head. "Probably not, but what else is there?"

That was a good question. I didn't think it would help to point out that Confucius would regard being overweight as extreme lack of virtue, so I took a different tack. "Most of the plant potatoes around here are men, right?" I said. She nodded. "What does a man want more of that he could have more of if he were in better shape?"

Dead silence. Wheels turned in her head for 30 or 40 seconds while I practiced my poker face. Finally, she gulped and said, "There's a real problem with that."

"I know," I said. "My wife talks to lots of women and she's explained it. It would be a burden, but it would shorten your widowhood." She sighed and walked away. The contest failed, plant potatoes stayed overweight, and medical costs kept going up.

Bottom Line

Government policy has enormous impact on manufacturing jobs. High-minded light bulb regulations have transferred manufacturing jobs to China because the "green" bulbs are too expensive to manufacture in the United States. Similarly, regulating by the EPA, OSHA, and a host of other regulators run up the cost of employing workers.

Most regulatory agencies start out with good intentions and may benefit society at first. Agency employees look for opportunities to write more rules that impose more and more costs. The net result? American factories shut down and foreign factories send goods here.

Bureaucrats and unions are skilled at manipulating their environment to increase their incomes and reduce their workload. Most bureaucrats are more loyal to their agency than to the nation; unions want workers to be more loyal to the union than to the employer. Bureaucrats and unions always want more money, regardless of performance. Bureaucrats revel in creating complexity; automotive union contracts are the size of telephone books and contain hundreds of job classifications. Getting anything unusual done in a unionized plant or in a bureaucracy involves complex negotiations.

Neither unions nor bureaucrats have evil intent. Like all of us, they seek to benefit themselves without having to add value. A business fails when unions or regulations take too much out. When a cancer gets too big, the cancer and the patient both die.

Machinist union demands for "full pay 'til the last day" felled Eastern Airlines. The union leaders got their wish: they received full paychecks without concessions or help for their struggling employer until the day they had no employer and no pay. The parasite destroyed its host and died in its turn.

Countless smaller and less well-known companies and unions have trod the Amoakeag path over the years. The UAW and the Big Three would have gone bankrupt if the federal government hadn't given them billions of our tax dollars.

Government bureaucrats aren't employed by a private business which can succumb to competitive pressure; they're paid by a government monopoly which raises taxes at will. Closing a business recycles assets into new businesses but recycling a failed bureaucracy is almost impossible. When bureaucrats take too much out of society, the only cure Confucius knew was for the entire society to fail.

As we watch the decline of America's union-encrusted industrial dinosaurs, it's sobering to consider that our national government, currently consuming 28% of the GNP directly and consuming far more through the costs of regulatory compliance, is in exactly the same predicament – but we're all "employees" of our government whether we want to pay taxes or not.

10 – Our Government-Sponsored Food Fight

The traditional Chinese diet was largely vegetarian in that 90% of calories came from cereal grains. Protein came from cereals, legumes, and protein-rich products such as bean curd (tofu) and soya sauce. Meat was rare. Only pork and poultry were popular, and there were no milk products.[200] Soya products supplied amino acids such as lysine which are lacking in many vegetarian diets.

The Chinese based medical practice on a particularly Chinese view of the body. Classical scholars had written of yin-yang, five phases, and fluid circulation to explain how people fell ill. Loss of virtue and harmony in bodily functions caused disease. Theories of circulation led physicians to map moxybustion and acupuncture points on the skin based on the flow of *qi* throughout the body.[201]

Whether theories about the flow of *qi* are scientifically correct or not, the Chinese worked out processes that had medical value. Although acupuncture roused skepticism among Western physicians when President Nixon's visit to China in 1972 brought it to their attention, recent studies have shown acupuncture to be 60 – 70% effective in granting relief from many types of pain.[202]

---

[200] Needham, Joseph, Bray, Francesca, *Science and civilization in China*, (Cambridge University Press, 1984) p 4

[201] Elman, Benjamin, *On their own terms: science in China, 1550-1900* (Harvard University Press, 2005) p 227

[202] Drum, David, *The Chronic Pain Management Sourcebook* (McGraw-Hill Professional, 1999) p 161 Acupuncture deniers assume that the Chinese used an ineffective practice for thousands of years without realizing it didn't work.

Bone carvings suggest that acupuncture was used as early as 1000 BC,[203] but the oldest known medical treatise, which relied on older writings, dates to around 100 BC.[204] The tradition of careful record keeping helped the pragmatic Chinese identify dozens of plants that had medicinal effects.

Recent studies have also shown that the Chinese diet was low in fat, high in plant fiber, contained adequate protein, and helped protect against heart disease.[205] Judicious use of traditional plants helped the Chinese enjoy good enough health that their country has been crowded since classical times.

The Chinese had no food surplus so there wasn't much debate about nutrition - people ate all of whatever they could afford. Most people either grew their own food or bought food at markets where they knew the farmers who'd grown it, so there was no need to regulate food quality.

Americans have so much food that the government pays farmers not to plant. Few city dwellers have any idea where food comes from or how it's produced. Their ignorance gives opportunities for non-virtuous behavior all along the food chain that necessitated the creation of agencies to regulate food quality and cleanliness. Abundance leads to arguments over what people should and shouldn't eat.

Nutrition advice in the press is contradictory, unreliable, and uncertain. We hear that caffeine is bad for the heart, then that it's good for the heart, then that it's bad in certain cases. Who knows?

For centuries, activists pontificated about the Evils of Drink. Then it turned out that red wine in moderation is good for the heart. Some say you can get the same effect by drinking the right kinds of grape juice, or maybe you can't. Who knows?

---

[203] Yelland, Sharon; Odent, Michel; *Acupuncture in midwifery* (Elsevier Health Sciences, 2005), p 2
[204] Ibid., pp 1-2
[205] "Traditional Chinese Diet Helps Ward Off Heart Disease," *ScienceDaily*, Nov. 16, 1999

The conflicting interests of those who profit from selling food and the bureaucrats who profit by writing more complex regulations increases confusion. The commendable regulatory goals of protecting public health are entangled in politics.

Our ongoing food fight confuses people who consume drugs, food, and food supplements. Manipulating the regulatory process brings great wealth for food companies and funds campaign contributions to politicians who participate in the manipulation.

There are huge amounts of money involved. Food supplements, also known as "functional foods," are a multi-billion dollar market.[206] Influencing new laws and getting help avoiding rules always offers opportunities for "campaign contributions." The food industry is so big that there's no chance of taking politics out of food regulation.

It Started with Farming

President Lincoln persuaded Congress to create the US Department of Agriculture in 1862. The new department received $172,000[207] to help farmers determine how best to use the unusual soils and weather conditions of the American West.

The Department's mandate was to a) insure a reliable food supply and b) spread useful information concerning agriculture. The agency interpreted part (a) as promoting agricultural interests and part (b) as requiring them to spread dietary advice. The USDA started studying the relationship between farms and nutrition in 1890.

Vitamins hadn't yet been isolated nor were the dietary causes of scurvy, beriberi, pellagra, goiter, and other such conditions

---

[206] Hui, Yui h. et al, *Handbook of Food Products Manufacturing: Principles, Bakery, Beverages, Cereals, Cheese, Confectionary, Fats, Fruits, and Functional Foods* (Wiley-Interscience, 2007) p 547 estimates that as of 2002, the US market was $18.25 billion followed by $15.4 billion in Europe and $11.8 billion in Japan.

[207] Towle, Nathaniel Carter, *A History and Analysis of the Constitution of the United States*, (Little, Brown, 1871) p 388-389

understood. Lacking information, it made sense for the department to encourage people to eat as wide a variety of foods as possible.

Food producers supported the resulting "eat more of everything" message. All foods were assumed to contain at least some nutrients and producers happily promoted their products as contributing to a healthful, high-variety diet. Any new product increased variety in your diet, a Good Thing endorsed by a government agency!

Increased scientific knowledge has brought ever-increasing complexity in food and drug regulation. This has led to pitched battles between regulators, producers, politicians, and consumers. The more we learn about how individual genetics and lifestyle affect medicine and nutrition, the worse the regulatory mess becomes.

The Big Food and Drug Fight

W. O. Atwater, the first USDA director of research, fired the first shot in the food fight in 1894. He wrote "The general impression of hygienists is that our diet is one-sided and that we eat too much ... fat, starch, and sugar. This is due partly to our large consumption of sugar and partly to our use of such large quantities of fat meats. ... How much harm is done to health by our one-sided and excessive diet no one can say. Physicians say that it is very great."[208]

In 1894, Atwater recommended a diet where 15% of the calories came from protein, 33% from fat, and 52% from carbohydrates. His recommendations are close to modern advice, but for years afterward, advisors kept saying, "eat more of everything." The Great Depression and World War II amplified this message because most people didn't have enough and gladly ate whatever they could get.

---

[208] Atwater, WO, *Foods: Nutritive Value and Cost*, (Washington DC:USDA 1894) p 25

"Eat more of everything" came under stress in the 1970's. Research had proved that eating too much fat, cholesterol, and sugar was harmed both health and the economy.[209]

Americans were getting fatter because they ate more calories than they burned through physical activity. The increased wealth of the 1950s and 60s meant that almost all Americans could afford to eat as much food of any sort they wished, limited only by what they could pack down.

This brought conflict between promoting farming and giving sound nutrition advice, of course. Food producers felt that "eat less" would target their foods as "bad" and hurt sales whereas consumer advocates and health professionals were enraged that the USDA kept the "eat more" mantra.

Recommendations were changed in the 1980's to accommodate industry's fears. For example, "avoid too much" became "choose a diet low in" and "choose lean meat" became "have two or three servings of meat." The guidelines tried to avoid classifying foods as "bad" by noting substances like salt and fat which could be harmful but did not name foods which contained them.

When the 1991 edition of the USDA's *Food Pyramid* was about to be published, the National Cattlemen's Association claimed that the *Pyramid* would cause people to eat less beef. They also objected that beef was so close to fats and sugars in the diagram that beef would become guilty by association.

When the *Pyramid* was delayed, national news media suddenly noticed that food producers had been influencing the USDA for 100 years. A new version of the *Pyramid* came out a year later.

The USDA tests about 1 percent of cattle for mad cow disease. One meat packer intended to test all its cattle. Arguing that full

---

[209] Researchers at the Centers for Disease Control and Prevention and RTI International found that medical expenditures caused by obesity during 2003 totaled $75 billion. According to the report published in the January, 2004 issue of Obesity Research, expenditures ranged from $7.7 billion in California to $87 million in Wyoming. Approximately half of these costs were paid from public sources such as Medicare and Medicaid.

testing would cause the public to question meat safety, USDA went political and forced the company to stop all testing.[210]

The thought process was similar to President Clinton's Surgeon General, Dr. Jocelyn Elders, refusing to warn people when Arkansas schools passed out defective condoms – she felt that admitting that condoms failed at about ten times the expected rate would cause people to lose faith in her program.[211]

The *Pyramid* caused heated controversy as food producers tried to avoid having the government urge people to eat less of their products. Popular interest in the *Pyramid* controversy showed that enough people were concerned about diet and health to make it a potent political issue. Manufacturers realized that they could make money by advertising foods as "good" or "healthy." Food producers making health claims brought the Food and Drug Administration into the food fight.

The Food Fight Widens

In 1906, President Roosevelt signed the Pure Food and Drugs Act. It tasked the Bureau of Chemistry within the Department of Agriculture with monitoring food and drugs.

The Bureau was renamed the Food and Drug Administration in 1931. This led to conflict between the producer-oriented Department of Agriculture and the consumer-protection role of the FDA within it. In 1940, the FDA moved to a department that became today's Department of Health and Human Services.[212]

The Food and Drug Administration is supposed to ban unsafe or ineffective medical products. The FDA interprets its mandate as requiring it to regulate marketing claims relating to health benefits

---

[210] "Free Market Myth," *Boston Review*, Jan-Feb 2009

[211] Geuras, Dean, Garofalo , Charles, *Practical Ethics in Public Administration* (Management Concepts, 2005) pp 78-79

[212] Pray, Steven, A *history of nonprescription product regulation* (Haworth Press, 2003) pp 74-75

of any device, drug, or food regardless of Constitutional support of Freedom of Speech.

The moment vitamins were discovered, profit-seeking companies started selling them as food supplements. Marketers focused on middle-class, educated women who probably didn't suffer vitamin deficiencies but could afford to worry that they might. Vitamin sales rose from $32 million in 1932 to $82 million in 1935, *during the Great Depression,* and when dollars were worth a lot more.

Over the years, the FDA has decided several times that vitamin supplements were drugs which fell under its regulatory umbrella. FDA staff believed that most people received enough vitamins in their food and didn't need supplements. On that basis, the FDA declared that businesses had to show scientific proof of a benefit before marketing a vitamin or any other nutritional supplement based on medical effectiveness. In other words, no one could take vitamins unless a physician determined that they suffered from a deficiency and wrote a prescription.

Manufacturers didn't want their potions regulated as prescription drugs which required FDA approval. Getting a drug approved cost millions of dollars and many years of medical trials. They argued that the American tradition of freedom of choice meant that anyone ought to be free to buy and consume any product if he or she believed that the benefits were worth the cost. They organized groups of their customers to "petition their elected representatives."

A glance at Wal-Mart's drug section shows that this point of view carried the day. It's possible to override a bureaucracy if enough people object. This would have astounded Confucius, who had no notion of the ruled being able to affect their rulers except by total, all-out rebellion.

All-Bran and the National Cancer Institute

The Kellogg Company struck the first major blow against the FDA's policy of regulating health claims in 1984. Kellogg worked closely with the National Cancer Institute, which, like the FDA, is part of the U.S. Department of Health and Human Services. Based on NCI approval, Kellogg put this message on All-Bran cereals:

> The National Cancer Institute believes eating the right foods may reduce your risk of cancer. Here are their recommendations: Eat high-fiber foods. A growing body of evidence says high-fiber foods are important to good health. That's why a healthy diet includes high-fiber foods like bran cereals.

The National Cancer Institute believed that Kellogg's advertisement was a public-spirited message about health based on well-demonstrated scientific fact. Kellogg's appeal to the NCI while making health claims in an advertising campaign surprised the FDA. The FDA realized that health claims would slip from its grasp unless they forced Kellogg to stop. Loss of bureaucratic turf was intolerable, of course, and they objected with all the vigor at their disposal.

The FDA lost. The Federal Trade Commission supported the NCI, reasoning that spreading facts about dietary health benefit everyone. Kellogg had realized that the NIC could help them influence the FDA. All-Bran increased its market share 47% in six months even though it tastes more like twigs and straw than food. Health claims sold ordinary food products! The food fight got wider.

Fighting Over Food And Vitamins

In 1993, the FDA declared all-out war on medical foods by broadening its definition of supplements from vitamins and minerals to include herbals, botanicals, and most other products sold in health food stores. They claimed jurisdiction over ingredients, packaging, and labels. If they'd won, all supplements would have required FDA approval and all factories making them would have been subject to the same FDA regulation and inspection as drug factories.

The FDA wanted manufacturers to demonstrate that their products were both effective and safe before selling them. This would ban supplements completely since it can cost as much as a billion dollars to shepherd a drug all the way through the approval process. Traditional herbal products can't be patented because they're found in nature so there would be no way for a manufacturer to recoup the immense cost of the clinical trials the FDA demands for drugs.

Even if people could report accurately on what they eat, it's impossible to determine what nutrients have been eaten. The USDA publishes data on the nutrition content of foods, but these data become outdated as new food products are invented, recipes change, or soil and weather affect vitamin content. It's pretty much impossible to demonstrate that a) the user wasn't getting enough of what's being tested and b) the user benefitted from taking the supplement.

Food supplement companies saw that the FDA would put them out of business if it was allowed to treat them as drug manufacturers. They lobbied Congress to limit the FDA's ability to police their marketing claims. They organized letter-writing campaigns, put up posters in health food stores, and exercised their constitutional right to petition their elected representatives for redress of grievances.

At the same time, people were beginning to demand the right to decide their own medical treatments.[213] Many supplement users believed that the FDA was a pawn of pharmaceutical firms and was trying to ban food supplements to force sick people to impoverish themselves by buying from Big Pharma.

---

[213] "More Information, Please" *Newsweek*, Oct. 20, 2007

Congress changed the law in 1994 to permit most of the health claims the FDA had tried to block. Court cases further limited the FDA's power to control marketing claims. As of now, food supplement manufacturers don't have to prove that their products are effective and they aren't required to ensure that labels accurately describe the ingredients in the product.

After the 1994 deregulation, supplement sales went from $4 billion to $15 billion in one year. Food companies started adding herbals to their foods so that they could make similar claims and drug companies considered selling their products as unregulated over-the-counter health foods instead of drugs.

The Battle of Cholestin and Tamoxifen

Cholestin, a traditional Asian health food, is made of milled rice fermented with red yeast.[214] Capsules sold in health-food stores can have as many as nine different compounds that lower cholesterol. One of these natural compounds is virtually identical to Lovastatin, a drug that had been through the high-cost FDA clinical trials.[215]

The FDA wanted to treat cholestin as a drug because of this similarity, but the courts ruled against them. Cholestin is cheaper because the manufacturer isn't subject to FDA regulations and need not recoup the cost of clinical trials. A month's supply of cholestin costs about $30 as opposed to $120-350 for prescription Lovastatin.

The FDA claims it's protecting public health, of course, but there would seem to be room for a degree of relaxation given the cost difference between cholestin and Lovastatin. Opponents see an overweening bureaucracy trampling public health to serve their political interests and enhance Big Pharma's profits.

---

[214] Durstine, J. Larry, *Action plan for high cholesterol* (Human Kinetics, 2005) p 154

[215] Ibid., p 159

Thalidomide

The ancient Greeks said, "the dose makes the poison." Many tranquilizers and painkillers have an effective dose that's close to the fatal dose. If you take a bit too much, you die, and if you don't take quite enough, the pill won't help.

Thalidomide was a tranquilizer and painkiller whose fatal dose was "incredibly high."[216] It would be difficult or impossible to kill anyone by overdosing thalidomide. Thalidomide also helped relieve morning sickness, and many pregnant women took it for that purpose. Germans were buying a million tablets per day by 1961.

At the time, doctors believed that drugs didn't pass through the placenta and affect babies. This view was wrong - babies were born with flippers instead of arms and legs. Thalidomide was taken off the market in 1961 because it caused birth defects.[217]

As horrible as this was, though, there was no scientific reason to take it off the market entirely. Yes, thalidomide causes birth defects when taken by pregnant women - but many drugs are dangerous to pregnant women. Thalidomide is useful for treating leprosy, some types of inflammation, and for certain forms of cancer.[218] Why deny thalidomide to male patients, or to women who aren't fertile? Reasonable men and women argue that the FDA and other regulatory bodies overreacted to the birth defects.

[216] Singleton, Carl, Wildin, Rowena, *The Sixties in America:* (Salem Press 1999) p 718
[217] Schardein , James L., Macina , Orest T., *Human developmental toxicants: aspects of toxicology and chemistry* (CRC Press, 2006) pp 130-131
[218] Davis, Darren W., Herbst , Roy, Abbruzzese , James L., *Antiangiogenic Cancer Therapy* (CRC Press 2007) pp 305-306

The Tryptophan Obfuscation

In 1989, at least 1,500 people who took tryptophan, an amino acid found in all food proteins, became seriously ill and about 40 died. The problem seemed to be related to taking the supplement.[219]

The FDA reflexively bans any drug that causes fatalities regardless of benefits, and banned tryptophan in 1991. However, it turned out the deaths had been caused by a contaminated batch from one manufacturer. After the problem was fixed, the FDA kept saying tryptophan was unsafe even though it's found naturally in foods.[220]

After much political argy-bargy, tryptophan was made available in its original form in 2001. The FDA lost credibility by taking a decade to undo an unjustified ban on a popular supplement. People who had benefited from tryptophan resented having to buy expensive drugs and suspected that the FDA was conspiring with the pharmaceutical industry. Others believe that the FDA needlessly delays the release of drugs that could save their lives and think the FDA is a collection of hidebound bureaucrats who kill people and waste precious research funds through obfuscation and inaction.[221]

The US Supreme Court upheld the FDA by deciding that the 5th amendment prohibition of depriving a person of life or liberty doesn't mean that patients may take drugs of which the FDA disapproves.[222] Those who regard this decision as a personal death sentence are making their views known in Washington insofar as their resources permit.

---

[219] Roufs, JB. *Review of L-tryptophan and eosinophilia-myalgia syndrome*, Journal of the American Dietary Association 1992 pp 844-850
[220] Sahelian, Ray, *5-HTP: Nature's Serotonin Solution* (Avery Pub. Group, 1998) pp 7, 30
[221] "The FDA Is Killing Chron's Patients" *Wall Street Journal.* Dec 30 2008, p A9
[222] Ibid.

Penicillin

I'm personally convinced that people should have the right to choose their own drugs; I'd be dead if the FDA had been permitted to apply its usual regulatory process to penicillin.

When my parents sailed from New York for the Chinese mission field in 1949, all four grandparents came to say "goodbye." They had heard, "The churches of Asia are built on the bones of the missionaries' wives." When we visited Singapore in 1959, we found a wall of memorials to women and children whose early deaths had created the need for that saying. My grandparents didn't expect to see my mother or me again.

I fell ill in the middle of the Pacific. There was no doctor aboard; the radio gave no clues. Parents can tell when a child turns the corner and is dying. In fear and prayer, my parents gave me some pills Dad had bought in a war surplus store before we sailed. He'd never heard of penicillin because it had been a war-time secret, but the clerk told him the pills were good for what ailed you. The next day, I was running around as if nothing had happened.

Throughout history, more soldiers died from infections than from enemy action. This well-known fact led to a massive research program to manufacture penicillin, which Alexander Fleming had discovered in 1928.[223] Researchers gathered molds and spores from all over the world, but the mold that led to mass production of penicillin was found on a melon in a market in Peoria, Ill.[224] The first penicillin from this mold resulted in a "miraculous" cure of a woman who was suffering from blood poisoning. Penicillin was rushed into production and was used in every theater of the war.

Penicillin produces allergic reactions in between .7% and 10% of most groups.[225] The normal FDA process would have banned it.

---

[223] Meyers, Morton, *Happy Accidents*, (Arcade Publishing, 2007) p 59
[224] Ibid., p 75
[225] Stewart, Gordon Thallon, McGovern, John P. *Penicillin allergy: clinical and immunological aspects* (Thomas, 1970) p 147

A larger percentage of wounded soldiers died from "jungle rot" in the Pacific theatre. Even if 1 in 10 died of penicillin allergy, saving 9 soldiers out of 10 was better than not using the drug. The military overrode the bureaucracy, a feat that is possible only in wartime. After the war, my dad found some surplus penicillin and bought enough to save my life without a prescription.

Doubts About Food Supplements

Penicillin was exceptional – the results were so spectacular that there was no denying that if it didn't kill, the results were "good enough" for the military. After the war, penicillin was known as a "wonder drug." The benefits, if any, from taking food supplements are harder to quantify but that doesn't inhibit marketing campaigns. Knowing that the benefits were questionable in many cases, the FDA fought making supplement labels less rigorous than drug labels. They feared that if they cut food supplements any slack, drug companies would go to court to win the same privileges for their products.

When the FDA wouldn't give supplement makers relief from their expensive clinical trial / inspection / control of labels / prescription use treadmill, supplement makers and users got a law passed forbidding the FDA to impose labeling requirements for food supplements. Having waged total war and won total victory, the supplement crowd is in no mood to compromise with a bureaucracy which they suspect of trying to put them out of business.

We shouldn't be surprised by advertisements for devices such as the Stirwand which embeds special minerals in plastic to enhance drinking water's effectiveness in the body. Their advertisement says:

> Make Your Own Quantum Age Drinking Water
> New clinical trials show substantial increase in hydration potential
> Use the Stirwand for great tasting, super-hydrating, energized water for you and your family.

> Great for all of your pets' water and watering
> livestock and for farm and agricultural
> applications.[226]

Stirring water with a plastic wand containing embedded minerals so that the water tastes better and energizes the body is reminiscent of Chinese theories about the flow of *qi*, but there were no bureaucrats regulating medical claims in those days.

Genetic Differences Complicate Nutrition

To be fair, nutrition is complex. Prescription drugs contain few active ingredients and generally only one, yet prescription drugs interact in subtle and ill-understood ways. Interactions between nutrients are far more complex because there are so many active compounds in food supplements and different plants vary so much. This makes the FDA's clinical-trial approach unsuitable for evaluating herbal medicines because there's no way to know how much of any ingredient a patient is actually receiving.

What's worse, people don't all react to seemingly clear-cut diseases in the same way. My son had a six-month bout of off-and-on illness. One week, he couldn't get out of bed, the next week he'd go to class. Medical centers told him to get more sleep. Digestive supplements didn't help.

After much testing, Mass General said to come back when it was bad enough that they could find it. A few days later, he got me out of bed. "Dad, I'm dying," he said, "get me to the hospital." We got.

More tests, no clues. Finally, one of the older doctors sucked air through her teeth, shook her head, and voted weakly for appendicitis. They got his appendix out just as it burst.

Appendicitis doesn't usually come and go for six months, but it can. A doctor told me they guess wrong about appendicitis about 20% of the time. So much for "medical science," it's a "healing art."

---

[226] http://www.quantumbalancing.com/stirwand.htm

Research shows that a patient's genetic makeup affects how a disease progresses and often determines whether FDA-approved drugs work or not. The *New York Times* wrote "Experts say that most drugs work for only about half the people who take them." The *Times* reported that tamoxifen, a drug which had passed clinical trials for helping prevent recurrence of breast cancer, works only on patients with the right genetic makeup.[227]

> In 2003, <u>more than 25 years after tamoxifen was introduced</u>, researchers led by Dr. David A. Flockhart at Indiana University School of Medicine figured out that the body coverts tamoxifen into another substance called endoxifen. It is endoxifen that actually exerts the cancer-fighting effect. The conversion is done by an enzyme in the body called CYP2D6, or 2D6 for short.
> But variations in people's 2D6 genes mean the enzymes have different levels of activity. Up to 7 percent of people, <u>depending on their ethnic group</u>, have an inactive enzyme, Dr. Flockhart said, while another 20 to 40 percent have an only modestly active enzyme. [emphasis added]

Tamoxifen was approved after the usual high-cost clinical trial regimen. Twenty-five years later, researchers find that 7% of patients don't benefit at all and that 20-40% benefit only a little. Patients who do benefit gain a lot; the drug was found to be effective even though the original studies probably included people who couldn't benefit at all due to their genetic makeup.

In spite of following the multi-million dollar drug trial protocol, nobody had a clue how tamoxifen worked even though the drug firm had studied it extensively before starting the clinical trials. Knowing

---

227 "Patient's DNA May Be Signal to Tailor Medication," *New York Times*, Dec. 29, 2008

that a drug works, at least in some people, isn't the same as knowing *why* it works; American skepticism of acupuncture comes to mind.

The benefits of herbal medicines are far more difficult to tease out because plants have so many ingredients which interact with nutrients in other foods. Not only that, the actual content of any specific dose of an herb depends on the soil where it was grown, the particular strain of seed, how it was watered and fertilized, when it was harvested, and a host of other environmental factors.

This variability is one reason Chinese and Japanese believe that the patient should consume the entire plant, root and branch. It's impossible to run clinical trials with plants whose ingredients vary so much, so American drug firms can't follow this methodology. They try to isolate the single "active ingredient" in each plant so that they can produce it in batches whose consistency and strength are controlled tightly enough to pass FDA muster.

Plant-based diet supplements can't be patented. That means there's no way for someone who pays for testing to get the money back. Requiring scientific proof of effectiveness would ban almost all food supplements, so the industry lobbied and mobilized customers to force the FDA to leave them alone. We ended up with "pretty much anything goes" with respect to supplements. This is good for business and liberty if not always for health.

What's more, it represents a defeat for a large, entrenched, well-funded bureaucracy. Public wrath can force bureaucrats to retreat, a lesson that should encourage us all.

And The Fight Plays On

It makes no sense to have "promote agriculture" and "promote healthy diets" in the same agency because of the inherent and irresolvable conflicts between the two. There's no way to reconcile "eat more" which pleases agribusiness and "eat less" which promotes better health by cutting sales.

The legislative committees that oversee the USDA are not interested in moving dietary functions to a different agency governed by a different committee. Losing influence over nutrition would reduce campaign contributions to agriculture committee members; they're as enthusiastic about that as cattlemen are about government advising "eat less beef."

Conflicting functions in the same committee might cause campaign contributions to cancel each other. We're reminded of a court transcript from the American West where the judge opened the trial with, "The court has in hand $10,000 from the plaintiff and $5,000 from the defendant. The court will return $5,000 to the plaintiff and try the case on its merits." Politicians never return campaign contributions except to avoid bad publicity.

We can draw a number of conclusions:

- The FDA's banning thalidomide when it posed no risk to the male half of the population and banning tryptophan for ten years because of one bad batch from one manufacturer shows that the agency operates without common sense.

- You can't believe what you read about health food products. Marketing generally trumps scientific accuracy and it's too expensive to verify claims for non-patentable compounds. What matters is whether it seems to work for you.

- The price difference between highly-regulated Lovastatin and unregulated cholestin suggests that there should be room for relaxing some FDA regulations. This will require another multi-year battle because bureaucracies give up regulatory turf as eagerly as food sellers give up market share.

- Diet supplements may confer benefits as cholestin reduces blood cholesterol, but nobody can afford to figure out how the nine active ingredients interact in different people. Studying Lovastatin was expensive enough; what would it cost to research eight other ingredients and all the combinations and permutations?

- Money and political pressure speak louder to legislators than facts. "Fact-finding" hearings generally end up browbeating witnesses to make committee members look good.
- We've found all the obvious supplements. Vitamin C deficiency causes scurvy in everyone, iodine deficiency causes goiter, etc. It's harder to figure out whether we need, say, zinc, copper, magnesium, or a zillion other compounds sold as nutraceuticals and if so, how much by whom. We can't prove whether these substances help or hinder health; the controversy will continue.
- There might be room for mechanisms for a) verifying that what's in the bottle matches the label and b) identifying dangerous compounds so that they can carry warnings, but there's not enough trust on either side to even talk about that.
- The billions and billions of dollars involved will fuel the food fight for years to come.

Deciding what government and industry are allowed to say about nutrition will continue to be part of the money and power-driven political process. As with all matters medical, each individual should learn as much as possible about medicines, food supplements, and medical treatment for any particular condition.

Health is far too important to be left to government. Why do we let government control whom we can ask for medical advice?

A Proposal to License Desperation

We could partially relieve the dilemma and take some of the venom out of the discussion by setting up a system for licensing desperate treatments. The FDA was given control of drug sales because so many non-virtuous merchants were selling dangerous or ineffective "snake oil." Over the years, they've expanded their mission to the point that it's becoming too costly to try new treatments.

In the early days, experiments could quickly verify that a new drug was both safe and effective, but we've already found all the easy drugs. The process has gotten more and more expensive and more and more people die waiting for new drugs to be approved.

Genetic makeup has a lot to do with how each person reacts to drugs. This invalidates the FDA's method of treating people as statistically equivalent, but they haven't come up with a substitute.

Fans of food supplements think that a chemical from a plant is "natural" and therefore less likely to do harm than a "drug" made in a chemical plant. That's silly – many medicines were discovered by analyzing plants to find "active ingredients" that had medical effects. The first poisons used by assassins were plant-based. A chemical is a chemical regardless of whether it comes from a plant in the ground or a plant in an industrial park, pun intended.

One way to break the log jam and strike a blow for freedom would be to decide that "pursuit of happiness" means that a dying person may have any treatment at all if conventional treatments have failed. Such a person could go to a licensed "desperation doctor" and take any treatment offered, subject to the following rules:

- There's no legal liability for what a "desperation doctor" does.
- The desperation doctor can charge whatever the patient will pay.
- The patient donates a blood and tissue sample before starting treatment so that genetic peculiarities can be explored later.
- The "desperation doctor" records every treatment administered to the patient to facilitate lessons learned.

- The "desperation doctor" win-lose record is on a web site.

A dying person should have the right to do anything that might help postpone death. Doctors will protest because this would dent their lucrative monopoly, but does society have the right to tell a dying person not to take laetrile? Or St. John's Wort? Or thalidomide? Or anything else they can afford?

Letting dying people choose their own treatments would give us medical data we'd not otherwise have. Setting up a licensing system would give the bureaucracy something to do and reduce the sting of their not being able to regulate what a "desperation doctor" does.

Medical advances can come from outside the profession. The Chamberlen family invented obstetrical forceps. Their rate of childbirth complications was lower than their competitors. They charged higher fees and guarded the secret for 150 years. This was good for them, but secrecy wasn't so good for womankind.

Letting desperate, dying people decide their own treatment would horrify bureaucrats, of course. Licensed "desperation doctors" won't come about unless people get motivated to whack back the bureaucrats, but we can dream, can't we?

Lack of Virtue

The FDA mess is due to lack of virtue. Virtuous businesses didn't sell harmful drugs, but there were so many snake oil salesmen that government pretty much had to get involved. Virtuous bureaucrats wouldn't have forbidden men to take Thalidomide or continued to ban Tryptophan once the real problem was known.

The FDA's failure to grab power over food supplements shows that citizens can change the course of government. This is as it should be in America where the Constitution declares the sovereignty of the people over the government.

We don't know whether our citizens will exert enough pressure to force enough spending cutbacks for our society to survive. The fact that merchants aroused enough citizens to overrule the FDA shows that it can be done, but we have a long way to go to get back to the path of virtue and prosperity.

11 – The United States Department of Injustice

Classical Chinese courts were utterly different from American courts. All authority was vested in the judge, who represented the Emperor's power to impose justice. A judge could order torture as needed to persuade a defendant to confess, for example. Neither defendant nor plaintiff had any rights whatsoever.

The court system started in the villages and ran all the way up to the Emperor. The "district magistrate" was lowest judge in the Chinese judicial system.

> From early times until the establishment of the Chinese republic in 1911, this government official united in his person the functions of judge, jury, prosecutor, and detective.
>
> The territory under his jurisdiction, a district, was the smallest administrative unit in the complicated Chinese government machine; it comprised one fairly large walled city, and all the countryside around it, say for sixty or seventy miles. The district magistrate was the highest civil authority in this unit; he was in charge of the town and land administration, the tribunal, the bureau for the collection of taxes, the register-office, while he was also generally responsible for the maintenance of public order in the entire district. Thus, he had practically full authority over all phases of the life of the people in his district, who called him, therefore, the "father-and-mother official." He was responsible

only to the higher authorities, viz. the prefect or governor of the province.

... Crimes are reported directly to him, it is he who is expected to collect and sift all evidence, find the criminal, arrest him, make him confess, sentence him, and finally administer to him the punishment for his crime.[228]

People called the magistrate the "father-and-mother official" because he acted as the official "head of household" for everyone in his district. Public court hearings offered a degree of accountability for the judge's actions. Everyone appreciated Confucius' assertion that the Emperor had to appoint judges who were paragons of virtue and punish those who weren't.

Finding Virtuous Judges

Chapter 2 introduced the legalists, rivals of Confucius, who believed that perfect laws could protect society when virtue ran out. The legalists forgot that imperfect men would administer their perfect laws. Imperfect men might be tempted to manipulate the law to further their own interests or to curry favor with the powerful.

The conflict between the Confucians and the legalists echo in the politicization of our modern Supreme Court. The belief that judges should follow the original intent of the Constitution rather than rule according to their personal philosophies is a profoundly legalistic idea. This view was expressed by US Supreme Court justice Antonin Scalia when he said, "...[T]he Constitution is not a living organism. It's a legal document."[229]

---

[228] Van Gulik, Robert, *Celebrated Cases of Judge Dee*, (Dover Publications, New York, 1976) p IX Mr. Van Gulik was a scholar of Chinese who translated a number of Chinese documents into English.
[229] Scalia, Antonin. Remarks in a speech in Puerto Rico, quoted in "Why Scalia Is Right" published in a *New York Times* blog by Stanley Fish, April 9, 2006

The "Impeach Earl Warren" bumper stickers of the 1960's and the fierce battle which ended in the US Senate rejecting Robert Bork for the US Supreme Court in 1987[230] show that Americans have two different views of "judicial virtue." One group wants judges who make decisions based on their own individual philosophy; another group wants judges to follow the original text of the Constitution. The personal philosophies of the Justices who "interpret" the Constitution matter far more than what the Constitution says because judges can twist the words to suit their beliefs.

Confucius wouldn't be surprised that Americans understand the importance of virtue in leaders. As Samuel Adams put it, "The public cannot be too curious concerning the character of public men."[231]

Choosing Chinese Judges

Classical Chinese chose entry-level judges by grading students on examinations of material taken from the nine volumes of Confucian classics. Being able to write a prize-winning essay about virtue didn't guarantee that the judge would be virtuous, of course, but the examination system worked quite well for millennia.

Examinations ensured that government officials were at least familiar with Confucian rules for ordering society. This gave them a common vocabulary and thought process, much as elite American universities spread their view of society throughout our government.

Chinese have studied hard for millennia because the only path to power was mastering the Confucian classics. This tradition continues in modern China with the annual examination that determines whether a student can attend college.

---

[230] "Bork's Nomination Is Rejected, 58-42; Reagan 'Saddened'," *New York Times*, October 24, 1987
[231] Adams, Samuel. Letter to James Warren, November 4, 1775

China may be changing at head-twirling speed, but the ritual of the gao kao (pronounced gow kow) remains as immutable as chopsticks. One Chinese saying compares the exam to a stampede of "a thousand soldiers and 10 horses across a single log bridge."

The Chinese test is in some ways like the American SAT, except that it lasts more than twice as long. The nine-hour test is offered once a year and is the sole determinant for admission to virtually all Chinese colleges and universities. About three in five students make the cut.[232]

The more things change in China, the more they remain the same. The examination content is the government's statement of what it takes to succeed in Chinese society and defines what the government regards as virtue.

For thousands of hears, Chinese society has selected powerful people based on ability to learn a large body of written material. As in all societies, powerful Chinese have more children than the less powerful. Natural selection rewards those who learn rapidly.

Duty to Rebel

Confucius saw that when greedy civil servants or judges became too numerous, they'd cover for each other so the Emperor couldn't find them. Once government as a whole became corrupt, there was no way to fix it other than to bring down the entire society and start over. At that point, he said, it was a citizen's duty to rebel.

Article 10 of the New Hampshire State Constitution defines revolution as a right instead of a duty, but the result is the same.

Government being instituted for the common benefit, protection, and security, of the whole

232 "China's College Entry Test Is An Obsession," *New York Times*, June 12, 2009

community, and not for the private interest or emolument of any one man, family, or class of men; therefore, whenever the ends of government are perverted, and public liberty manifestly endangered, and all other means of redress are ineffectual, the people may, and of right ought to reform the old, or establish a new government. The doctrine of nonresistance against arbitrary power, and oppression, is absurd, slavish, and destructive of the good and happiness of mankind.

Confucius anticipated the American right of revolution when he said, "... if the people have no faith (in their rulers), then there is no standing (for the state)."[233]

When he said that rulers had to serve people well enough to keep their loyalty and support, Confucius asserted that people are the ultimate source of actual power. History demonstrates that any government that loses the trust and confidence of its people falls eventually, either by conquest from outside or from internal rebellion.

The American Declaration of Independence places sovereignty with the people but goes beyond Confucius in arguing that common people have rights instead of only duties. "Governments are instituted among Men, deriving their just powers from the consent of the governed, — that whenever any Form of Government becomes destructive of these ends, it is the Right of the People to alter or to abolish it, and to institute new Government."

No Due Process

The Chinese legal system had no notion of due process. Although the court system administered cases partly on written law, partly on tradition, and partly on the judge's common sense, a higher-level official might intervene and direct the verdict at any time.

---

[233] Confucius, *Analects*, XII, vii

The case of Yang Bin shows that nothing has changed. Yang Bin became one of China's first billionaires. He flaunted his wealth, got involved in relationships between China and North Korea, and was sentenced to 18 years in jail for bribery and forgery.

In the West, the Industrial Revolution created an entire new "merchant class" who rapidly became far wealthier than the old-time noble families. It took several generations to work out how to share power with the new millionaires and billionaires.

The ancient Chinese government didn't have to cope with a great deal of wealth that was outside direct government control. Opening the Chinese economy to world markets has created vast wealth in China. The modern Chinese government hasn't figured out a constructive way to handle wealthy individuals who've become far more numerous and powerful than at any time in China's past:

> "A few people in China have gotten rich beyond imagination, and the government needs to show that it controls rich people, too," said Liu Huan, a finance expert at the Central University of Finance and Economics in Beijing. "Private entrepreneurs have higher status now than before, but they also have more demands on them."
>
> The crackdown on industry titans shows how China's economy -- however robust and Westernized it appears on the surface -- still answers to an ossified political system. The country has a growing number of multimillionaires and even a few billionaires, but <u>their fortunes depend on the whims of a handful of Communist Party officials</u>. [emphasis added]
>
> China recognizes that private enterprise, long the most dynamic part of the economy, has become its mainstay. As state-run companies continue to shrink and lay off workers, the private sector has surged ahead, increasing efficiency and production as well as the personal wealth of an entrepreneurial elite.

Privately run businesses now account for just over half of the gross domestic product and employ 130 million people -- the lion's share of industrial workers, but only about one-fifth the total work force.

At least on paper, China has built the legal infrastructure to enforce commercial laws much as the United States does. The difference is that real enforcement occurs only when party bosses in Beijing decide that the time has come, and when they identify capitalists who have fallen from favor.[234]

The American concept of "equality before the law" means that no one should be above the law regardless of wealth or position. This sounds good in theory – Leona Helmsley went to jail for income tax evasion even though she was an extremely wealthy woman[235] – but as the *New York Times* states, law enforcement is more of a political matter than a legal matter in China.

Western economic history shows that having a well-working, predictable justice system affects the economy:

The rule of law is held to be not only good in itself, because it embodies and encourages a just society, but also a cause of other good things, notably growth. "No other single political ideal has ever achieved global endorsement," says Brian Tamanaha, a legal scholar at St John's University, New York.[236]

---

234 "To Be Rich, Chinese and in Trouble: 3 Tales," *New York Times*, October 13, 2002

235 Markham, Jerry, *A financial history of modern U.S. corporate scandals: from Enron to reform* (M.E. Sharpe, 2005) p 392

236 "Economics and the rule of law," *Economist*, Mar 13, 2008

The Perception of Justice

Wise governments try to encourage taxable economic activity by creating institutions stable enough and predictable enough that sellers have confidence that they'll get paid. A business can't grow beyond the size a family can administer in a single location without an efficient banking system to handle payment, borrow money against receivables, and supply credit.

Societies also need courts to resolve disputes and deter lawbreakers. Courts and banks can take many forms, but without reliable law enforcement, commerce is held back when people can't enforce contracts or can't transfer money. Without commerce, there's nothing to tax except the rice crop. If rice taxes were too high, the farmer starved and there was nothing to tax next year.

A Chinese magistrate was so visible to townspeople that a corrupt magistrate could get an entire district irritated at the government. This led to problems collecting taxes and in getting cooperation. One reason Chinese court proceedings were open to the public was that the Chinese understood the ancient axiom, "Justice must not only be done, justice must be seen to be done."[237]

President Obama has had difficulty finding competent, virtuous cabinet officials who were sympathetic to his policies. Just a day before Senator Tom Daschle withdrew his nomination to be Secretary of Health and Human Services thanks to public revelations of his tax evasions, Mr. Obama reminded us of the importance of maintaining at least the appearance of impartial justice:

> I've got to own up to my mistake, which is that ultimately it's important for this administration to send a message that there aren't two sets of rules. You know, one for prominent people and one for ordinary folks who have to pay their taxes.[238]

[237] Rosenthal, Joel H., Barry, *Christian, Ethics & International Affairs: A Reader* (Georgetown University Press, 2009) p 288
[238] President Barack Obama, *New York Times* quote of the day, Feb. 4, 2009

Mr. Obama was correct in saying that it's important for people to believe that everyone plays by the same set of rules. When Sen. Daschle failed to pay more than $100,000 in taxes on time, he had to pay once his omission came to light but suffered no further penalties.[239] Charlie Rangel, who chaired the House committee that writes tax law, only had to apologize and resign his chairmanship for "forgetting" to pay taxes on foreign income. [240] He didn't go to jail either.

Lenient treatment of politicians contrasts with Leona Helmsley's jail term for not declaring income when she received services from her business' employees whose salaries were tax-deductible. That's the same way Sen. Daschle evaded taxes but he too didn't go to jail. [241]

Given such high-level tax cheating, normal folks feel that there are in fact two sets of rules: easy rules for big-shot politicians and harder, more expensive rules for everyone else. This is what Confucius said would happen when government officials lose virtue.

How Many Sets of Rules?

Our Founders understood the importance of making sure that government officials were bound by the law in the same way as everyone else; they knew how the British and French kings had jailed people whom they disliked.[242] The term "letter de cachet," which means "signed letter," referred to the King of France's practice of giving his friends signed arrest warrants with a blank

---

[239] "Obama on Defense as Daschle Withdraws," *Wall Street Journal*, Feb 4, 2009

[240] "Censured Charles Rangel can't help himself," *The Washington Post*, April 25, 2013

[241] Harnden, Toby "Barack Obama nominees forced to quit over taxes," The *Daily Telegraph* (London), (February 3, 2009.

[242] Alexander Dumas' *The Count of Monte Christo* is a fictional account of a man who'd been wrongly imprisoned in the Chateau d'If off Marseilles. Arbitrary imprisonments were common enough not to arouse readers' disbelief.

spot for the name of the arrestee. These warrants could jail anyone simply by filling in the name.

The Constitution insists on "due process" before imprisoning someone or taking his property. The Founders wanted to outlaw the abuse of government authority that was common everywhere in the world at the time. Despite their best intentions, however, America had a long and bitter experience with having two sets of rules.

For example, when Thomas Jefferson wrote "All men are created equal," an entire category of men and women weren't equal at all – blacks. Many of the Founders recognized the irony and injustice of fighting for their own liberty while enslaving others. John Jay, whom President Washington appointed to be the first Chief Justice of our Supreme Court, wrote in the *Federalist Papers:*

> It is much to be wished that slavery may be abolished. The honor of the States, as well as justice and humanity, in my opinion, loudly call upon them to emancipate these unhappy people. To contend for our own liberty, and to deny that blessing to others, involves an inconsistency not to be excused.[243]

Why didn't the Founders outlaw slavery? They were concerned about the upheaval that would be involved in moving from a slave society to a society without slavery. Benjamin Franklin wrote:

> Slavery is such an atrocious debasement of human nature, that its very extirpation, if not performed with solicitous care, may sometimes open a source of serious evils.[244]

Mr. Franklin's fear of "serious evils" was correct: it took the "serious evil" and bloodshed of the Civil War to abolish the injustice of slavery and another full century of racial discrimination before American blacks began to receive the equality to which they were entitled under the law.

---

[243] Letter to R. Lushington, March 15, 1786
[244] Isaacson , Walter, *Benjamin Franklin* (Simon and Schuster, 2003) p 465

Dr. Martin Luther King Jr. appealed to Americans' heritage in our Constitution and Declaration of Independence in his "I Have a Dream" speech where he defined justice as people being judged by their character rather than by their color or by who they were.[245]

Statues of Justice show a blindfolded lady holding a sword and a set of balances. Count verdicts shouldn't depend on whether a defendant is rich or poor, powerful or weak, male or female, black or white, but on the law as written and the facts of the case or, as Dr. King put it, the content of the defendant's character. Only if courts and the law work in this way can people hope to understand the law well enough to obey it. If what happens in court depends on who you are or on whom you know, how can you know how to act or know how to expect others to behave?

As in America, getting caught up in the court system was expensive for Chinese commoners lacking political power.[246] The Chinese understood the desirability of justice being predictable but they had no Constitution. With no institutional checks on government, Chinese citizens were protected only by the personal virtue of local officials.

A widespread sense of predictable and consistent "equal justice under law" also helps affects society's prosperity or lack thereof. During the period 946-1087, for example, the economy of South Fukien, one of the Chinese Maritime Provinces, grew rapidly. Government encouraged the boom via streamlined, predictable justice and support of the banking system.[247] Today, we see a vast difference in prosperity between countries with predictable legal and financial systems and those with capricious courts where property rights are not protected,[248] just as Mr. Obama said.

---

[245] Delivered at the Lincoln Memorial on August 28, 1963
[246] So, Billy, Su, Jilang, *Prosperity, region, and institutions in maritime China: the South Fukien pattern, 946-1368* (Harvard Univ Asia Center, 2000) p 249
[247] Ibid., p 27
[248] Aghion, Philippe , Durlauf, Steven N., *Handbook of economic growth* (Elsevier, 2005) p 277

The Khans and the Necessity of Law

Genghis Khan, who united the Mongol tribes and conquered an empire that reached from northern China to the gates of Vienna, was born at a time when the Mongolian tribes had essentially no legal system beyond "might makes right." His mother was kidnapped from her first husband before he was conceived and his father abandoned the family. He was enslaved in his youth. His wife was stolen for long enough that his oldest son's paternity was in question.

Genghis realized that he had to stop his tribes from fighting each other for his regime to survive. He instituted laws that even he had to obey. The tribes weren't used to the idea of laws. It took years of persuasion backed by execution, but Genghis left a stable, unified nation that was loyal to one set of laws.

Business prospered under stable laws combined with paper money and other financial documents that were recognized over a 3,000 mile span. The economy expanded fast enough that government spending could pay his warriors enough to keep them contented.

After Genghis died, his youngest son's wife proved to be the best politician and the Mongol empire ended up divided among her four sons. Her youngest son Kublai inherited the smallest piece, the part of northern China which Genghis had conquered.

Kublai was a better politician than warrior. Instead of challenging his relatives, he took the rest of China away from the ruling Sung dynasty through diplomacy, propaganda, and encouraging businesses. His scheming took advantage of the legal system his grandfather had instituted. Ordinary Chinese who feared the Sung's reputation for arbitrary decrees moved to Kublai's domain to take advantages of his predictable business environment.

The first concern in doing business is finding customers. After the sale, the problem changes to getting paid. From a business point of view, government should offer swift, predictable answers to payment disputes. Getting paid is fundamental – no one starts a business unless they're convinced they'll get paid.[249]

When businessmen seeking assurance of payment moved to his territory, their taxes helped fund his imperialistic notions.[250] This virtuous cycle made his eventual victory seem more and more inevitable. When Kublai finally stormed the Sung's capital city in 1276 after nearly two decades of scheming, his army had more Chinese allies than Mongol soldiers.[251]

The 5th amendment to the US Constitution placed the protection of property on the same level of importance as life and liberty:

> ... nor be deprived of life, liberty, or property, without due process of law – moreover, the 14th amendment extends this restriction on government action to the states.

The Emperors who came after Kublai didn't maintain the practice of subordinating themselves to well-defined laws. They discarded Genghis' labors, reverted to "might makes right," and ruled by arbitrary decree. Court officials copied the Emperor in violating the law and their bad example spread all the way down the system. The dynasty ended when virtue ran out and their subjects rebelled.

---

[249] This illustrates the basic law of capitalism – nothing happens unless it's more wonderful than money. You don't buy something unless it's more wonderful to you than what you pay. If the product doesn't meet that standard, you keep your money and the store loses a sale. The business challenge is to figure out how to be perceived as more wonderful than money at low cost to you.

[250] Azfar, Omar, Cadwell, Charles, *Market-augmenting Government: The Institutional Foundations for Prosperity* (Univ. of Michigan Press, 2003) p 33

[251] Jack Weatherford, *Genghis Khan and the Making of the Modern World*, Three Rivers Press (New York, 2004) Chapter 8

When Virtue Runs Out

The people who operate the American legal system no longer seek consistent, predictable justice and pursue personal gain instead. I saw this in 1989 when police took four children from friends of mine on false child abuse charges. His mother-in-law got angry and spouted an exaggerated tale about his spanking his kids. The story went to the local police.

My friend always spoke out against buying the cops new toys at town meeting so they were glad to swoop down on him even though New Hampshire law specifically permitted parents to spank their children. One officer testified in court that they responded vigorously against him because he was "vocal in the community."

Aren't freedom of speech and freedom from fear two of the Four Freedoms lauded by FDR and immortalized in a painting by Norman Rockwell, the patron saint of Americana? "Four freedoms" is a good sound-bite, but freedom suffers when officials lose virtue.

My friend spent more than his net worth on lawyers. The Child Protection Agency spent money on lawyers, counselors, therapists, guardians, and all kinds of hangers-on. He got his children back after his youngest child suffered two broken arms and a worm infection while in state custody. His marriage was placed under great strain. Financially, he never recovered.

The Terminated Contract

Some years later, the government railroaded my employer into jail because the Navy didn't want to pay termination fees for ending a contract. His story illustrates one way you can protect yourself if the government ever starts asking you questions.

Warship crew training was found to be inadequate in the late 1980s. The USS *Stark* was nearly sunk by an airborne missile fired by Iraq, and the USS *Vincennes* shot down a civilian airliner by mistake. My company won the contract to deliver a more realistic naval combat trainer.

The contracting office wanted to award the contract to a large firm that had promised to hire the contract administrators when they retired. Politicians can direct money via earmarks, but the bureaucrats couldn't just give the money to their friends. My company won with a price so low that the rules forced the bureaucrats to buy the trainer from us and watch their cushy post-retirement jobs fluttering away into the distance.

We didn't find out that we weren't supposed to have won the contract for a year or so. We were continually frustrated as the government stalled instead of providing the detailed data we needed to model the weapons, ships, airplanes, bombs, and other items students had to learn to use. Understanding the performance of weapons, radar, engines, and other equipment was crucial to developing a computer system accurate enough to meet the training requirements for realistic combat.

I hadn't yet applied what I knew of the Confucian Cycle to the US government. I naively thought the contracting office wanted a good trainer. In reality, they didn't care if the trainer worked - they had wanted the money to go to someone else all along. We saw a similar situation when Sen. John McCain stopped the fraudulent Boeing airborne-tanker contract in 2004.[252]

The Reckoning

When President Reagan bankrupted the "Evil Empire" by funding Star Wars at a level the Soviets couldn't match, our deep-water trainer wasn't needed for the irregular conflicts we're in now. The contracting office used the changed international situation as an excuse to terminate our contract.

The government could terminate the project at any time, of course, but the contract said the government owed us about $8 million in termination payments. When they wouldn't pay, we filed

---

[252] "McCain Advisers Lobbied for Europeans to Win Air Force Tanker Deal", *New York Times*, March 12, 2008

a claim with the Contract Board of Appeals, a court-like system which is supposed to resolve conflicts more cheaply than a real court.

The Board of Appeals requires that everybody turn over all the evidence; this is known as "discovery." During discovery, we received a government Power Point that admitted that they might owe us as much as $11 million. We thought we'd get paid.

It was a year before we got to the board. As our Hearing Master gaveled the session to order, a government employee ran in and said that the US Attorney had charged my boss with fraud in connection with the contract. The hearing master noted the strange coincidence with respect to timing, but he had to suspend the hearing because criminal charges take precedence over contract appeals.

We later found that the "Justice" Department not only ranked lawyers by how much jail time they got, they gave extra points for helping other government agencies save money. Ranking lawyers by jail time means that once a Justice Department official has invested enough time or effort investigating someone, his career is damaged if he can't inflict at least some jail time on the target.[253]

Rudy Giuliani had not yet shown everyone how to get elected mayor by bringing spectacular charges to collect headlines, but our US attorney wanted a promotion to Washington. He thought he could earn points by saving the Navy money even though there was no evidence that any fraud had been committed.

My Friend from the Concentration Camp

One of my friends who'd worked on the contract knew that he had to protect himself. He was a 3rd-generation Japanese-American who'd been born in a Wyoming concentration camp. Our government had rounded up his parents early in World War II. They met and married in the camp; he was born there. He

---

[253] "White Collar Gestapo," *Forbes*, Dec. 1, 1997, p 82

understandably grew up with a somewhat cynical view of "truth, justice, and the American way."

He refused to talk to the government without an "immunity letter." He explained how it worked. "You testify for hours under oath," he said. "It's perjury if you lie. Nobody can remember every detail of this mess. They go over what you say with a fine-tooth comb. If they don't like what you say, they tell you that you don't agree with something. You stick with what you said and they hammer you. If you admit you might be wrong, they gotcha. They can charge you with perjury, which means jail. They bend your testimony to get what they want. If you complain, it's jail."

His letter granted him immunity from any charges coming out of whatever he said. That protected him from threats which might manipulate his testimony. "How did you make them write the letter?" I wanted to know.

"I asked if I was a target, a suspect, or a witness. They said I was a witness, so I asked for the letter. They said the judge would force me to talk. I told them to get ready for two or three days instead of a half-day or so. They asked 'Why?' Because, I told them, every question you ask, including my name, I'll plead the 5th amendment against self-incrimination.[254] The only way to break the 5th is for the judge to grant me immunity for my answer. I answer. You ask me another question, I take the 5th, you ask the judge to grant me immunity, and so it goes. The grand jury will get bored."

I asked how his name could incriminate him. "The Census Bureau claims answers are confidential," he told me. "During WW II, the Bureau gave the Army a list of people with Japanese names or

---

[254] No person shall be held to answer for a capital, or otherwise infamous crime, unless on presentment or indictment of a Grand Jury, except in cases arising in the land or naval forces, or in the Militia, when in actual service in time of War or public danger; nor shall any person be subject for the same offense to be twice put in jeopardy of life or limb; **nor shall be compelled in any criminal case to be a witness against himself**, nor be deprived of life, liberty, or property, without due process of law; nor shall private property be taken for public use, without just compensation. Fifth Amendment, United States Constitution [emphasis added]

who lived in Japanese neighborhoods. So much for government promises. My parents were locked up for their names; they could have been locked up for where they lived. I could take the 5th on my name and on my address and on anything else they asked. So they gave me the letter."

Scooter Libby and Martha Stewart would have avoided serious problems if they'd simply refused to talk to the feds. The amendment says, "No person," it's available to anyone.

Six Months in Club Fed

When the government called me before the grand jury, I asked for, and got, the same immunity letter. I could testify without fear of getting caught up in the government's political games.

It didn't work out so well for my boss. Having invested so much time investigating him, the government employees had to get *something* for Attorney General Janet Reno, even though their victim was no more guilty than the alleged sex abusers Reno had persecuted in Florida on her way to being nominated by President Clinton.

They accused him of "mail fraud" for a "misleading" letter to a major Swiss investor in spite of an affidavit from the investor saying that he had not been misled. The investor wouldn't come to the US to testify for fear that he might not be allowed to return home.

They also invented bogus money-laundering charges. To pressure my boss, the investigators had the IRS seize our corporate bank accounts. He beat those charges and the IRS gave money back, but it was hard to meet payroll with an empty bank account. Government control over the banking system gives regulatory officials great power that is ripe for abuse.

State law makes it a serious offense not to meet payroll; he paid us in cash. The amounts involved let the feds charge him with money laundering.[255]

Money laundering is defined as taking cash from outside the banking system and converting it to deposits in the banking system. For this to be a crime there has to be a "predicate act," that is, the money has to be the proceeds of a crime. My boss was doing the exact opposite of money laundering – he was converting bank deposits to cash, not the other way 'round – but the feds added money laundering to the list of charges.

He accepted a six-month sentence in a "Club Fed" minimum security prison despite having spent more than a million dollars on legal fees. The Navy paid $2 million for the cancellation instead of their own $11 million estimate. My boss didn't want to lie, so he refused the "mail fraud" charges and confessed to one count of money laundering without a predicate act which made it no crime at all.

He had to cave because the charges added up to more than 150 years in jail. At that time, judges could sentence someone based on all charges even if the jury acquitted the defendant of all but one charge. This was 150 years in jail in his case. This abusive tactic makes it difficult for an innocent defendant to do anything other than plead guilty – the downside risk of not copping a plea is too great.

The judge let him out of Club Fed early; the prison counseling bureaucracy claimed credit for "rehabilitating" him.

Some months later, an army general phoned and told him that the Navy procurement command that had cheated us had been shut down and its functions had been transferred to the US Army. After some thought, he realized that this was the only apology he'd ever receive from a government he'd done his best to serve, not only as a civilian, but as a Marine officer sent in harm's way to recover our freighter the *Mayaguez* under President Ford.

---

[255] Androphy, Joe, "The Government's Dirty Laundry," *Forbes*, April 7, 2008 describes many cases where government abused the term "money laundering."

Injustice Has Become Normal

On March 12, 2008, the *New York Times* reported the resignation of Governor Eliot Spitzer (D-NY) because he'd been a customer of a prostitution ring. Gov. Spitzer's fall removed a powerful man who had perfected the art of destroying people without a shred of criminal evidence.

Spitzer's technique was to accuse a business or a highly visible person of some ill-defined crime, reap publicity and name recognition, preen for the press, and move on. The accused usually copped a plea for a trifling amount of money just to get the matter to go away. By that time, the issue was forgotten; only the charges were remembered. Spitzer rode the publicity into the governor's office, only to see the same process destroy him as Robespierre died in the same guillotine to which he had sent so many.

American politicians don't traditionally like to completely destroy each other; the fact that a wealthy, powerful, well-connected man like Spitzer was hounded out of office shows that none of us are safe. Shortly after his resignation, we learned that he had been investigated with unusual intensity:

> The scale and intensity of the investigation of Mr. Spitzer, then the governor of New York, seemed on its face to be a departure for the Justice Department, which aggressively investigates allegations of wrongdoing by public officials, but almost never investigates people who pay prostitutes for sex.[256]

The *Times* noted that the Justice Department "almost never" spends resources investigating prostitution. The Department justified their investigation of Mr. Spitzer by pointing out that they might be accused of a cover-up if they hadn't followed up the matter, but other Justice officials acknowledged that they rarely chase

---

[256] "U.S. Defends Tough Tactics on Spitzer", *New York Times*, March 21, 2008

clients of prostitution rings. This illustrates how government officials can pick and choose whom to pursue and whom to destroy. The Justice Department might have been egged on by some powerful person who'd been annoyed by Mr. Spitzer. We may never know.

Abuse of power is as old as power. Governor Spitzer wasn't alone in abusing prosecutorial power for personal gain. Durham County District Attorney Mike Nifong charged Duke University lacrosse players with rape on false evidence partly to help win re-election.[257] He won, but was eventually disbarred after his victims were vindicated. His fraud came out because his victims' families believed their sons and mortgaged their homes to hire investigators and lawyers.

Ambitious prosecutors won't refrain from abusing their powers to win publicity just because Mr. Nifong was disbarred and Mr. Spitzer was forced to resign in disgrace. South Carolina Attorney General Henry McMaster gained publicity by accusing Craigslist of facilitating prostitution by letting people post ads in their "adult services" section. Craigslist management changed their operations and claimed to be in full compliance with all applicable laws. When McMaster continued to threaten the site's management with prosecution, Craigslist sued him,[258] but how many of us have the money to take a government official to court?

There are tens of thousands of prosecutors working for federal, state, and local departments of justice and they all need something to do. The Justice Department ranks lawyers by how much jail time they inflict[259] although they don't admit that any more than the IRS admits ranking investigators by how much money they get.

The Department doesn't care whether the accused are guilty or innocent. There are individual lawyers and judges who care about justice, but the system doesn't care because doing justice isn't

[257] "Former Duke Prosecutor Nifong Disbarred," *ABC News*, June 16, 2007
[258] "Craigslist Ready to Sue, McMaster Claims Victory," *Charlestown City Paper*, May 20, 2009
[259] "White Collar Gestapo," *Forbes*, Dec. 1, 1997, p 82

rewarded by increased budgets or promotions. As a well-known governor once asked during a capital criminal trial, "What is truth?"[260]

Perverse Incentives Drive Perverse Actions

In 1976, the Supreme Court ruled that prosecutors have absolute immunity from civil lawsuits. They acknowledged that their ruling left a defendant who'd been wronged with no means to obtain justice, but said that the alternative of prosecutors facing lawsuits every time they lost a case was worse. Thus, although the 5th Circuit ruled in 1992 in *Sanders v English*[261] that your rights could be violated by prosecutorial misconduct, the earlier Supreme Court ruling meant that there was nothing you could do about it.[262]

The perverse incentives in our justice system have led to precisely the results we'd expect – justice is systematically perverted in favor of bureaucratic self-interest. *USA Today* told how Nino Lyons spent three years in jail for dealing in drugs.[263] Witnesses testified that Lyons had sold them drugs, but the prosecutors never revealed that a) most of the witnesses were prison inmates and b) some of the inmates were promised early release if they testified against Lyons.

In another case, prosecutors gave green cards to illegal immigrants when they testified against an accused government employee.

Although federal prosecutors are supposed to seek justice instead of merely maximizing jail time, *USA Today* found that the incentives which have been put in place by the bureaucracy led more than 200 cases where judges determined that federal prosecutors violated either the law or legal ethics to secure convictions.

---

[260] John 18:38
[261] *Sanders v English*, 950 F.2d 1152, 1163 (5th Cir 1992)
[262] *Imbler v. Pachtman*, 424 U.S. 409 (1976)
[263] "Prosecutor's conduct can tip the scales," *USA Today*, Sept. 23, 2010, p. 1A

The *Wall Street Journal* reported that the Northern California innocence Project found that prosecutors were punished in only about 1% of the 600 cases of proven prosecutorial misconduct. The *Journal* quoted the study's authors, "[Prosecutorial misconduct] fundamentally perverts the course of justice" and "undermines our trust in the reliability of the justice system."[264]

Confucius expected the Emperor to correct such problems by decapitating the unjust. Once citizens lost confidence in state institutions, rebellion in the form of lack of cooperation, lying to the government, and tax cheating inevitably followed.

A Multitude of New Offices

Mens rea, which is Latin for "guilty mind," is an important part of the "due process" our Constitution requires before anyone can be convicted of a crime. Criminal intent is obvious when someone smashes into your house and steals something. In cases involving Byzantine government regulations, however, it's hard to convince a jury that the defendant intended to commit a crime that the jurors have probably never heard of and can barely understand.

Criminal laws that nobody can figure out and which anyone can trip over should be repealed. A law that can't get conviction in court is no law at all. Instead of repealing such incomprehensible laws, however, Congress is removing *mens rea* protection.

Our elected representatives have not only defined violating an agency's rules as crimes, they're also saying that the agency needn't prove that the accused intended to commit a crime. The *Wall Street Journal* estimates that the federal criminal code occupies 27 feet of shelf space.[265] It's impossible for anyone, even lawyers, to know what all the federal crimes are.

---

[264] "Punishment Found Lacking in Prosecutor Misconduct," *Wall Street Journal*, 10/5/2010, p A6

[265] "Federal Police Ranks Swell to Enforce a Widening Array of Criminal Laws," *Wall Street Journal*, Dec 17, 2011

This makes bureaucrats happy – the more "criminals" they catch, the more money they ask for. Having rule-violations defined as crimes makes them seem more important. Like Child Protection agencies, they've been given perverse incentives to boost their statistics – they create "criminals" by defining honest mistakes as crimes.

As soon as rules carried criminal penalties, agencies got permission to fund their own police forces. A Federal SWAT team from the Environmental Protection Agency, the Labor or Education departments, the National Park Service, the Bureau of Land Management or even the National Oceanic and Atmospheric Administration that forecasts weather (!) can bust down your door.

> Agents from NOAA along with the Fish and Wildlife Service raided the Miami business of Morgan Mok in 2008, seeking evidence she had broken the Endangered Species Act trading in coral.
>
> The agents had assault rifles and the case documents indicated her house and business records had been under surveillance over a six-month period, says Ms. Mok. Under the 1973 law, the departments of Interior and Commerce (home to NOAA) must write regulations to define what is endangered and how it must be protected. One of those regulations specifies coral. ...
>
> Ms. Mok says she showed that her coral had been properly obtained. She paid a $500 fine and served one year of probation for failing to complete paperwork for an otherwise legal transaction.[266]

NOAA didn't have to show that Ms. Mok intended to break their rules, they only needed to show that she hadn't done the paperwork

---

[266] "Federal Police Ranks Swell to Enforce a Widening Array of Criminal Laws," *Wall Street Journal*, Dec 17, 2011

correctly. Once exempt from *mens rea*, improper paperwork became a criminal act which could have earned her jail time.

The *Journal* also told of Lawrence Lewis, a maintenance engineer who was jailed when a blocked toilet sent sewage into a creek. He worked at a nursing home where elderly residents often flushed adult diapers down the toilets, jamming the sewers and flooding the facility. Long before Mr. Lewis started there, standard practice was to divert overflow into a storm drain to protect low-lying apartments full of sick people.

Nobody knew the drain led to the creek until a jogger noticed murky water on March 29, 2007 and the EPA brought criminal charges. Mr. Lewis' lawyer told him his intentions and his ignorance didn't matter – any violation was a crime regardless of intent, and he'd admitted starting the pump which fed the storm drain. He went to jail for mishandling a blocked-up toilet.[267]

Any offense against any rule can be treated as a criminal matter regardless of intent, so it's best to say nothing at all to any government employee at any level. Anything you say will be used against you because the agency wants a bigger budget. Just plead the 5th!

King George Strikes Again

The Declaration of Independence complained about King George III. "He has erected a multitude of New Offices, and sent hither swarms of Officers to harass our people, and eat out their substance."

The King's men wanted revenue; they didn't want to put people in jail. Convicts don't have income from which to pay taxes and they consume resources because they have to be fed.

Our Congress is stupider than King George's revenue agents. By lowering legal standards for putting people in jail, Congress does more than "eat out our substance." People in jail have no substance

---

[267] "A Sewage Blunder Earns Engineer a Criminal Record," *Wall Street Journal*, Dec 12, 2011, p A1

with which to pay taxes, and criminal records make it impossible to get jobs. There's no substance for anyone to eat.

The Roman aristocracy kept laws secret and enforced them severely against the lower classes. Opportunities for abuse abounded because only judges were familiar with the law. After decades of protest, Roman law was posted in the forum around 450 BC for anyone to read.[268] We're submitting once again to the tyranny of secret, unknowable, incomprehensible criminal laws.

King George merely multiplied offices, but there's no way to become familiar with 27 feet of fine print listing tens of thousands of federal crimes. The only way to restore justice is to whack government back to size, which we ought to do anyway.

The first step is to restore *mens rea!* It's OK to fine people for mistakes when they aren't trying to commit crimes, but mistakes or well-intended actions such as any rational person might do should never bring jail time.

How We Got Here

Our Founders knew that there was no way to guarantee virtue in government officials. They divided government power because only government can keep government in check. They hoped that the legislative, judicial, and executive branches of government would keep an eye on each other.

The Founders hoped that states could serve as an additional check on the central government. State legislators appointed US Senators until we changed the Constitution in 1913. A Senator's was appointed to make sure that the federal government didn't usurp power from state governments.

People could move to another state if any state government became abusive. The fact that more Americans move from high-tax to low-tax states than in the other direction shows the wisdom of

---

[268] Roth, Mitchel P., *Crime and Punishment: A History of the Criminal Justice System,* (Cengage Learning, 2005) p 13

the Founders' model of state governments competing for citizens' favor.

The 10th Amendment put strict limits on the federal government:

> The powers not delegated to the United States by the Constitution, nor prohibited by it to the States, are reserved to the States respectively, or to the people. – US Constitution, Article X.

The federal government has no Constitutional power to involve itself in education, old age pensions, drug regulation, or welfare. The Constitution forbids most of what the federal government does. The court system was supposed to protect citizens from the legislature's desire to grab power or spend money on their friends, but the Supreme Court gave up the battle in 1937.

Up until that time, the Court had voided most of President Roosevelt's "New Deal" legislation on the unarguable grounds that the Constitution did not permit the Federal government to do what Roosevelt wanted to do. The Constitution doesn't specify how many judges should serve on the Supreme Court, however. Roosevelt threatened to "pack the court" by using his Democratic majority in the Senate to appoint extra judges who would see things his way.

Though FDR's scheme to "pack the court" failed in a public relations disaster, he won because Justice Owen Roberts switched sides. Instead of 5-4 majorities ruling against bigger government, the court issued 5-4 rulings in favor. From then on, the Court upheld essentially any program the federal legislature wished.[269]

The 18 clauses of Article I, Section 8 of the Constitution list all legitimate legislative powers of the Federal government. The "Commerce Clause" describes one of these powers:

---

[269] O'Toole, Randal, *The Best-Laid Plans*, (Cato Institute, 2007) p 307

> 3: To regulate Commerce with foreign Nations, and among the several States, and with the Indian Tribes;

Justice Roberts interpreted the "commerce clause" more broadly than in the past. The ruling in *Wicard v Filburn* illustrates the destruction of state power in favor of the federal government. A farmer named Filburn grew grain to feed his animals. Since his grain was eaten on his farm and did not enter interstate commerce, Filburn argued, the government had no right to tell him how much he could grow. The Department of Agriculture wanted to limit the grain farmers grew to keep prices high.

The court ruled against Filburn, pointing out that he would have bought grain if he hadn't grown his own. The grain he would have bought might have been grown in another state. His not buying grain affected interstate commerce and the government had the right to tell him how much grain he could grow.[270]

Similar logic was used to rule that the State of California could not allow California citizens to use "medical marijuana" which had been grown in California – their legal pot couldn't be distinguished from illegal pot grown in other states and was therefore part of interstate commerce just as Filburn's home-grown and home-eaten grain was part of interstate commerce. In essence, all drugs are part of interstate commerce and are subject to federal regulation.[271]

When you breathe in oxygen and exhale carbon dioxide, your CO_2 might drift to another state. Every breath you take is part of interstate commerce and is subject to regulations relating to CO_2 emissions; so says our Supreme Court.

The State of Montana is responding to these federal power grabs by considering a law declaring that guns made and kept in Montana are not involved in interstate commerce and are not subject to

---

[270] *Wicard v Filburn*, 317 U.S. 111 (1942)
[271] *Gonzales v Raich*, 352 F. 3d 1222

federal gun control laws.[272] A "Made in Montana" stamp takes them out of interstate commerce until they cross a state line.

Only a few black-powder and high-end hunting rifles are produced in Montana. Someone in Montana may start making .22 caliber rifles or automatic pistols without applying for a manufacturing license from the Bureau of Alcohol, Tobacco, and Firearms.

What will the feds do if Montana police arrest federal officers for harassing gun owners whose actions are legal under Montana law? The feds could go to federal court, but what if the state denies federal jurisdiction because the right to regulate guns in the state of Montana is "reserved to the states, or to the people" per the 10th Amendment? What then? Will the feds arrest the governor? Will state police or county sheriffs arrest the feds? Do we want to find out?

Back to the Confucian Path of Virtue

Our Founders did their best, but their failure to specify the number of Supreme Court judges gave President Roosevelt a way to destroy their system of limited Federal government. His threat to "pack the court" made Justice Roberts yield to his demands. This opened the way for "more than one hundred agencies and sub-agencies" as mentioned in Chapter 3 to write rules which take control of larger and larger portions of our lives and impose criminal sanctions on us.

Enacting laws to set up government agencies wouldn't be of much use if the Federal government couldn't pay the agencies' expenses; few bureaucrats are willing to write rules for free.

The Founders intended that the Federal government be under-funded – the Constitution limited the Federal government to collecting taxes on imports. The Founders believed that tariffs would encourage domestic manufacturing, which it did, and that import duties couldn't provide enough to support the Federal

---

[272] House Bill 246, Montana Legislature, 2009 session

government in the style to which it would want to become accustomed.

The Federal government imposed an income tax and an excise tax to pay for the Civil War, but these were repealed after the war ended. An income tax established in 1894 was ruled unconstitutional. Instead of threatening the Supreme Court, the legislature amended the Constitution so that an income tax came into being in 1913.

Without the vast sums of money yielded by the income tax, the Supreme Court decisions permitting the New Deal laws that so greatly expanded government would have had no effect. Sen. Moynihan's "Professionalization of reform" would have been impossible because of lack of money.

The best way to coax government back to the path of virtue is to "starve the beast," as President Reagan put it, through tax cuts and by abolishing the federal agencies that are not permitted under the enumerated powers given Congress under Article 1 Section 8.

The charts showing the number of government employees in Chapter 3 illustrates that cutting taxes only slows government growth. Although the only hope for cutting the bureaucracy is to un-elect politicians who keep voting for bigger government, there's another change which would make the system less damaging.

When they divided our government, our Founders neglected to point out that because lawyers are officers of the court, they are members of the judicial branch of government by definition. It's a conflict of interest for lawyers to run for office so they can write laws and charge us money to help us cope with the laws they write.

It's probably too late to correct this omission to the Constitution because there are too many lawyers in various legislatures who won't vote themselves out of office. If we could cut back the number and complexity of our laws, however, we'd have fewer people quoting ol' Will Shakespeare out of context:

The first thing we do, let's kill all the lawyers[273].

---

[273] Shakespeare , William, *Henry The Sixth*, Part 2 Act 4, scene 2, 71–78

12 – Bureaucratic Evil in the Guise of Liberalism

America's Declaration of Independence listed "life, liberty, and the pursuit of happiness" as rights endowed by our creator. "Pursuit of happiness" wasn't meant as a guarantee that everyone would *achieve* happiness, but times have changed. Many voters feel that government should guarantee happiness regardless of cost. Obama supporter Peggy Joseph expected to gain from the 2008 election:

> I never thought this day would happen. I won't have to work on puttin' gas in my car. I won't have to work at payin' my mortgage.
> You know. If I help him [Obama], he's gonna help me.[274]

Government efforts to supply happiness always lead to loss of liberty – even when they don't actually accomplish any happiness, as Ms. Joseph admitted several years later. [275] We'll see that this was especially true when politicians decided to take extraordinary measures to protect children from abuse.

China in Confucius' day had no notion of "inalienable rights." Although family stability was important to the state, the Emperor or his minions could intervene arbitrarily in what Americans have traditionally considered private family matters.

---

[274] "Campaign winner is ... Peggy the Moocher," *San Angelo Standard Times*, Nov. 5, 2008

[275] "Hey, Obama! Where's my mortgage payment?" *World Net Daily*, July. 14, 2014

The Chinese had little notion of individuality. Every person was part of a family, clan, or village. Everything a person did reflected on everyone else. Everyone was collectively responsible for anything anyone connected to him or her did.

The Japanese expressed this notion of collective responsibility in the word *"tonari."* Your *tonari* was the houses on either side and the three houses across the street. If anyone in your family committed a crime, your family was punished. The adjoining houses and the house directly across the street were punished less severely. The houses diagonally across the street received a lighter punishment yet. All these people were required to help you encourage all of your family members to behave virtuously.

There were no individual crimes. Although perpetrators received the heaviest punishment, crimes were the fault of some group or other. Crime was not society's responsibility as Western liberals argue when they speak about "root causes." Crimes were the responsibility of the perpetrator and his nearest neighbors and kinfolk.

The Japanese never asked Cain's question, "Am I my brother's keeper?"[276] You'd better be your brother's keeper and your neighbor's too. If they messed up, you'd be in trouble along with them.

The Soft Approach to Family Matters

One day in rural Japan, my mother received an unexpected visit from a dignified Japanese gentleman. His calling card said he was "head of the block." She later learned that most towns had a "head of the block" for every so many families. This was a wise, tactful, volunteer who had a record of achieving consensus on knotty problems.

After the obligatory cups of tea and talk about the weather, he explained his mission: my younger brothers weren't bringing

---

[276] Genesis 4:9 ~ 4004 BC

toothbrushes to school. Despite the teacher's best efforts to persuade them to walk the path of virtue, they couldn't brush their teeth after lunch as required by the rules of hygiene. This lack of virtue had to be remedied. Had my mom seen the notes about toothbrushes?

My mother was apologetic. The notes had come home, but she didn't read Japanese very well. She thought she was supposed to ensure that my brothers brushed their teeth *before* going to school.

The head of the block lit up with a huge smile. "We had a meeting," he told her. "We thought it must be something like that." A few more cups of tea and he bowed himself out, problem solved!

Think about the social safety net this implies. The teacher sent a note home. Nothing happened. She met with the head of the PTA who bucked the matter to the head of the block who brought harmony, peace, and consensus all 'round without shaming anyone. Now that she understood, however, woe to my mother if she violated consensus and let my siblings go to school without their toothbrushes!

Child Protection and Coercive Intervention

While child abuse has always been with us and people of good will have always tried to intervene on the child's behalf, the last fifty years have seen much more forced official involvement in family affairs. This is the sort of bureaucratic growth Confucius predicted.

The Asian approach to achieving virtue involves discussion, explanation, conciliation, and consensus. While no Asian government ever hesitated to deal forcefully with the non-virtuous,[277] they knew it's better to achieve compliance through persuasion. Emperors required Confucius' writings to be taught in school because Confucius taught that God wanted citizens to obey.

---

[277] The Chinese government's "one child policy" involves persuasion, fines, involuntary abortions, and escalates to forced sterilization.

The notion that God demanded obedience was a good opening to a chat with a recalcitrant citizen.

The American process is different. When a family doesn't raise children to the satisfaction of the local child protection bureaucracy, the first contact with the family is often a social worker at the door with an armed policeman in tow. Under threat of a court order, the social worker demands to search the house and interview the children without the parents' being present. Government interference over parents' objection is called "coercive intervention." This heavy-handed approach to virtue upsets parents, harms children, and benefits lawyers, counselors, and entities that profit from conflict.

Chapter 2 compared two bureaucracies' responses when they made obvious mistakes. The private company fixed its error because bad publicity would drive customers away. The child "protection" agency doesn't wait for customers to seek their services; it gathers children into the system by force whenever it can warp the law or procedures to "justify" removal or other coercive intervention without worrying about public perception.

It may be shocking to realize that our government snatches children from their parents for no good reason, but many abuses like the attack on the Ratte family described in Chapter 2 have been documented. A government can commit no worse offense against a family than tearing it apart. It's worth examining the legislative and procedural history of child abuse agencies to show how they ended up abusing children instead of protecting them.

Sen. Walter Mondale, for whom the child protection law is named, said he was proud of his efforts to "protect children" while he was running for President against Ronald Reagan. Alas, results count more than intent. In reality, the results of government involvement in family operation are generally bad and sometimes evil.

Child Abuse Prevention and Treatment Act

Bureaucracies can't simply create a new agency on their own authority; a legislative body must pass a law setting up the agency of their dreams. The law is named after its sponsors so lawmakers can claim credit for serving the people. Lawmakers get credit, bureaucrats get money and power, taxpayers get the bill, and we lose more freedom.

On January 31st, 1974, President Nixon signed Public Law 93-247, The Child Abuse Prevention and Treatment Act (CAPTA). Although social engineering wasn't popular, child abuse was regarded as abhorrent even though nobody had any idea how much actual abuse needed prevention. As Senator Mondale said while running for the Presidency, "Not even Richard Nixon is in favor of child abuse."[278] Twenty years later, Janet Reno's popularity soared when she claimed child abuse prevention as the purpose for the Waco, Texas raid that incinerated more than 80 children and adults.[279]

When lawmakers coupled the protective instincts most adults have towards children with every agency's hunger for funds, it's no surprise that every state has an agency to collect federal grants to help protect children. Names and abbreviations vary, but the function is usually described as Child Protection Services or CPS.

There is no problem so horrible that government can't make it worse. With vague definitions, relaxed standards of evidence, secret hearings, and large sums of money, CAPTA was a bureaucrat's dream. Here are some of its less well-publicized rules:

---

[278] Nelson, Barbara J. *Making an Issue of Child Abuse*, (University of Chicago Press, 1986) p 102

[279] Manel, Jon. "Surviving Waco." *BBC News*, October 7, 2008, available online at http://news.bbc.co.uk/today/hi/today/newsid_7654000/7654418.stm see also "Jury clears US over Waco deaths" *BBC News*, July 15, 2000 available online at http://news.bbc.co.uk/2/hi/americas/834416.stm

- Child abuse hearings must be held in secret "to protect the privacy of the child."[280] States without a "confidentiality provision" in their CPS laws didn't get federal funds, so it's no surprise that all states immediately enacted secrecy laws. While it makes sense for government not to talk about accusations, CAPTA bars the accused from going public. We abhor secret trials; secrecy is the handmaid of injustice and the first tool of tyranny.

- Child abuse hearings can admit anonymous hearsay evidence.[281] CAPTA denies you the right to know who's accused you. How can you question your accuser's credibility? You can cross-examine the social worker about what your accuser said, but you can't cross-examine your accuser to show bias or to show that the accuser doesn't know what happened.

- There's a very low standard for convicting parents of abuse – a state judge can order permanent removal if he finds that it's more likely than not that abuse occurred.[282] This "preponderance of the evidence" standard is far below "beyond any reasonable doubt" needed for criminal conviction. Many people consider

---

[280] Child Abuse Prevention and Treatment Act (CAPTA), as amended (42 U.S.C. 5101 et seq.) – sections 106 (b)(2)(B)(viii), (ix), and (x)

[281] National Study of Child Protective Services Systems and Reform Efforts (U.S. Department of Health and Human Services, 2003) ... standards for nonprofessionals and <u>anonymous reporting sources</u> vary. [emphasis added]

[282] National Study of Child Protective Services Systems and Reform Efforts (U.S. Department of Health and Human Services, 2003) says "Standards of evidence: Relatively high evidentiary standards (preponderance, material, or clear and convincing) are necessary to substantiate abuse in 23 states. In 19 states, lower standards were specified (credible, reasonable, or probable cause). Nine states do not specify a standard of evidence." HHS states that "preponderance of the evidence" is a "relatively high" standard of proof!

arbitrary removal of their children to be worse than imprisonment, but the level of proof required is far lower.

- Thirty-two states accept anonymous reports.[283] Some state agencies not only accept anonymous accusations and use them in court, they actually reach out to find potential accusers and publicize the fact that hot-line accusations can remain secret.

- Failure to report suspected child abuse can lead to felony conviction.[284] Physicians, teachers and other professionals report trivial matters because they may be prosecuted for covering up child abuse. This blocks communications between parents and professionals who're involved in their children's lives.

- There are no penalties for making false abuse accusations. This protects people who use government as a weapon. In 1992, *Playboy* warned that lawyers were advising divorcing wives who wanted custody to charge husbands with abuse.[285] Judges generally gave custody to the mother while sorting this out, by which time

---

[283] National Study of Child Protective Services Systems and Reform Efforts, (U.S. Department of Health and Human Services, 2003) Chapter 3, "Screening and Intake."

[284] National Study of Child Protective Services Systems and Reform Efforts (U.S. Department of Health and Human Services, 2003) Mandatory reporting: Nearly all states require professionals who work with children (i.e. social workers, medical personnel, educators, and child daycare providers) to report suspected child maltreatment.

[285] "Presumed Guilty," *Playboy*, June 1992 p 74. "Almost always, you find kids who are three or four years old. The two year olds are no good because they can't speak well enough and are totally unreliable in what they do say. The five- and six-year-olds are already old enough to say 'He didn't do that, lady, and nothing you say is going to convince me.' But threes and fours are perfect. After they've been worked over by a parent or zealous validator, they can be counted on because they believe it and will testify accordingly."

---

the relationship between the father and his children was damaged beyond repair. The mother could tell the children anything she wanted and they couldn't see him to hear his side of the story. CPS workers are happy to count such accusations in their statistics at budget review time, of course.[286]

Although CAPTA proceedings take place in courtrooms before judges, they bear no resemblance to trials in which justice is seen to be done. CAPTA exempted CPS proceedings from protections against judicial abuse that Americans regard as vital to our legal system. Child advocates felt that child abuse was *so* horrible that the accused should be denied the customary rights granted to those accused of mass murder; after all, observing defendant's rights slows down prosecutions.

CAPTA abandoning due process should be disturbing enough, but the remedies are worse. CAPTA requires removal of children to a foster or group home for a state to receive Title IV-E Federal funds.[287] Treatment without removal is paid for by the state budget; treatment after removal is paid for by the feds.

This is a powerful incentive for states and CPS employees to gravitate instantly to the most intrusive possible action. If they snatch the children, expenses are paid by someone else and parents will submit to nearly anything CPS wants to get their children back. As a social worker put it, "It's a lot easier to work with the family after removal because it gives us a bargaining tool."[288]

[286] "Child-Abuse Charges Ensnare Some Parents In Baseless Proceedings," *Wall Street Journal*, 4/23/89 p 1 explains the motivations behind many false abuse reports.
[287] "Florida Shifts Child-Welfare System's Focus to Saving Families," *New York Times*, July 25, 2009 "Ordinarily, federal aid is determined by how many children are in custody."
[288] Pride, Mary. *The Child Abuse Industry*. (Crossway Books, 1986), p 67

The Texas Polygamy Outrage

A case involving accusations of polygamy and statutory rape showed the child "protection" system at its worst. Someone claiming to be a 16-year-old girl called the Texas CPS and said she'd been forced to marry a 50 year old against her will. She said she was a member of a religious cult whose members lived in a large compound. Officials searched the compound and couldn't find the caller, but many girls appeared to have been made pregnant when they were too young to have had legal sex with anyone.[289]

Concluding that the compound was a hotbed of child abuse, officials rounded up 462 children and put them in state custody. They took this extreme action even though Texas CPS staff members were well aware of the evil they were doing. On April 8, 2008, *Fox News* reported:[290]

> Children's Protective Services (CPS) spokeswoman Marleigh Meisner said each child will get an advocate and an attorney. But she said they would have a tough time adjusting to modern life if they are permanently separated from their families.

This case was so spectacular that questions were asked. On April 26, 2008, *USA Today* posted an API report:[291]

> The state of Texas made a damning accusation when it rounded up 462 children at a polygamous

---

[289] "All Texas Polygamist Sect Children Reunited With Parents" *Fox News – Associated Press*, June 4 2008,
http://www.foxnews.com/story/0,2933,362816,00.html

[290] "Abuse Investigated at Polygamist Compound After 400 Removed" *Fox News – Associated Press* April 8, 2008
http://www.foxnews.com/story/0,2933,346959,00.html

[291] "Sweep of FLDS Kids Raises Legal Questions" *USA Today* April 26, 2008
http://www.usatoday.com/news/nation/2008-04-26-polygamist-retreat_N.htm

sect's ranch: The adults are forcing teenage girls into marriage and sex, creating a culture so poisonous that none should be allowed to keep their children.

But the broad sweep — from nursing infants to teenagers — is raising constitutional questions, even in a state where authorities have wide latitude for taking a family's children.

"Of course, we condemn child abuse and we don't stand up for the perpetration of that," said Lisa Graybill, legal director of the American Civil Liberties Union of Texas. But "what the state has done has offended a pretty wide swath of the American people with what appears to be an overreaching action to sweep up all these children."

Removing 462 children led to a massive federal windfall. The children should have been returned when the state found no evidence of abuse, but giving children back would end federal reimbursement and take 462 clients from court-appointed lawyers, child advocates, therapists, and other parasitic hangers-on.

Removal is often the first response of CPS agencies to any report of abuse or neglect no matter how ill-founded or malicious. The phone call which triggered the invasion was later found to have been made by a person who had a history of making false accusations,[292] but the state kept the children anyway.

If a CPS agency can't find evidence of abuse after removing the children, the only way to keep their victims in the system is an evaluation which finds that the children need counseling because their parents messed them up through "psychological abuse."

The agency subcontracts the evaluation to someone on their "certified counselor" list. The counselor can declare that there's nothing wrong with the child or intone, "This child needs therapy"

---

[292] "Texas had no right to seize sect children, appellate court says" *Los Angeles Times*, May 23, 2008, http://www.latimes.com/features/religion/la-na-polygamy23-2008may23,0,5363805.story

for which the agency will pay. What's he going to do? Embarrass his best customer, give up a patient, and risk being thrown off the counselor list? Or collect hourly fees for years to come, paid for by a government which never runs out of money? Nobody in the system seems disturbed by this conflict of interest between counselors telling the truth or staying on the approved list and making money.

In the Texas case, a number of parents who were living in the compound brought suit to have their children returned. The judge agreed with the parents that the state had overstepped its bounds and issued an order to return all but a few of the children who had plainly had sex before the age of consent.[293]

The facts are plain: a) the state kept the federal reimbursement even though their actions in taking the children were illegal and b) nobody even criticized agency employees who abused so many children. This reinforces perverse incentives to remove children – if you grab children illegally, the worst that can happen is that courts might order you to give them back. There's no punishment. You, your agency, and your subcontractors can ride the federal gravy train as long as the case lasts.

Follow the Money

On April 6, 2005, the Congressional Research Service submitted a document "Child Welfare Financing: An Issue Overview."[294] It lists many categories of CPS expenses beyond foster care costs which are eligible for federal reimbursement. The document says:

---

[293] "Texas had no right to seize sect children, appellate court says" *Los Angeles Times*, May 23, 2008, available online at
http://www.latimes.com/features/religion/la-na-polygamy23-2008may23,0,5363805.story

[294] Child Welfare Financing: An Issue Overview. Congressional Research Service, Library of Congress, April 6, 2005
http://digital.library.unt.edu/govdocs/crs//data/2005/upl-meta-crs-7687/meta-crs-7687.ocr

States seek federal reimbursement for eligible foster care expenses by submitting claims in several program categories, including foster care room and board (maintenance payments), program administration (including case planning), training, and data system development and operation (i.e., State Automated Child Welfare Information System, SACWIS). When viewed as federal cost per eligible child, claims for foster care maintenance payments have been relatively stable for more than 15 years, while claims for administration have risen significantly over the same time period. [emphasis added]

In FY1987 states made foster care administrative claims worth $506 million compared to administrative claims worth $2.2 billion in FY2003. The average monthly cost per eligible child for these administrative claims was $373 in FY1987 compared to $773 in FY2003. [emphasis added]

While expenses for caring for children have remained pretty much the same despite inflation, money for "administrative claims" nearly doubled between 1987 and 2003.

According to the Congressional Research Service, each child CPS removes from home is worth an average of $773 per month in federal reimbursement of administrative expenses, which is that much less money they need from the state budget. The document says that "claims for foster care maintenance payments have been relatively stable for more than 15 years" whereas administrative expenses for each child have increased steadily.

With such perverse incentives in place, is it any wonder that CPS agencies find so much "abuse?"

CPS agencies protest that the federal government no longer reimburses state agencies on a per-child basis. They assert that federal funds are given as "block grants" in which the agency gets a fixed amount of money each year. CPS apologists claim that there's no incentive to grab a child because that won't result in more money. The *New York Times* reported that this defense is false:

> Ordinarily, federal aid is determined by how many children are in custody.[295]

The more children an agency grabs, the more success they claim in fighting child abuse and the more money they request. The Texas agency strained their budget by snatching 462 children, giving them a story to tell their state legislators and the federal bureaucracy. Grabbing children lays the foundation for getting more money.

The Texas CPS didn't want to end the federal revenue stream. 462 kids at $750 each is $346,500 per month for "administrative costs and training" on top of reimbursement for child care expenses.

What will happen if parents who sued to get their children back win damages? The taxpayers will pay and CPS will ask for a budget increase to cover the expense. They'll never reform their system because the feds pay extra as long as they can hold on to the children.

Any agency will lie, cheat, and steal to get federal funds because state politicians don't like raising state taxes to get more money from their voters. The feds won't deny funds because of procedural errors; the more money federal bureaucrats shovel out, the more money they can ask for next year.[296]

What if it's found that CPS violated the law in snatching and abusing these children? They'll say that the error was due to overwork caused by lack of funds and ask for more. The worse job they do, the more children they abuse, the more money they get. That's how this bureaucracy is dragging us into the Confucian abyss.

---

[295] "Florida Shifts Child-Welfare System's Focus to Saving Families," *New York Times*, July 25, 2009

[296] "Housing agencies faulted in audits to get $300M of stimulus" *USA Today*, April 8, 2009, p 1 "The federal government will soon send more than $300 million in stimulus funds to 61 housing agencies that have been repeatedly faulted by auditors for mishandling government aid, a USA TODAY review has found."

Government Makes a Lousy Parent

In a long-term study of childcare outcomes, MIT researchers found that even when a child's biological family was in bad shape with drug abuse, violence, whatever, removing the child to foster care almost always made the outcome worse. The *MIT News* article "Kids gain more from family than foster care" says:[297]

> An MIT Sloan School of Management professor has for the first time used the analytic tools of applied economics to show that children faced with two options – being allowed to stay at home or being placed into foster care – have generally better life outcomes when they remain with their families.
>
> "While much has been written about the trade-off between family preservation and child protection, little empirical work has been able to support a greater emphasis on either one," said Joseph Doyle Jr., assistant professor of applied economics at Sloan. "My research suggests that children on the margin of foster care placement have better employment, delinquency, and teen motherhood outcomes when they remain at home."

Doyle, the Jon D. Gruber Career Development Assistant Professor of Applied Economics, said his study is the first to empirically demonstrate causal effects between placement decisions and long-term outcomes.

The article ends:

> But if keeping children who stay with their families generally fare better, that will mean a

---

[297] Doyle, Jr., Joseph J. "Kids gain more from family than foster care" *MIT News*, July 3, 2007 http://web.mit.edu/newsoffice/2007/sloan-fostercare-study-0703.html

greater need for services to help keep families intact. "Our research generally supports the current direction toward family preservation," said Doyle. "Future research should consider an even wider set of childhood outcomes." [emphasis added]

This was reported in *USA Today* on July 3, 2007, and it wasn't the first such report. Douglas J. Besharov, former head of the National Center on Child Abuse and Neglect, wrote:

> The reason for intervention in most cumulatively harmful situations is emotional harm to the child. ... ironically, placing the child to safeguard his health often leads to greater emotional harm, as the child is taken out of the family environment.[298] ... much of the present high level of intervention is unwarranted and some is demonstrably harmful to the children and families involved. More than sixty-five percent of all reports of suspected child maltreatment--involving over 750,000 children per year--turn out to be unfounded. [emphasis added][299]

Public education studies show that government employees have trouble teaching kids to read, how can we expect bureaucrats to be good parents? There's no doubt that children should almost always be raised by their parents instead of being yanked out in return for federal funds. The system that should protect children from abuse ends up abusing children instead of helping them.

Even though they know this, judges issue removal orders and the federal government picks up the costs. Social workers remove children because the federal government pays them to remove children. They won't change their *modus operandi* without changes

---

[298] "'Doing Something' about Child Abuse: The Need to Narrow the Grounds for State Intervention," *Harvard Journal of Law and Public Policy Vol 8*, 1985 p. 560 & 586 Douglas J. Besharov

[299] Ibid., p 556

to the funding mechanism. Bureaucracies always fight changes to their rice bowls and the legions of counselors and lawyers who've grown fat off the feds would find themselves unemployed if fewer children were removed.

Removing children generally leads to other income streams. It's extremely traumatic for children to be abruptly snatched from their homes. A child who's damaged badly enough becomes a Child In Need of Services (CHINS) who's eligible for even more federal money. How convenient! Destruction continues because funding and procedures are in place. Bureaucrats prefer to continue with business as usual whether their activities help or not.

When bureaucrats who know better damage children, their actions become evil.

What CPS Insiders Say

Twenty-one years after CAPTA was passed and ten years after Dr. Besharov warned against harming children by unneeded removal, Theresa Reid, Executive Director of the American Professional Society on the Abuse of Children, addressed the Child Abuse Prevention Symposium at the University of Minnesota.[300] Her November 30, 1995 speech summarized changes in child abuse prevention since the law was passed. The next several paragraphs are quotes from her talk and comments about underlying realities she didn't mention.

> It is impossible to mention all the very important advances in knowledge that have been made in the last 10 years, but let me mention a few:
> There is the work of John McCann, Jan Bays, and other physicians revealing that medical evidence of sexual abuse is rarer than we thought; that

---

[300] The transcript of her talk is available online at http://www.cyfc.umn.edu/family/research/tr_kn.htm

anomalies once thought to testify to sexual molestation are often found in normal children; that most sexual abuse leaves no medical evidence.

Ms. Reid didn't mention the parents who'd been jailed for abuse based on anomalies "often found in normal children" nor did she address children who were torn from their parents when they hadn't been abused at all. She expressed no regrets, no sorrow at the evils she and her colleagues had committed against innocent parents and traumatized children. Being a bureaucrat means never having to say you're sorry no matter how much evil you bring about.

She said, "most sexual abuse leaves no medical evidence." If there's no evidence, how can anyone be certain that abuse occurred? How do CPS workers get convictions? As in the Texas false abuse alarm, CPS workers ask judges to order "psychological evaluations" which create conflicts of interest as explained above.

Ms. Reid said that the child abuse fraternity couldn't define the conditions they were trying to treat:

> Furthermore, there was a lack of consensus in definitions for sexual and physical abuse--the most studied areas--and virtually no consensus in defining neglect and psychological abuse.

How can you treat a condition you can't define? How can you jail parents on such ill-defined charges? Vague definitions make it easier for bureaucrats to extend their reach and boost their budgets. Ms. Reid said that CPS agencies were running into opposition:

> This latest swing corresponds with the founding, in 1992, of the False Memory Syndrome Foundation. FMSF has been very effective in persuading the media to change its story from the suffering of victims of incest to the suffering of fathers, mothers,

and families whose grown daughters have made false accusations of incest.[301]

The False Memory Syndrome Foundation (FMSF) was founded after psychologists started suggesting that incest victims blocked out memories of abuse, but that a skilled mental health worker could uncover these hidden memories.

Many parents were jailed after psychologists persuaded judges to use such "memories" in court. The FMSF tried to defend the accused and discredit the psychologists. Ms. Reid noted that enough parents were jailed that mass-circulation magazines became alarmed.

> The same period has seen a shift in many stories about physical abuse as well, with the focus increasingly often on the pain of parents whose families are ripped apart by overzealous social workers. This scenario is being pitched very successfully to media reaching middle America. *Family Circle, Reader's Digest,*[302] *Ladies Home Journal,* and *Woman's Day*[303] have all recently featured stories of poorly trained CPS workers who yank

---

[301] "Childhood Trauma: Memory or Invention?" *New York Times*, 7/12/92 p C1 explains how false memories of abuse can be planted by misguided therapists. It quotes Dr. Khilstrom of the University of Arizona, "Everything we know about the memory of events says it is highly susceptible to reinvention." It also describes research efforts which show that many people can be induced to believe totally false memories. Since adults are so easy to manipulate, shouldn't the testimony of children who have been interrogated repeatedly by social workers be viewed with suspicion? *see also* "Rush to Judgement," *Newsweek*, 4/19/93 p 54 which explains how a couple was convicted of abuse after one of their daughters dreamed she'd been abused as a child.

[302] "When Parents Become Victims," *Reader's Digest*, April 1993 p 101 explains how easily any parent can be falsely accused of sexual abuse.

[303] "Could The State Take Your Child?" *Woman's Day*, 5/18/93 p 54 explains how easily social workers can take children from their parents. The article includes two pages of advice on how to protect your family from government "help." There's something seriously wrong when parents band together to protect themselves from government agents who're supposed to help them.

children from families on the basis of malicious reports or for behavior most people consider clearly non-abusive--such as a swat on the behind in a grocery store.

This fear of jack-booted government social workers <u>ripping up innocent families</u> has penetrated well beyond the readership of Family Circle and into the offices of highly educated congressional staff. I have had conversations this year with two influential staff members of different U.S. Senators ... Both were new mothers<u>, terrified at the prospect of having their babies taken away from them by strangers working for the government</u>. And guess what? For the first time, the nation's major piece of child abuse legislation requires states to provide detailed information about false accusations of abuse. [emphasis added]

Two new mothers were terrified of having their children taken from them. Ms. Reid's only touch of regret, if it could be called that, was concern that states now had to provide detailed information on false accusations. The agencies would have to hire more people to collect the new data. That's not punishment, it's a reward – budgets would go up because of the extra reporting requirements.

Ms. Reid ended her speech by urging professionalism:

... there is no doubt that errors in professional practice <u>have been made</u>, and that these errors always have the potential for causing <u>very great harm</u>, and sometimes have done so.

... many of those knowledge gains undermine what we thought we knew 10 years ago: when, for instance, we thought <u>children never lied or made misstatements about sexual abuse</u>; that certain genital anomalies were clear evidence of abuse; that certain sexual behaviors were evidence of abuse, when in fact they turn out to be fairly common in children.

Any parent knows that a child can lie and that a child's grasp on reality can be tenuous, yet Ms. Reid admits that social workers were convinced that "children never lied or made misstatements about sexual abuse." How could any childcare professional not know that children are easily confused and sometimes lie? How many innocent parents went to jail when social workers led children to make false charges of sexual abuse? How many were jailed because their children had genital anomalies that were "fairly common in children?"

Having restated her point that CPS agencies hadn't known what they were doing 10 years ago, Ms. Reid ended with a plea for higher standards of professional conduct:

> We need to ensure that we are rigorously self-policing: because lives are in the balance, this is a moral imperative. ... If adequate structures are not in place for this self-policing, we need to build them, and enforce them.

Ms. Reid declared that her colleagues had a "moral imperative" to be self-policing in 1995. Fifteen years later, Prof. Ratte's son was removed from his home when a concession stand employee accidentally gave him alcoholic lemonade. Shortly after that, the Texas CPS rounded up 462 kids on grounds that were so flimsy that a judge ordered that the children be returned. CPS agencies don't share Ms. Reid's concern for professional standards. As with any bureaucracy, boosting the budget trumps professionalism any day of the week.

CPS Agencies Do Evil

Mary Pride, who wrote *The Child Abuse Industry*,[304] was one of the first to point out the dangers of letting bureaucracies get involved in removing children from their families. She quoted Aleksandr Solzhenitsyn, famous Soviet dissident and author of *The Gulag Archipelago*, who said, "In order for men to commit great evil, they must first be convinced that they are doing good." Ms. Reid must be convinced that she and her colleagues are doing great good in order to feel good about the evil that they commit.

Although Ms. Reid declared that CPS "errors always have the potential for causing very great harm, and sometimes have done so," she was plainly convinced that child abuse is so monstrous, so bad, so evil - that all the harm done to children and the widespread fear of mothers that their children will be removed is justified to protect children from abuse. She assumes that abuse exists when there's no evidence and she believes that removal helps children, or is at least harmless enough that when in doubt, yank 'em out!

Her benign view of removal is contradicted by the MIT study that found that outcomes for children who're removed are generally worse than for children who're left in their homes even when the homes are less than ideal. She also ignored Dr. Besharov's 1985 article that told how removal harms children and reported that 65% of abuse accusations are unfounded.

Ms. Reid spoke favorably of new knowledge that had been gained, but her colleagues and the judges who sign removal orders haven't accepted the MIT study. They continue to damage children and families in the name of child "protection."

In discussing threats to the West,[305] Solzhenitsyn warned of "an atmosphere of moral mediocrity, paralyzing man's noblest

---

[304] Pride, Mary. *The Child Abuse Industry* (Crossway Books, 1986)

[305] "Is Solzhenitsyn Right?" *Time Magazine*, June 26, 1978. Mr. Solzhenitsyn made this point in his Harvard commencement address of June 8, 1978, quoted in Kelly K. Monroe, Kelly Monroe Kullberg *Finding God At Harvard*, (Zondervan: 1996) pp 97, 98

impulses" and a "tilt of freedom in the direction of evil ... It stems primarily out of a humanistic and benevolent concept according to which there is no evil inherent in human nature."[306]

Even if the ideas behind the Mondale Act were "humanistic and benevolent," outcomes show that CPS agencies are tilting our society further and further in the direction of evil. It's bad enough for government to waste our money; it's far worse for government agencies to lay waste our families. Knowledgeable parents would sooner face a tiger than a child "protection" bureaucrat.

Abusing Fewer Children

A few changes would help. First, the federal government should get out of the child removal business. Child protection is not, and was never intended to be, among the enumerated powers given in the U.S. Constitution, Article 1, Section 8. The Constitution reserves child protection to the states.

Second, if the federal government must violate the Constitution in this way, if the feds paid to treat families instead of paying only when children were removed, states would have fewer incentives for removal. The State of Florida had great success with this approach:

> Ordinarily, federal aid is determined by how many children are in custody. Florida asked to receive a flat fee that it could spend on counseling and other aid instead of foster care when it wished. The shift was seen as <u>fiscally risky — an increase in foster children would not bring more money</u> — but it has paid off. "The new system is not only better for the children but it also saves money," said George

---

[306] Mr. Solzhenitsyn made this point in his Harvard commencement address of June 8, 1978, quoted in Kelly K. Monroe, Kelly Monroe Kullberg *Finding God At Harvard*, (Zondervan: 1996) p 98

Sheldon, secretary of children and family services.[307]
[emphasis added]

The *Times* didn't think it odd that agencies are paid according to the number of children they remove and finds it newsworthy that keeping children in their homes is better for them. The MIT report and the *Times* article suggest that keeping families together instead of paying agencies to pull families apart would help children even if state governments might think it "fiscally risky" to have states pay for removal instead of billing the federal government.

Third, secret child abuse hearings encourage lying. It may be reasonable to protect the privacy of an abused child, but what about cases where no abuse has occurred? Secret trials lead to injustice for innocent parties. The law should be changed so that persons accused of abuse have the option to open the proceedings to the public. Few would do this because the disgrace of being accused of child abuse is so great, but the fact that a defendant could open the proceedings to public scrutiny would make everyone more careful.

Fourth, it's utterly unjust not to be permitted to cross-examine your accuser to show bias. Anonymous accusations are an invitation to use government power as a weapon in private quarrels. Child abuse is obviously a crime and should be treated as a crime with the rules of evidence that are expected in criminal matters. False accusations should be prosecuted as severely as any form of perjury.

Absent such changes, child protection agencies will continue to damage children and be rewarded with bigger budgets the more kids they damage. It's similar to teachers who get paid extra for summer school classes when they don't teach the material during the school year. As Solzhenitsyn said, the liberal illusion that human nature is not evil leads both to great evil and to bureaucratic bloat.

The problem we've been exploring is that nobody enforces virtuous behavior in our bureaucracies, but all bureaucrats are human beings subject to the influences they grew up under. This

---

[307] "Florida Shifts Child-Welfare System's Focus to Saving Families," *New York Times*, July 25, 2009

compounds the problem: the next chapter explores loss of virtue in our families.

13 – Our Farewell to Duty

Confucius believed that virtue flows from rulers down to citizens; he never considered democracy or the idea that people could control their government. In a democracy, virtue can flow from citizens up to rulers if citizens vote non-virtuous rulers out of office, but voters are more likely to vote themselves benefits than to enforce virtue. That's why our Founders gave us "A republic, if you can keep it."[308]

Getting rid of non-virtuous officials requires virtuous voters. This universal truth is rediscovered whenever things go wrong in a democracy. George Soros recently realized that virtue had to flow from the electorate up into the government:

> Popper [a philosopher who advocated the creation of the "open society" and who wrote about the limitations of the scientific method] assumed that the purpose of critical thinking is to gain a better understanding of reality. That is true in science but not in politics. The primary purpose of political discourse is to gain power and to stay in power. Those who fail to recognize this are unlikely to *be* in power. The only way in which politicians can be persuaded to pay more respect to reality is by the electorate insisting on it, rewarding those whom it considers truthful and insightful, and punishing those who engage in deliberate deception. In other words, the electorate needs to be more committed to the pursuit of truth than it is at present. Without such a commitment, democratic politics will not

---

[308] Benjamin Franklin as he left Independence Hall after the Constitutional Convention of 1787

produce the desired results. <u>An open society can be only as virtuous as the people living in it</u>.[309] [emphasis added]

Mr. Soros, an extremely successful financial trader, recognized the importance of individual and collective virtue in society. The Chinese term "virtue" is extremely broad; the closest English approximation combines "morality," "duty," and "responsibility."

Confucius believed that children are born selfish; an infant's only concern is to have its needs met without regard to whether it's convenient for someone else to feed it or change its diaper. Confucius taught that parents and teachers are duty-bound to teach children to be willing, if not eager, to assume the responsibilities, requirements, and duties of adulthood, the sooner the better.

Americans once shared that view. During my Boy Scout years, we recited the Boy Scout Oath in unison at every meeting. It begins, "On my honor, I will do my best to do my duty to God and my country..." The oath identifies three duties which Scouts swear to fulfill:

- Duty to God and to country
- Duty to others
- Duty to self

The oath says nothing about self-gratification, pleasure, or self-esteem. The oath speaks of duty a Scout gives to others; it says nothing of what the Scout gets from others. Duty to God, country, and to others are easy to understand but hard to do. Duty to self meant keeping yourself healthy, developing yourself by study, and maintaining character through honesty and cleanliness of speech.

Developing yourself wasn't for self-gratification, self-improvement made it possible for you to fulfill your duty to others

---

[309] Soros, George, *The New Paradigm for Financial Markets*, (Perseus Books Group, 2008) p. 39

instead of burdening society. The Scout's emphasis on clean speech is like Confucius' describing the importance of politeness.[310]

Our Duty-Bound Past

American society was once based on duty. Students had a duty to learn whatever the school taught whether they were interested in the subject or not. Teachers had a duty to impart knowledge to their students whether the students wanted to learn or not.

I have a friend who found old records in a forgotten archive. When his town hired their first teacher well over a century ago, some of the first-grade students were 16 or 17 because they'd never had a school. The men who hired the teacher told her to let them know immediately if any student gave any trouble.

Whenever one of those oversized first graders gave the teacher lip, the selectmen took him behind the barn and explained his duty to learn whatever the teacher wanted to teach. They beat the rebellion out of him because he'd wasted the town's money by making it hard for other students to learn. The first graders eventually recognized their duty to learn and graduated; teachers who proved unable or unwilling to impart knowledge were fired.

My high school had guidance counselors in the early 1960's, but nobody mentioned self-esteem. Counselors found out what students wanted to do after graduation and helped choose courses and activities to prepare them as well as possible. College-bound students took advanced courses; students who didn't want to go to college took shop or vocational ed, and so on. The goal was to prepare students to take their places in the ranks of virtuous adult taxpayers so society could recover its investment in educating them.

Everybody knew that true self-esteem came from mastery of the material. Any student whom the staff felt wasn't doing his or her best was made to feel inferior and urged to get with the program.

---

[310] Durant, William. *Our Oriental Heritage*, (New York, Simon and Schuster, 1954), p 673

Everybody knew, and occasionally sang, this song from 1907:

> School days, school days, dear old golden rule days
> Readin' and 'ritin' and 'rithmetic,
> Taught to the tune of the hickory stick

Learning was enhanced by applying the board of education vigorously to the seat of learning, repeat as needed. Children are born with no connection between the ears and the brain; most of what adults say goes in one ear and out the other. Pounding the bottom enough establishes a connection between the ears and the brain after which virtuous learning can take place.

Duty-Bound Families

The concept of students and teachers fulfilling their duties in school was based on duty in marriage and in families. "Duty of marriage" was written into Jewish law around 1,500 BC,[311] 1,000 years before Confucius. Getting married meant taking up one's duty as an adult; any pleasure or gratification that came with marriage was incidental.

The responsibilities of duty-based marriage started long before the wedding. Men and women had a duty to prepare themselves through study and through learning the skills to support and maintain their home. They had a duty to keep themselves pure so that their future spouses could have confidence in sexual fidelity in marriage.

Duty-based marriage is illustrated in the musical "Fiddler on the Roof," starring Zero Mostel, which was set in Tsarist Russia in 1905. The musical opened in 1964 and ran for a record-setting 3,242 performances, returning $1,574 for every dollar invested in it.[312]

---

[311] Exodus 21:10 ~ 1500 BC
[312] *Fiddler on the Roof* Jerry Bock, Joseph Stein, Sheldon Harnick, Sholem Aleichem, Hal Leonard Corporation, 1990

The song "Do You Love Me?"[313] illustrates a time when couples focused on duty in marriage. Tevye, the husband, asks his wife Golde, "Do you love me?" She has trouble taking his question seriously or even understanding it. After some talk, she declares,

Do I love you?

For twenty-five years I've washed your clothes

Cooked your meals, cleaned your house

Given you children, milked the cow

After twenty-five years, why talk about love right now?

Golde hadn't thought about love. She was focused on her duty to her husband and to her family. Love hadn't entered her mind; she couldn't talk about love when she had so much work to do. They talk a bit more, and she says:

Do I love him?

For twenty-five years I've lived with him

Fought him, starved with him

Twenty-five years my bed is his

If that's not love, what is?

After more talk, they realize that they do love each other because true love means fulfilling your duty to serve spouse, family, and society. Although it's nice to be loved, duty was more important:

It doesn't change a thing

But even so

After twenty-five years

It's nice to know[314]

---

313 Jerry Bock p. 112
314 Ibid.

The idea of basing marriage, family, education, and government on duty is similar to Confucius' teaching that society is based on virtue. Our tradition of duty is captured in the song "America the Beautiful," which describes what used to be expected of *all* citizens, "who more than self their country loved, and duty more than life."[315] Americans used to sing that from their hearts; our military still do. The pattern of Western society up until the 1950's or early 1960's was Confucian in its emphasis on duty throughout society.

Our Farewell to Duty

How things have changed! As Robert Samuelson put it, "We gradually moved from an era in which people did not want to use government for anything to today when people use government for almost everything."[316]

The song "School Days" is immortalized on a US Government web site maintained by the National Institute of Health.[317] Despite this implicit government endorsement of corporal punishment as a means of encouraging students to learn virtue, the days when teachers could punish students who won't learn are long gone.

Instead of promoting self-esteem through mastery of the material, schools have absorbed the edubabble fallacy that self-esteem can be given by telling students how wonderful they are. Recognizing students who do well harms the self-esteem of those who're failing, so good work is ignored and sometimes discouraged.

The decline in our educational system was facilitated by the philosophies of John Dewey, a proponent of "progressive education," who believed teachers should concentrate on social engineering instead of on imparting knowledge. Instead of directing the curriculum and calling on assistance when students were unwilling

---

[315] You'll find the song on a number of web sites by searching for that phrase.
[316] Robert Samuelson, "Clinton's Nemesis," *Newsweek*, Feb 1, 1993 p. 51
[317] "School Days," Music by Gus Edwards; Lyrics by Will D. Cobb, 1907. Referenced on http://kids.niehs.nih.gov/lyrics/schooldays.htm

to learn what was required, teachers have to come to view themselves as "facilitators" who help their students achieve self-actualization.

"Self-actualization" was coined by Abraham Maslow, who defined it as "the full use and exploitation of talents, capacities, potentialities, etc."[318] Self-actualization is a process which can continue throughout life. Another researcher said, "Putting it in personal terms, self-actualization is the developmental process of becoming or actualizing the 'real you.'"[319]

The goal of helping students achieve self-actualization caught hold among American educators. Schools abandoned the idea that teachers had a duty to impart knowledge from the curriculum; now teachers were supposed to help each student find the "real you."

The difficulty is that for many students, the "real you" is a lazy bum who doesn't want to learn. A teacher who encourages students to strive for the best instead of accepting them as they are often finds a "better you." Worthwhile self-actualization is a result of achievement and fulfilled responsibility; it's not a goal in itself. Tevye and Golde found self-actualization in shared duty well done. Students used to find self-actualization and genuine self-esteem through virtuously learning the material. Confucius would approve.

Confucian Parenting

Confucius would have had no sympathy for the idea of unguided self-actualization. Most children grow up to be self-actualized oafs and barbarians unless they're forced to practice virtue. Although government and society could help, Chinese parents had the primary duty to teach their children virtue and found themselves in big trouble if their children weren't virtuous.

---

[318] Maslow, Abraham H., *Motivation and Personality*, Harper and row, 1970 p 150.
[319] DB Wolfe, R. Sisodia, "Marketing to the self-actualizing customer" *Journal of Consumer Marketing*, Volume 20, Number 6, 2003 pp 555-569

The Chinese economy offered a concrete reason for Chinese parents to invest great effort in raising virtuous children. Most Chinese were farmers. Growing rice supports a dense population, but rice farming requires huge amounts of backbreaking labor. The Chinese had no machinery, so the effort of pumping water, maintaining dikes, planting, weeding, harvesting, and threshing had to be powered by human muscle because there were few animals. Muscle-powered agriculture wears people out and they die young.

There is no investment besides children that can hold value for 30 to 50 years without the government or someone else stealing it. Farmers avoided starvation by teaching their children to be virtuous enough to feed them when they got too old to farm. One of Confucius' arguments for taking care of the aged was that your parents' spirits would hang around and cause you trouble if you didn't take care of them during their declining years. Avoiding starvation is a practical benefit from investing effort in raising virtuous children.

My mother took a Confucian approach to dealing with the "real me." I read one of her "child development" textbooks when I was in 5th grade. "Mom," I said, "you're raising me all wrong. This book says spanking me bruises my tender, delicate psyche."

Mom put her hands on her hips and gave me "that look." "I've two things to say. The guy who wrote that never had any children, he doesn't know what he's talking about. Second, I want to damage your psyche, it's unacceptable. If I leave your psyche alone, you'll burn the house down or worse. My duty as your parent is to eliminate unacceptable childish behavior and replace it with acceptable adult behavior as fast as I can. Spanking you helps me do that."

Mom didn't have that idea just because she lived in Japan. Long before I was born, her mother taught her that she had a duty to correct the "real me" so that I'd carry out my duties when I grew up. Mom put great effort into molding me into a virtuous adult. She wasn't satisfied with the "real me" or even a "better me," she wanted the "best possible me" she could find. If I didn't want to help around the house, if I didn't want to learn something she and dad thought I ought to know, too bad. Her mantra was, "You can, and you must, so you will." No "self-actualization" for me, it was "parental-actualization."

Under the American educational philosophy enforced by teachers' unions, there's no way to make a student learn. Schools have no punishments for students who refuse to learn and aren't permitted to honor those who do. Instead of holding back the ignorant which might harm their self-esteem, schools promote them until they graduate without knowing how to function in adult society.

Emphasis on self-esteem cheats students by violating the implied contract between the parents and the school. The agreement is that if students come to school, put in their time, and do what they're told, they'll be taught how to become functioning members of adult society. We taxpayers fund schools so that teachers can fulfill their duty to teach children to become adult taxpayers.

Boosting self-esteem is less work than imparting knowledge, but unearned self-esteem not only defrauds students, it turns out to be bad for them. *Science Daily* published in an article called "High Self-esteem Is Not Always What It's Cracked Up To Be":[320]

> It was once thought that more self-esteem necessarily is better self-esteem. In recent years, however, high self-esteem per se has come under attack on several fronts, especially in areas such as aggressive behavior. Also, individuals with high self-esteem sometimes become <u>very unlikable</u> when others or events threaten their egos. [emphasis added]
> One of the ways in which high self-esteem can turn bad is when it is accompanied by verbal defensiveness--lashing out at others when a person's

---

[320] "High Self-esteem Is Not Always What It's Cracked Up To Be." staff writer *Science Daily* April 28, 2008

opinions, beliefs, statements or values are threatened. So Kernis and his colleagues designed a study, reported in the current article, to see if respondents whose self-esteem is "fragile" were more verbally defensive than those whose self-esteem was "secure."

The difference between "fragile" self-esteem and "secure" self-esteem is obvious; only in modern America is government money needed to research it. My high school teachers recognized that "secure" self-esteem came only from mastery of the material; they expended every effort to help, tutor, bully, persuade, cajole, pester, harass, and otherwise inspire each student to the point of mastery whether students wanted to learn or not. At graduation, almost all my classmates had "secure" self-esteem which they'd earned through virtuous duty done to the best of their abilities; nobody wasted time imparting fragile, unearned self-esteem.

Today's educators, in contrast, impart "fragile" self-esteem by telling lies to make students feel good about themselves. Fragile students lash out in attempts to protect their self-esteem when their ignorance shows and they end up unemployable because they aren't worth the minimum wage.

In ducking their duty to impart knowledge, educators defraud students and defraud the taxpayers who pay their salaries. As children see that teachers' promises aren't trustworthy, as they observe adults around them shirking duty, why should they submit to the unpleasant parts of duty? If we don't force kids to do their homework, how can we expect them to fill out tax returns? Not all of us can be politicians like Sen. Tom Daschle or Rep. Charlie Rangel whose exalted status means that they needn't worry about such trivia as filling out income tax returns properly.[321]

---

[321] Kocieniewski, David "Rangel Tries to Explain Back Taxes on Villa." *New York Times* Sept 10, 2008

Churches Turn Duty to Delight

As might be expected, the loss of any sense of duty in our schools followed the loss of duty in marriage and in family affairs. When Confucius spoke of the "Mandate of Heaven," he invoked the authority of God to explain how things should be done.

Religion has always played a major role in ordering human affairs. People seem to act better when they think God cares what they do. The pronouncements of authoritative ecclesiastics have been given extra weight in our society, particularly in matters pertaining to marriage, family, and other areas of morality, because many people still believe that, in some sense, God stands behind the church.

Divorce was forbidden for the first 1,600 years of the Christian era, but allowance for divorce was written into the Westminster Confession of Faith almost 400 years ago. The 1646 edition says: "Nothing but adultery, or such willful desertion as can no way be remedied by the church, or civil magistrate, is cause sufficient of dissolving the bond of marriage." Instead of no divorce ever, Protestants permitted divorce and remarriage after adultery or desertion. Giving married people a way to escape marriage was new.

In the 1930's, the Presbyterian Church began a discussion of divorce which lasted 20 years. The church decided to permit divorce for the "moral equivalent of adultery;" they changed the Confession to permit remarriage after divorce "when sufficient penitence for sin and failure is evident, and a firm purpose of and endeavor after Christian marriage is manifested." Four centuries after divorce was first permitted on narrow grounds, remarriage after divorce became OK if you're sorry and promise to try harder next time.

In the 1950's, the Presbyterians reversed their definition of marriage. As Eric Mount Jr. and Johanna W. H. Bos wrote, "The primary purpose of marriage was no longer the benefit of society but the benefit of the people entering the marriage covenant."[322] The church changed from teaching duty and responsibility in marriage to teaching delight and the right to self-gratification. Instead of a right to the pursuit of happiness and duty to give your spouse happiness, you had a right to receive happiness from your spouse whether you fulfilled your duty or not. Instead of having to meet your spouse's needs, you expected your spouse or anyone else to meet your needs.

This changed the whole basis of marriage. The state of California passed the first no-fault divorce law in 1970, twenty years after the church had, in effect, redefined the goal of marriage from duty to delight. As no-fault divorce swept the nation, it became easier to get out of the obligation to fulfill the duties of the marriage covenant than to get out of paying for a refrigerator.

Duty-free marriage couldn't have been implemented without birth control, of course. Back in the days of duty, when a man and woman came together, they'd be parents within a year. People didn't marry until they were ready to assume the duties of parenthood; they knew that as night follows day, "first comes love, then comes marriage, then comes a baby in a baby-carriage."

Most women were sensible enough not to want to assume the risks of a pregnancy or the duties of motherhood without some sort of commitment from a man who was prepared to assume the duties of fatherhood. Most women want a man in their lives badly enough that they're willing to live with a man without marriage if they aren't likely to get pregnant, but this wasn't clear until childless cohabitation became possible thanks to the Pill.

Before the pill, women had a closed shop in that most women agreed that they wouldn't sleep with a man without marriage. There were bad girls, of course, but men knew how to tell the difference. If a woman would sleep with him without marriage, she was a bad girl and he shouldn't marry her. If she wouldn't, she was

---

[322] Mount, Jr., Eric and Bos, Johanna W. H. "Scripture on Sexuality, Shifting Authority," *Journal of Presbyterian History* 59 no. 2, (Summer 1981): 224

a good girl and it was OK to marry her. Now that most American girls act like bad girls, men are confused about whom to marry.

What's more, today's legal climate places American men at a severe disadvantage. Enough women are willing to live with men without marriage that a man can enjoy the delights of female companionship without any commitments. If she stops taking her pills, becomes pregnant, and decides not to exercise her right to choose an abortion, the worst that can happen is that he can get tagged for child support until the child is 18.

If he marries her, however, she can walk out at any time for any reason or for no reason at all under no-fault divorce laws. In that case, he'll not only have to pay child support, he'll have to pay alimony, too, which unlike child support does not end when the child turns 18. If she moves in with a new boyfriend instead of marrying again, he'll pay alimony 'til death do them finally part.

Having married her, the man has a duty to support her, but, having married him, she has a duty to fulfill the wife's responsibilities. Our legal system has made it possible for either party to avoid their responsibilities to each other and to society at a whim, but in a disproportionate way: men are far more frequently forced to support their ex-wives than the other way around. Is it any wonder that men aren't eager to assume the responsibilities of marriage when they can enjoy female companionship without marriage? What's surprising is that some men still get married at all.

The Catholic Church never recognized no-fault divorce and continues to teach against sexual promiscuity. This isn't the first time in history that religious leaders have lamented the breakdown of marriages and of sexual morality. Jewish history records that the nation of Israel was hauled off to captivity in Babylon around 606 BC. After some of the exiles returned, they asked why they weren't prospering. The prophet Malachi explained that society had been weakened because marriages had broken down. He gave a Confucian-sounding analysis of the purpose and importance of virtuous families:

Yet ye say, Wherefore? Because the LORD hath been witness between thee and the wife of thy youth, <u>against whom thou hast dealt treacherously: yet is she thy companion, and the wife of thy covenant</u>. And did not he make one? Yet had he the residue of the spirit. And wherefore one? That <u>he might seek a godly seed</u>. Therefore take heed to your spirit, and let none deal treacherously against the wife of his youth. For the LORD, the God of Israel, saith that he hateth putting away: for one covereth violence with his garment, saith the LORD of hosts: therefore take heed to your spirit, that ye deal not treacherously. **Malachi 2:14-16** ~ 400 BC

Like Confucius, Malachi blamed family breakdown for the collapse of the Nation of Israel and for the exile's weakness after their return. Failing to do your duty to your family was treachery!

No-Fault Divorce Makes Logical Sense

If marriage is a matter of fulfilling duty, divorce isn't possible – your duties to your spouse cannot end until one of you dies. As Jack Benny put it, "My wife Mary and I have been married for forty-seven years and not once have we had an argument serious enough to consider divorce. Murder, yes, but divorce, never."

If, in contrast, marriage is for the purpose of delight, you ought to be able to get a divorce any time you're no longer delighted. It was reasonable to pass no-fault divorce laws once churches changed the driving force of marriage from duty to delight.

Changing the basis of satisfaction in marriage from responsibility to a right made a legal change seem reasonable for legislators. Not having read Confucius, they didn't understand the long-term implications of weakening people's sense of responsibility toward their families. Over time, the law was changed to eliminate any duty to treat wedding vows as an enforceable contract.

The flaw in this reasoning is that delight can't keep a couple together for the decades needed to teach children enough virtue for them to fulfill their duties to society, to their future spouses, and to their aging parents. Addicts learn that as pleasurable substances are ingested over time, it takes more and more to get the same good feeling. The limits of pleasure were documented long ago:

> Hast thou found honey? eat so much as is sufficient for thee, lest thou be filled therewith, <u>and vomit it</u>. **Proverbs 25:16** ~1,000 BC, 500 years before Confucius

Confucius' concept of "virtue" permitted pleasure, but not as an end in itself. Pleasure came from doing one's duty and from moderate engagement in activities which brought pleasure for the sake of pleasure. He realized that pleasure fades when overused.

The delights of inter-gender interaction are subject to the same limitations; if a couple seeks delight for its own sake, no pleasure can ever be enough. If husband and wife jointly seek satisfaction through mutual duty well done, however, they can be content while enjoying the pleasures of marriage. Contentment through duty well done is no longer taught in our society, we're taught to demand our rights instead of doing our duty.

Confucian Families

In muscle-powered societies, most people are farmers. Dry farming requires plowing, planting, weeding, harvesting, and threshing. Rice farming required even more labor to maintain dikes and pump water to the rice fields, so around 80% of all Chinese have been farmers since the beginning of Chinese history around 2,850 BC.[323]

Chinese women couldn't produce food because they weren't strong enough to do the work needed to grow rice and do all the domestic work needed to maintain a house and get the rice ready to

---

[323] Durant, Will, *Our Oriental Heritage*, (Simon and Schuster 1954) p 636

eat. The Chinese pictograph for "man" combines the picture for "field" and the picture for "strength," indicating that the man provides strength in the field. A woman had to have a man feed her or she couldn't survive long enough to raise children. As discussed in Chapter 6, American women were in the same situation until Amoskeag Mills started hiring women workers around 1850.

A woman and her children could starve to death if she lost her relationship to a man; natural selection favored women who focused great effort and skill on maintaining family ties. Once a woman established a stable family, her reproductive success was as assured as it was possible to be, but her husband's success depended on her children being his. Natural selection favored men who were possessive and jealous. A man who didn't keep other men away from his wife raised other men's children and was bred out of the gene pool.

The more often a man has sex, the more children he has. Each time he has sex, he might get another child. Although his dating style was a bit abrupt for modern tastes, Genghis Khan's success as a warrior led to his having an estimated 16 million living descendants because he got first pick of the women whenever his army captured a town or village.[324]

Having sex isn't nearly as important to a woman's reproductive success. Having sex while pregnant doesn't make her any more pregnant, and she had to nurse each child for a year or two to keep it alive. Nursing made her less fertile, but it wasn't a perfect contraceptive. If she became pregnant before her child was old enough for solid food, the child might die, so it was better to avoid sex until the child was weaned. A woman needs to have sex only 2 or 3 times every two or three years to achieve maximum reproductive success.

Natural selection makes people enjoy doing what's needed for survival. That's one reason men and women both enjoy eating. Women aren't generally as driven to have sex as men are; women

---

[324] "Genghis Khan a Prolific Lover, DNA Data Suggests," *National Geographic*, February 14, 2003

are driven to have relationships because relationships are more important to a woman's reproductive success than sex.

The better a woman relates to her infant, the faster she can figure out why it's crying – wet? Cold? Hot? Whatever? – and get it to go back to sleep. The better she relates to other women, the more they help her keep her babies alive. "I use honey for that cough." "Mine walked at 12 months." Women also share hints how to keep husbands from wandering.

The better she relates to her husband, the more likely he is to stick around and feed her. If the relationship breaks down and he runs off, she may starve to death. Women are driven to have relationships as powerfully as men are driven to have sex.

In classical China, the only old-age pension system available was to have enough sons. Sons carried on the family name and supported the parents when they became old.[325] A girl joined her husband's family and helped take care of her in-laws; raising a girl and providing her dowry brought no benefit to her parents. Lacking effective contraception, parents put female infants to death to save food or to stop the woman from nursing so that she could have a son.[326]

When the Communist government instituted the one-child policy in 1979 to reduce population growth,[327] parents chose to use ultrasound to determine sex and aborted girls. This led to a "bride shortage"[328] which could lead to disorder. Societies seem to become unstable when sex ratios reach something like 120 males to 100 females: in other words, when one-sixth of the men are surplus on the marriage market. [329]

---

[325] "A Slow-burning Fuse," The *Economist* June 27, 2009 p 13 points out that supporting one's aged parents is not only required by Confucian tradition, a 1996 law requires it and permits parents to sue if they aren't supported. This system gets unworkable if couples have only one child, of course.

[326] Mjngello, David E., *Drowning Girls in Ancient China: female infanticide since 1650* (Rowman & Littlefield, 2008) p 21

[327] Gilbert, Geoffrey, *World Population, 2nd ed.* (ABC-CLIO 2006) p 24-25

[328] Ibid., p 112

[329] "Forbidden No More," *Smithsonian Magazine*, March 2008 pp 80-90

In 19th century China, as many as 25 percent of men were unable to marry. "These young men became natural recruits for bandit gangs and local militia,"[330] and nearly toppled the government. Confucius was entirely correct in pointing out that family stability has a profound effect on the stability of the society.

Given the woman shortage, any woman can find plenty of men who'll be glad to follow Genghis Khan's "love 'em and leave 'em" dating strategy. This does not bode well for future family stability.

A modern Chinese girl can get a job and avoid depending on a man. If she can afford birth control, she can enjoy male companionship without pregnancy and the government would praise her for having an abortion should contraception fail. As long as she trusts the government to take care of her old age, she needn't take on the burden of caring for a child. If she has no children, she'll be out of the gene pool and will leave no footprints on the sands of time.[331]

Back to the Confucian Path

In America, so many men have become accustomed to relating physically to women without marrying that it's hard for a woman who wants to get married and have children to get a man to take her seriously. Once a man gets in the habit of treating women as disposable toys, it's hard for him to settle down with a treasure.

When a woman begins to relate to a man, her most important decision is whether she wants to be his treasure or to be his toy. This determines whether he plays with her or stays with her.

It hurts a woman to be a man's toy. Watch a little boy play with a toy truck – he rolls it this way and that, he focuses all his attention on it until he gets tired of the truck. Then he dumps it and runs off

---

[330] Little, Daniel, *Understanding Peasant China*, (Yale University Press, 1989) p 172
[331] The Chinese say, "If you're planning for next year, plant rice. For 20 years, plant trees. If you're planning for 100 years, plant men."

to some other toy. Sometimes he'll hit the truck or throw it against the wall. Does a woman want to be treated as a boy's toy?

A boy may choose a favorite toy that becomes his treasure. A boy never hurts his treasure, he takes *good* care of it, and his treasure gets *huge* amounts of attention for years and years.

Grandmothers say, "The difference between men and boys is the size of their toys." When a man plays with a woman, she gets attention for a while but it seldom ends well. Women write to blogs, "Why doesn't he call me anymore?" It's simple – he got tired of playing with her and moved on to another toy; at least he didn't throw her against the wall. The solution is not to wish men were different, the solution is for a woman to position herself so that she becomes a man's treasure instead of being his toy.

Boys are taught to play with toys; a man won't expect to find a treasure. A woman should take herself out of the "toy" category *before* the first date. When a man asks her out, a woman should say something like:

> "Before you spend any money on me, I want you to understand that I want to get married. I'm looking for a husband; I'm not looking for a good time. I'm not saying you have to agree to marry me now, but I want you to agree that our purpose in being together is to decide whether we should get married."

In today's "hookup" culture, that'll boggle his mind. A woman might explain:

> "God made me to be a treasure for some man. I want to be such a treasure for my husband that he'll value me so much that he likes being with me and enjoys talking to me. If you're not that man, we can part friends, but I'm not a toy. I want a man to stay with me; I don't want a man to play with me. You're a nice guy and I could easily fall in love with you. If I

end up loving you and you won't marry me, I'll be hurt.

The marriage vows say, "To have and to hold." I expect my husband to have me; I plan to belong to my husband. If that's you, I'll do my best to be a real treasure for you, but I don't want a man to just take me. Being your treasure means I give myself to you when you want me. I give myself because I know that giving myself to you makes you happy with me. You'll want to make love five times before breakfast and start in again when you get home from work. That's a bit much from my point of view, but that's what men think "to have and to hold" means.

If I'm yours, though, I expect you to be mine. I want to have my husband, but men don't like being taken any more than women do. Your being mine means you want to open your heart to me. You open yourself to me because you know that giving yourself to me makes me happy with you. I want you to open your heart to me five times before breakfast and talk more when you get back from work. I want to know what you're doing and how you feel about it. I want to know what's on your heart. Opening your heart to me bores and humbles you just as opening my body to you bores and humbles me. My emotions are made so that it's hard for me to be yours if you aren't mine. Opening my body to you makes me yours; opening your heart to me makes you mine. That's how we float each other's boats.

If you belong to me while treating me as your very own special treasure, I'll be *glad* to be yours. If I enjoy giving myself to you and being yours, you'll be glad to belong to me. Being glad to belong to each other will bring us joy all our days. If you won't at least *consider* marriage, please don't waste my time."

I know women who've done that; it works. When their husbands tell the story, other men agree that they'd be interested in marrying a woman who wanted to be God's treasure for her husband. A treasure he'd marry; why marry a used toy? Why wipe his face with someone else's used Kleenex?

This speech addresses many of a man's natural selection hot-buttons:

- Her not sleeping around calms his fear of raising other men's children. Putting herself in the "good girl" category makes him more likely to marry her. A woman who says she wants marriage but goes to bed without marriage is a liar. Given that she can walk out at any time, her character is the only guarantee that the marriage will last. Why would a man commit himself to a woman who lies about something as important as marriage?

- Saying that she expects him to have her when he wants her addresses his possessiveness. Men know that most women feel that most men are too possessive. Telling him she plans to encourage his possessiveness makes him more willing to give up his right to pursue all the women in the entire world and focus on her alone.

- She addresses her fears of his paying attention to other women. Women have far more sexual capacity than men do. A man is always interested, but can't have sex for a while after making love. If she takes everything he can make, she makes it harder for other women to get his attention. He won't be interested in them because she's drained off his energy. A man turns to pornography, other women, or other men when he's sexually frustrated. If his wife lets him leave home every morning with his shirt soaked in gasoline, he'll eventually get too near a fire and they'll both be burned.

- Making love brings out his protective instincts. Men aren't bound to women by sex nearly as strongly as sex binds women to men, but taking care of a woman increased a man's reproductive success. Some bonding occurs when a man makes love, particularly if she thanks him for wanting her. The more often they make love, the stronger his bond.

- Putting talk on the table addresses her need to communicate and to build her relationship with him through talk. Men talk to teach; they build relationships through shared experiences. By telling him how much she expects to talk, she can use the dating period to make sure he's glad to open his heart to her. Opening his heart to her makes him hers as opening her body to him makes her his. Natural selection has made women sensitive to whether men are happy with them; an unhappy man is likely to abandon her and her children. Opening his heart to her makes her confident that he really is happy with her. If he can't or won't be happy to be hers, she can back out before she's gotten too emotionally involved to walk away.

- Getting him used to talking to her before anything happens makes it easier to make decisions peacefully. A woman had a lot more to lose when a relationship broke down than a man did – he'd be lonely, she'd starve. Natural selection made women care more about relationships and favoured women who were inclined to go along with men. When a man and a woman are together in a car, the man's usually driving, even if it's her car. Having had to guard women closely to avoid raising other men's children, men are selected to want to be in charge, or at least to cast the tie-breaking vote. Getting a man used to talking to her means he'll understand her better which makes it more likely that she'll be able to put up with his wanting to lead.

Sex and speech are the two sides of the arch that holds up a family. Talking helps women share tips on keeping babies alive and keeping men from running off; natural selection favors women who're driven to talk. When a man encourages a woman to talk and thanks her for her speech, she feels loved, valued, honored and appreciated. When a woman thanks a man for their sex life, he feels loved, honored, valued, and appreciated.

Talking scares away animals so a hunter can't catch them. Natural selection favors men who don't talk. Talking enough to satisfy a woman is learned behavior; making love enough to satisfy a man is learned behavior. Meeting each other's needs establishes a strong family that fulfills its duty to their children and to society. Being happy with each other makes it easier for them to be virtuous and teach their children to be virtuous. Government tries to force people to be virtuous, but virtue imposed from outside doesn't work nearly as well as virtue that comes from within or is taught by example.

By Bible or By Bayonet

Governments throughout history have used drastic punishment as a means of making citizens fulfill government's definition of virtue, but all rulers recognize that it's better to persuade citizens if possible. It's easier for the rulers if citizens go along voluntarily than if they have to be forced. Most people have some sort of belief in God, so appealing to religion is a popular way to persuade people to obey.

Confucius stated explicitly that God expected everyone to obey government and that "virtue" must be taught because people were naturally too selfish to behave virtuously on their own. His belief that every person needs training is similar to the Christian idea of "original sin." Unlike Christianity, however, Confucius believed that men could become perfect through education, self-cultivation, and by performing rituals. His concept of "perfectibility of man" is more optimistic than the Christian doctrine of "original sin" which holds that people can't become perfect until after death.

Government is responsible to enlighten people through education and by setting good examples.[332] Modern social workers believe that people would grow up to be virtuous if only we could place them in virtuous environments. This is similar to Confucius' view on perfectibility, but today's thinkers overlook Confucius' emphasis on the importance of setting good examples.

Although many of Confucius' rules for ordering society, including his statement that citizens have a duty to obey their government, are found in the Bible, the Bible is not as popular with tyrants because the Bible teaches that a citizen's duty to obey God is more important than obeying government. Confucius thought that virtue flowed top-down; citizens behave badly unless given constant examples and exhortation from on high. Western thinkers such as Rep. Robert Winthrop, in contrast, believed that a virtuous citizenry could work bottom-up to create a virtuous society with little need for government:

> All societies of men must be governed in some way or other. The less they may have of stringent State Government, the more they must have of individual self-government. The less they rely on public law or physical force, the more they must rely on private moral restraint. Men, in a word, must

---

[332] Embree, Ainslee Thomas, Gluck, Carol, *Asia in Western and World History*, (Sharpe, 1995) p 702-703 The concept of the perfectibility of man was introduced by the ancient Greeks. The idea is popular with intellectual elites who see themselves as the only force which can uplifting the benighted masses and help them get closer to the perfection of the elites who've already arrived. The benighted masses sometimes beg to differ.

necessarily be controlled, either by a power within them, or by a power without them; either by the Word of God, or by the strong arm of man; <u>either by the Bible, or by the bayonet</u>. It may do for other countries and other governments to talk about the State supporting religion. Here, under our own free institutions, it is Religion which must support the State.[333] [emphasis added]

Rep. Winthrop echoed the US Constitution in saying that when men are self-ruled and follow natural law, which is another way to describe "virtue," government is more or less unnecessary.

The Founders limited the federal government because they didn't trust government and they didn't think much government would be needed so long as citizens were virtuous. We're seeing, however, that when people abandon their duties and demand benefits from government, candidates for office promise to give them everything they want if people turn power over to the government.

Confucius believed that the Emperor had to be tyrannical because common people couldn't govern themselves. The downside of his system was that there was no way to repair a government that lost virtue. Where the American Founders believed that power had to stay in the hands of the people because only the people could keep government virtuous, Confucius believed that ordinary citizens could never be virtuous enough to force government to be virtuous. The Founders believed that virtue flowed from the people up to government via the ballot box; Confucius believed that virtue flowed from government down to the people via good examples and the bayonet.

---

[333] Robert Charles Winthrop, "Either by the Bible or the Bayonet," as quoted in Federer, William J., *America's God and Country* (St. Louis, MO: Amerisearch, 2000), 701-702. Rep. Winthrop was Speaker of the US House of Representatives 1847-1849. The quote is also in Stanley, Charles F., *Charles Stanley's Handbook for Christian Living* (Thomas Nelson) p 103

Confucius was correct about the influence of leaders as examples of virtue or lack thereof. It was big news when Henry Ford II, grandson of the founder of Ford Motor Company, divorced in 1964. Until then, any Ford employee who divorced was fired. "If you can't keep your promises to your spouse," Henry I who founded the company used to say, "you can't keep your promises to me."

Henry Ford shared Confucius' belief that private conduct affects public actions and that leaders set standards for followers. Duty-free marriages teach children that they're on their own and have to look out for #1. Duty-free politicians set examples of stealing and of looking out for #1.

If everybody's looking out for #1, if everybody's more interested in taking out than in putting in, if married people are more concerned with having their own needs met than with meeting each others' needs, society becomes virtue-free and can't last long. As more and more people refuse to do their duty voluntarily, government steps in to keep order, but non-virtuous politicians can't enforce virtue.

Bad Leaders and Collapse

Confucius said that collapse comes when leaders set bad examples. People are always aware of leaders' behavior. When local bigwigs act without virtue and don't do their duty to society, people lose virtue and stop doing their duty. Powerful people cheat on taxes and profit unfairly; lesser people feel they've no stake in society.

In our system, the people on the bottom of the pile elect leaders. Our leaders don't like being subject to the will of the people and use tricks such as gerrymandering, manipulating the news, swapping earmarks for campaign contributions, and padding voting lists to stay in office. Despite its imperfections, however, enough of our republic remains that voters can and occasionally do get rid of elected officials who betray their duty to us.

The problem is that we Americans have lost enough of our own sense of virtue that we no longer demand virtue from our leaders.

In the past, the path to success was to go to work and earn what you wanted. Our leaders now pay off supporters so it's often easier to get what we want by lobbying government instead of working. As we no longer require virtue in our leaders, crooked leaders set worse and worse examples. We're losing virtue all up and down the line.

History verifies Confucius' statements about the vital role that virtuous families play in the strength of a society. Spartan parents taught every son to lay his life on the line to defend the nation as required. When they left for the front, mothers said, "Come back carrying your shield or on it." The only way a Spartan would return without his shield was if he threw it away to run from the battle, in which case he might as well not come home at all. Spartans were duty-bound to stand their ground to the death.

The Roman republic adopted this Greek tradition of duty and was able to protect the largest empire the world had known up to that time. They based their military on "If you wish for peace, prepare for war.[334]" Because they were ready and willing to defend their society regardless of cost, Rome enjoyed a 200-year period of peace.

In the late Roman Empire, this duty-based custom declined. So did Rome. Rome fell because its citizens lost virtue and abandoned duty. As Will Durant put it, "A great civilization is not conquered from without until it has destroyed itself within."[335]

[334] Renatus, Publius Flavius *De Re Militari*, book 3, 4th of 5th century. Quoted in Milner, N.P, *Vegetius: epitome of military science*, (Liverpool University Press, 1996)

[335] Durant, Will. *Caesar and Christ*, (1944, New York) p 665

14 – Other Thinkers

Scholars, philosophers, and thinkers everywhere have written rules for managing society. No set of rules survives for very long if it's based on an unrealistic view of human nature; groups whose practices get too far from Confucius' rules go extinct.

Members of the United Society of Believers in Christ's Second Appearing were called Shakers because of their peculiar behavior during worship services. Starting in the 1700s, the American Shakers attracted 20,000 converts over the next century. The Shakers practiced celibacy because of the Biblical statement that people would neither marry nor be given in marriage in heaven (Mark 12:25). Their community gained members only through conversion or by adopting orphans. Today, there are only a handful of elderly Shakers left. Communities that don't encourage reproduction tend to die out.

Many utopian, communitarian, or isolationist societies have come and gone. Few philosophies have lasted as long as Confucianism which was documented 2,500 years ago:

- Children have a duty to serve and obey their parents
- Citizens have a duty to serve and obey the government
- Government has a duty to serve the welfare of the people.

Confucius taught that from the Emperor down to the lowliest peasant head of household, virtuous leaders must always look out for their followers' best interest.

Confucius didn't invent the rules; he called himself "a transmitter, not a maker."[336] He presented self-evident rules that God had put in place, much as Sir Isaac Newton described God's laws of gravity which he hadn't invented.

The Dustbins of History

Social structures have to be tested for many generations to see if they work in the long term. The better they sound, the more testing they need. Karl Marx's formula, "From each according to his ability, to each according to his need" would work in a perfectly virtuous society. Society would prosper greatly if each person contributed as much as possible and took only what was necessary. The early Christian church operated this way:

> And all that believed were together, and had all things common; And sold their possessions and goods, and parted them to all men, as every man had need. **Acts 2:44-45** ~50 AD

Unselfish generosity that lets a group practice this degree of sharing is so unusual that it's documented twice:

> And the multitude of them that believed were of one heart and of one soul: neither said any of them that ought of the things which he possessed was his own; but they had all things common. **Acts 4:32** ~50 AD

The church was neither communist nor socialist in that every individual was at liberty either to contribute property or not (Acts 5:4). The practice of having property and money in common died out early in church history, probably due to insufficient virtue.

---

[336] Confucius, *Analects*, VII, I

The 20th century Israeli kibbutz movement was based on Marx's rule. Unfortunately, human nature contains enough greed that this organization doesn't last long – kibbutzes break down over time as the most capable members seek better opportunities elsewhere.

The Pilgrims risked their lives sailing from Holland to Massachusetts in 1620. They had fled England because the king wouldn't let them worship as they chose and left Holland for better economic opportunity and because their children were adopting Dutch culture.

They tried the "all things in common" philosophy described in the Book of Acts. They soon found, however, that despite being isolated in a hostile wilderness, many wouldn't work hard because the community as a whole would get the benefit. When the Pilgrims changed their policies so that each person kept the fruits of his or her labor, productivity increased and starvation was avoided. The colonists at Jamestown had a similar learning experience.

Many utopias based on sharing everything have been tried; all such societies have disappeared. Enforcing economic equality in the name of some warped view of "fairness" sounds so attractive, however, that governments and societies keep trying variants of Marx's principle even though it's failed everywhere it's been tried.

The idea that government should always seek to do "the greatest good for the greatest number"[337] is similar to Confucius' view that government had a duty to look out for everyone's welfare.

Although "greatest good" doesn't include direct economic implications, it's often been used to justify taxing the better-off to support the poor. Carried too far, this leads to the same economic disaster experienced by the Pilgrims as people lose all incentive to work.

---

[337] Bentham, Jeremy, quoted in Bowie and Simon, *The Individual and the Political Order*, (Lanham, Md, Rowman & Littlefield, 2008) p 30

The Mandate of Heaven

Confucius stated that God had put the Emperor in place and that God expected people to obey the Emperor and anyone whom he appointed - as long as he kept the "Mandate of Heaven." Depending on how you count, 10-15 dynasties lost the "Mandate of Heaven" and fell during China's 5000-year history.[338]

The Bible says that it's fatal to stray too far from God's rules:

> For the nation and kingdom that will not serve thee shall perish; yea, those nations shall <u>utterly be wasted</u>. **Isaiah 60:12** ~700 BC
> Except the LORD build the house, they labour in vain that build it: except the LORD keep the city, the watchman waketh but in vain. **Psalm 127:1**

Other sources express similar rules for ordering society based on God's will, pure reason, or practical experience. Organizational principles that worked over multiple generations survived; systems which didn't work faded away.

All successful formulas bear a striking resemblance to Confucius' rules. The long-term survival of Confucius' ideas suggest that he found the core principles of how to manage a society made up of greedy, selfish, lazy human beings, all of whom must be taught virtue for society to survive over the long term.

The Pilgrims' experience shows that no society can survive if too many focus on taking resources out of society or too few work to put resources in. The idea that all people have a duty to contribute as

---

[338] Durant, William. *Our Oriental Heritage,* (New York, Simon and Schuster, 1954) p. 636 has a dynastic chart which starts with "Legendary rulers" in 2,800 BC, about 4,800 years ago. There are indications that Chinese rulers had well-developed organizational systems before that. The figure of 5,000 years is more or less traditional. The Chinese bureaucratic system is far older than the 200-year-old republican form of government as practiced in America or communism which collapsed before reaching its first century.

much to society as they can is the core of Confucian virtue and of all successful systems. Many writers invoke God's will to reinforce their definitions of virtue as Confucius did.

Duties of Children

The Bible commands children to obey their parents just as Confucius did. Disobeying parents could be punished by death; obedience was rewarded with long life. Public stoning encouraged virtue in others:

> If a man have a stubborn and rebellious son, which will not obey the voice of his father, or the voice of his mother, and that, when they have chastened him, will not hearken unto them: Then shall his father and his mother lay hold on him, and bring him out unto the elders of his city, and unto the gate of his place; And they shall say unto the elders of his city, This our son is stubborn and rebellious, he will not obey our voice; he is a glutton, and a drunkard. And all the men of his city shall stone him with stones, <u>that he die</u>: so shalt thou put evil away from among you; and all Israel shall hear, and fear. **Deuteronomy 21:18-21** ~1500 BC
>
> Honour thy father and thy mother: that thy days may be long upon the land which the LORD thy God giveth thee. **Exodus 20:12** ~1500 BC
>
> For Moses said, Honour thy father and thy mother; and, Whoso curseth father or mother, <u>let him die the death</u>: **Mark 7:10** ~50 AD
>
> Children, obey your parents in the Lord: for this is right. **Ephesians 6:1** ~50 AD
>
> Children, obey your parents in all things: for this is well pleasing unto the Lord. **Colossians 3:20** ~50 AD

Max Hasting's description of the collapse of social order in England shows what happens when children get out of control:

> A key factor in delinquency is lack of effective sanctions to deter it. From an early stage, feral children discover that they can bully fellow pupils at school, shout abuse at people in the streets, urinate outside pubs, hurl litter from car windows, play car radios at deafening volumes, and, indeed, commit casual assaults with only a negligible prospect of facing rebuke, far less retribution. John Stuart Mill wrote in his great 1859 essay, *On Liberty*: 'The liberty of the individual must be thus far limited; he must not make himself a nuisance to other people.'
>
> Yet every day up and down the land, this vital principle of civilized societies is breached with impunity. Anyone who reproaches a child, far less an adult, for discarding rubbish, making a racket, committing vandalism or driving unsociably will receive in return a torrent of obscenities, if not violence.[339]

Civilization is fragile – children who don't obey parents don't obey anyone and grow up to be barbarians. That's why ancient law commanded that extremely disobedient sons to be put to death.

Duties of Parents

A mother pulled off the road to spank her son. A policeman was worried about abuse and asked her if anything was wrong. "No, officer," she said, "I'm dealing with him when he's 6 so you won't have to deal with him when he's 16." Confucius taught that parents

---

[339] Hastings, Max, "Years of liberal dogma have spawned a generation of amoral, uneducated, welfare dependent, brutalized youngsters" *Daily Mail*, August 9, 2011

must instill virtue into their children. The Bible also assigns that responsibility to parents:

> And these words, which I command thee this day, shall be in thine heart: And thou shalt teach them diligently unto thy children, and shalt talk of them when thou sittest in thine house, and when thou walkest by the way, and when thou liest down, and when thou risest up. **Deuteronomy 6:6-7** ~1500 BC

Parents not only had to obey God's law, they were to teach it constantly to their children. Parents had to teach virtue without abuse, however. The Bible teaches that rulers generally oppress subjects instead of benefiting them:

> And Samuel told all the words of the LORD unto the people that asked of him a king. And he said, This will be the manner of the king that shall reign over you: He will take your sons, and appoint them for himself, for his chariots, and to be his horsemen; and some shall run before his chariots. And he will appoint him captains over thousands, and captains over fifties; and will set them to ear his ground, and to reap his harvest, and to make his instruments of war, and instruments of his chariots. And he will take your daughters to be confectionaries, and to be cooks, and to be bakers. And he will take your fields, and your vineyards, and your oliveyards, even the best of them, and give them to his servants. And he will take the tenth of your seed, and of your vineyards, and give to his officers, and to his servants. And he will take your menservants, and your maidservants, and your goodliest young men, and your asses, and put them to his work. He will take the tenth of your sheep: and ye shall be his servants. And ye shall cry out in that day because of

your king which ye shall have chosen you; and the LORD will not hear you in that day. **I Samuel 8:10-18** ~1200 BC

The people wanted a king to be like other nations. They got a king, but their kings didn't teach their own sons virtue. Four kings and two civil wars later, the people had had enough and rebelled.

The Bible assigns mothers day-to-day duty of handling children:

I will therefore that the younger women marry, bear children, guide the house, give none occasion to the adversary to speak reproachfully. **I Timothy 5:14** ~50 AD

Urging women to bear children echoes Confucius' directive that people have a duty to bear children so that their ancestors continue to have descendants.

The Biblical writers also wrote that children should be treated like servants in order to teach them how to serve. They're to be kept under control until they learn virtue:

Now I say, That the heir, as long as he is a child, <u>differeth nothing from a servant</u>, though he be lord of all; But is under tutors and governors until the time appointed of the father. **Galatians 4:1-2** ~50 AD

Abuse of authority is so common, however, that the Bible warns fathers not to overdo:

And, ye fathers, provoke not your children to wrath: but bring them up in the nurture and admonition of the Lord. **Ephesians 6:4** ~50 AD

As with nations, abuse of authority drives family members to anger and rebellion.

Duties of Husbands

Like Confucius, the Bible states that a husband leads his household:

> But I would have you know, <u>that the head of
> every man is Christ</u>; and the head of the woman is
> the man; and the head of Christ is God. I
> **Corinthians 11:3** ~50 AD

A virtuous husband must obey God to keep the "Mandate of Heaven" in his household. The Bible also commands husbands:

> Husbands, love your wives, and be not bitter
> against them. **Colossians 3:19** ~50 AD

The Greek word translated "love" is *agapao* which is not an emotion or feeling; it's an act of will. A husband must choose to actively and consistently nourish his wife and look out for her best interest as government must actively look out for the public interest.

> Husbands, love your wives, even as Christ also
> loved the church, and gave himself for it; That he
> might sanctify and cleanse it with the washing of
> water by the word, That he might present it to
> himself a glorious church, not having spot, or
> wrinkle, or any such thing; but that it should be holy
> and without blemish. So ought men to love their
> wives as their own bodies. He that loveth his wife
> loveth himself. **Ephesians 5:25-28** ~50 AD

As Christ gave His life to save His people, a husband should give his life to take care of his wife. Christ forgives our sins so that He can present His church to Himself as "holy and without blemish." A man must love his wife as God's perfect gift for him. Marriage prospers if a man appreciates and honors his wife as God's perfect gift for him and she acts like God's perfect gift for him.

Confucius observed that society is based on families. When families are virtuous, society is strong. When families lose virtue and fall apart, society falls. As with any organization, a family stands or falls on the virtue of its members.

A man's virtue sets the tone for his relationship with his wife. Men may or may not understand women very well, but they all know that a woman can give a man a taste of the joys of heaven. A man pursues a woman hoping that she'll become his treasure.

Few men realize that being God's treasure for a man is emotionally demanding – a woman burns out if her husband doesn't meet her emotional needs. A virtuous husband treats his wife so well that she likes belonging to him and delights in his desire for her:

> I am my beloved's, and his desire is toward me.
> **Song 7:10**
> His left hand should be under my head, and his right hand should embrace me. **Song 8:3** ~1000 BC

Why is she happy to belong to him? Why does she encourage his desire for her? Because he's exercised virtue – he belongs to her:

> My beloved is mine, and I am his: **Song 2:16**
> I am my beloved's, and my beloved is mine:
> **Song 6:3**

She's happy to belong to him because she knows that he belongs to her. How does a man show a woman that he belongs to her? By opening his heart to her as often, as sincerely, and as lovingly as he expects her to open herself to him.

A wife can give her husband a taste of the joys of heaven, but she can't make him any happier than he makes her.

The Wisdom of Wives

The Bible describes wifely virtue and teaches that a virtuous wife should be praised and appreciated:

> She openeth her mouth with wisdom; and in her tongue is the law of kindness. She looketh well to the ways of her household, and eateth not the bread of idleness. **Proverbs 31:26-27**
>
> Give her of the fruit of her hands; and <u>let her own works praise her in the gates</u>. **Proverbs 31:31** ~1000 BC
>
> Her children arise up, and call her blessed; her husband also, and he praiseth her. Many daughters have done virtuously, but thou excellest them all. **Proverbs 31:28-29** ~1000 BC

That last passage is vital. Confucius observed that children are born selfish and must be taught virtue. Children don't naturally "arise up and call her blessed." Instead of expressing gratitude, children tend to take whatever parents give and demand more.

A father must teach his children to respect, honor, and appreciate their mother. If she hadn't put her life on the line giving birth, they wouldn't exist.[340] If she hadn't spent years changing diapers and feeding them, they'd have died.

After children learn to appreciate their mother, they can learn virtue from her. Most of the Book of Proverbs is passed from a father to his children, but this bit of wisdom came from a mother:

---

[340] It's difficult estimate how many women die during pregnancy or while giving birth. Records suggest that during the seventeenth and eighteenth centuries, 1-1.5% of births led to the mother's death. A woman who had the usual 5-8 children had a 1 in 8 chance of dying during one of her pregnancies. To this day, a pregnant woman walks the shadow of the valley of death.

¹The words of king Lemuel, the prophecy that <u>his mother taught him</u>. ²What, my son? and what, the son of my womb? and what, the son of my vows? ³Give not thy strength unto women, nor thy ways to that which destroyeth kings. ⁴It is not for kings, O Lemuel, it is not for kings to drink wine; nor for princes strong drink: ⁵Lest they drink, and forget the law, and pervert the judgment of any of the afflicted. ⁶Give strong drink unto him that is ready to perish, and wine unto those that be of heavy hearts. ⁷Let him drink, and forget his poverty, and remember his misery no more. ⁸Open thy mouth for the dumb in the cause of all such as are appointed to destruction. ⁹Open thy mouth, judge righteously, and plead the cause of the poor and needy. **Proverbs 31:1-9**

Knowing that her son would become King, Mrs. Lemuel did her best to teach him how to rule virtuously. Her guidance is the same as Confucius' formula telling rulers how to keep subjects' loyalty:

- V3 – Don't mess with women
- V4-5 – Don't be a drunk – it leads to unjust behaviour. Nothing undermines subjects' loyalty faster than a perception of unjust rule. Justice must not only be done, justice must be seen to be done.
- V6-7 – Take care of your people when they're hurting.
- V8 – Look out for people who're headed for destruction. Warn others about unwise behaviour. Set an example of virtue and teach virtue.
- V9 – Be fair at all times. Teach everyone to look out for the poor and for everybody else.

Machiavelli extended Mrs. Lemuel's advice about doing justice and avoiding unwise involvement with women:

Still, a prince should make himself feared in such a way that if he does not gain love, he at any rate avoids hatred; for fear and the absence of hatred may well go together, and will always be attained by one who abstains from interfering with the property of his citizens and subjects or with their women.

He also agreed with Confucius about capital punishment:

And when he is obliged to take the life of anyone, let him do so when there is proper justification and manifest reason for it; but above all he must abstain from taking the property of others, for men forget more easily the death of their father than the loss of their patrimony. Then also pretexts for seizing property are never wanting, and one who begins to live by rapine will always find some reason for taking the goods of others, whereas causes for taking life are rarer and more fleeting.[341]

Duties of Leaders to Their Followers

Confucius declared that virtuous leaders must strive to benefit followers. Adam Smith listed three responsibilities of national leaders:

The sovereign has only three duties to attend to; three duties of great importance, indeed, but plain and intelligible to common understandings: first, the duty of protecting the society from the violence and invasion of other independent societies; secondly, the duty of protecting, as far as possible, every

---

[341] Machiavelli, *The Prince*, Of Cruelty and Clemency, and Whether It Is Better to be Loved or Feared

member of the society from the injustice and oppression of every other member of it, or the duty of establishing an exact administration of justice; and, thirdly, the duty of erecting and maintaining certain public works and certain public institutions.
Adam Smith, *The Wealth of Nations*

Adam Smith and Confucius agree that virtuous leadership is essential for any enterprise to survive. This applies to business, government, and families. At the family level, for example, parents must keep kids from abusing each other and must organize meals, sleep, housing, clothing and other matters of shared importance.
Napoleon Bonaparte said:

One must serve a nation worthily, but not take pains to flatter people. To win them, you must do them good. For nothing is more dangerous than to echo people's opinions and say just what they want to hear. When afterwards, they do not get all they want, they get restless and believe you have broken your word.[342]

Leaders must do what's good for their followers instead of always doing what their followers want. This requires servant leadership. The Bible commands leaders to lead by serving:

So after he [Jesus] had washed their feet, and had taken his garments, and was set down again, he said unto them, Know ye what I have done to you? Ye call me Master and Lord: and ye say well; for so I am. If I then, your Lord and Master, have washed your feet; ye also ought to wash one another's feet. For I have given you an example, that ye should do as I have done to you. **John 13:12-15** ~50 AD

[342] Jerry Manas, *Napoleon on Project Management: Timeless Lessons in Planning, Execution, and Leadership*, (Nashville, Tn, Thomas Nelson, Inc., 2006) p 14

Foot-washing was the lowliest job imaginable. When Jesus washed His followers' feet, He set a powerful example of servant leadership. Confucius' pointing out that virtuous leaders take care of their followers is another way of describing "servant leadership."

Parents must teach their children to serve other people by commanding them, requiring them to serve the family as soon as they are able, and by setting examples of virtuous service.

On another occasion, Jesus' disciples argued over which of them was most important. Jesus rebuked them and explained how a virtuous leader should lead by serving:

> But Jesus called them to him, and saith unto them, Ye know that they which are accounted to rule over the Gentiles exercise lordship over them; and their great ones exercise authority upon them. But so shall it not be among you: but whosoever will be great among you, shall be your minister: And whosoever of you will be the chiefest, shall be servant of all. For even the Son of man came not to be ministered unto, but to minister, and to give his life a ransom for many. **Mark 10:42-45** ~50 AD

Jesus pointed out that leaders "exercise authority." He forbade this, commanding that His disciples follow His example and serve others. Whoever desires to lead the most must serve the most.

Duties of Citizens to Government

The Bible says rulers are put in place by God and must be obeyed. Verse 4 of this passage says God expects rulers to benefit their subjects and punish evildoers as Confucius said. Verse 6 tells people to pay taxes:

> ¹Let every soul be subject unto the higher powers. For there is no power but of God: the

powers that be are ordained of God. ²Whosoever therefore resisteth the power, resisteth the ordinance of God: and they that resist shall receive to themselves damnation. ³For rulers are not a terror to good works, but to the evil. Wilt thou then not be afraid of the power? Do that which is good, and thou shalt have praise of the same: ⁴For he is the minister of God to thee for good. But if thou do that which is evil, be afraid; for he beareth not the sword in vain: for he is the minister of God, a revenger to execute wrath upon him that doeth evil. ⁵Wherefore ye must needs be subject, not only for wrath, but also for conscience sake. ⁶For for this cause pay ye tribute also: for they are God's ministers, attending continually upon this very thing. ⁷Render therefore to all their dues: tribute to whom tribute is due; custom to whom custom; fear to whom fear; honour to whom honour. **Romans 13:1-7** ~50 AD

Given Confucius' declaration that God Himself wanted citizens to obey government, it's no wonder his teachings became the foundation of a state religion – what better endorsement could a ruler want? Many Western rulers have cited this passage out of similar motivations. Emperors, as much as kings and presidents, often forgot that Confucius said they had to rule virtuously and that they governed with the consent of the people.

The Consent of the Governed

The American Declaration of Independence says,

"Governments are instituted among Men, deriving their just powers from the consent of the governed, — that whenever any Form of Government becomes destructive of these ends, it is the <u>Right of the People</u> to alter or to abolish it, and to institute new Government."

Confucius didn't believe in Democracy – citizens had no rights and the Emperor's power was absolute. He knew, however, that rulers need the people's consent and said that society could not survive if people lost faith in government. Confucius anticipated the "right of revolution" when he said,

> "Before the sovereigns of the Shang (Dynasty) had lost (the hearts of) the people, they were the mates of God. Take warning from the house of Shang."[343]

When greedy civil servants or corrupt judges became too numerous, they hide each other so that the Emperor couldn't find them to kill them. At that point, Confucius said, it was not just a citizen's right, but a citizen's duty to rebel. Once government as a whole became selfish or corrupt, there was no way to fix it other than to bring down the entire society and start over.

In advising a local ruler, he said, "... if the people have no faith (in their rulers), then there is no standing (for the state)."[344]

When the Declaration of Independence was written, one of the chief complaints against King George was that

> He has erected a multitude of New Offices, and sent hither swarms of Officers to <u>harass our people and eat out their substance</u>.

King George lost his American colonies when the colonists lost faith in his government.

In saying that rulers had to serve people well enough to keep their support, Confucius recognized that people are the ultimate

---

[343] *Great Learning* in Legge, *Life*, X, 5
[344] Confucius, *Analects*, XII, vii

source of all power. History shows repeatedly that any government that loses trust falls, either by conquest or from internal rebellion.

As Confucius cited the fall of the Shang dynasty, the Bible tells how Samuel's sons didn't learn his virtue. Instead of accepting their rule after their father, the people asked Samuel to appoint a king.

> And it came to pass, when Samuel was old, that he made his sons judges over Israel. Now the name of his firstborn was Joel; and the name of his second, Abiah: they were judges in Beersheba. And his sons walked not in his ways, <u>but turned aside after lucre, and took bribes, and perverted judgment</u>. Then all the elders of Israel gathered themselves together, and came to Samuel unto Ramah, And said unto him, Behold, <u>thou art old, and thy sons walk not in thy ways: now make us a king to judge us like all the nations</u>. **I Samuel 8:1-5** ~1100 BC

Samuel was unable to pass on his leadership position because his sons weren't virtuous and people lost faith in them. Saul was the first king, followed by David and then Solomon who taxed the people heavily. About 500 years before Confucius was born, the nation rebelled against Solomon's son Rehoboam, murdered the head of the Internal Revenue Service, and made Jeroboam king because Rehoboam refused to cut taxes as they had asked:

> And Rehoboam went to Shechem: for to Shechem were <u>all Israel come to make him king</u>. And it came to pass, when Jeroboam the son of Nebat, who was in Egypt, whither he fled from the presence of Solomon the king, heard it, that Jeroboam returned out of Egypt. And they sent and called him. So Jeroboam and all Israel came and spake to Rehoboam, saying, Thy father made our yoke grievous: <u>now therefore ease thou somewhat the grievous servitude of thy father, and his heavy yoke that he put upon us, and we will serve thee</u>. And he said unto them, Come

again unto me after three days. And the people departed. And king Rehoboam took counsel with the old men that had stood before Solomon his father while he yet lived, saying, What counsel give ye me to return answer to this people? And they spake unto him, saying, If thou be kind to this people, and please them, and speak good words to them, they will be thy servants for ever. But he forsook the counsel which the old men gave him, and took counsel with the young men that were brought up with him, that stood before him. And he said unto them, What advice give ye that we may return answer to this people, which have spoken to me, saying, Ease somewhat the yoke that thy father did put upon us? And the young men that were brought up with him spake unto him, saying, Thus shalt thou answer the people that spake unto thee, saying, Thy father made our yoke heavy, but make thou it somewhat lighter for us; thus shalt thou say unto them, My little finger shall be thicker than my father's loins. For whereas my father put a heavy yoke upon you, I will put more to your yoke: my father chastised you with whips, but I will chastise you with scorpions. So Jeroboam and all the people came to Rehoboam on the third day, as the king bade, saying, Come again to me on the third day. And the <u>king answered them roughly</u>; and king Rehoboam forsook the counsel of the old men, And answered them after the advice of the young men, saying, My father made your yoke heavy, but I will add thereto: my father chastised you with whips, but I will chastise you with scorpions. So the king hearkened not unto the people: for the cause was of God, that the LORD might perform his word, which he spake by the hand of Ahijah the Shilonite to Jeroboam the son of Nebat. And when all Israel saw that the king would not hearken unto them, the people answered the king, saying, What portion have we in David? and we have none inheritance in the son of Jesse: every man to your tents, O Israel: and now, David, see to thine own house. So all Israel went to their tents. But as for the children of Israel that dwelt in the cities of Judah, Rehoboam reigned over them. Then king Rehoboam sent Hadoram that was over the tribute; and <u>the children of Israel stoned him with stones, that he died</u>. But king Rehoboam made speed to get him up to his chariot, to flee to Jerusalem. And Israel rebelled against the house of David unto this day. **II Chronicles 10:1-19** ~950 BC

Confucius could have cited the "house of David" or the "house of Samuel" as he cited the "house of Shang"; the lesson is the same.

Characteristics of Good Government

Plato recognized the value of virtuous rule and justice. He valued the ideal "philosopher-king" instead of "virtue" specifically, but had the same insight that prosperity required wise, just rule:

> "...true pilot must of necessity pay attention to the seasons, the heavens, the stars, the winds, and everything proper to the craft if he is really to rule a ship"[345]
> "philosophers [must] become kings... or those now called kings [must] ... genuinely and adequately philosophize"[346]

The Bible describes a virtuous ruler – he takes care of the poor, does justice, and punishes evildoers:

---

[345] Plato, *The Republic*, 6.488d ~380 BC
[346] Ibid., 5.473d

He shall judge thy people with righteousness, and thy poor with judgment. **Psalm 72:2** ~1000 BC

He shall judge the poor of the people, he shall save the children of the needy, and shall break in pieces the oppressor. **Psalm 72:4**

For he shall deliver the needy when he crieth; the poor also, and him that hath no helper. He shall spare the poor and needy, and shall save the souls of the needy. He shall redeem their soul from deceit and violence: and precious shall their blood be in his sight. **Psalm 72:12-14**

Doing justice and taking care of the poor stabilizes society and helps a ruler know the mind of God.

He judged the cause of the poor and needy; then it was well with him: was not this to know me? saith the LORD. **Jeremiah 22:16** ~590 BC

A virtuous ruler will have success in international affairs:

He shall have dominion also from sea to sea, and from the river unto the ends of the earth. They that dwell in the wilderness shall bow before him; and his enemies shall lick the dust. The kings of Tarshish and of the isles shall bring presents: the kings of Sheba and Seba shall offer gifts. Yea, all kings shall fall down before him: all nations shall serve him. **Psalm 72:8-11**

Citizens support virtuous rulers who can then conduct relations with other nations. The ruler can speak in confidence that citizens will support his policies.

Rulers answer to God to keep the "Mandate of Heaven":

Let us hear the conclusion of the whole matter: Fear God, and keep his commandments: for this is the whole <u>duty of man</u>. For God shall bring every work into judgment, with every secret thing, whether it be good, or whether it be evil. **Ecclesiastes 12:13-14** ~970 BC

The Bible points out that all men are equal before God. Even though the Bible commands citizens to obey their governments, many rulers have sought to suppress the Bible because they resent being placed on the same level as their followers.

Some leaders assert the importance of applying the law equally to everyone. Early in his administration, President Obama said:

"I've got to own up to my mistake, which is that ultimately it's important for this administration to send a message that there aren't two sets of rules. You know, one for prominent people and one for ordinary folks who have to pay their taxes."[347]

The Bible and Confucius both teach that God's laws apply to everyone; non-virtuous rulers see themselves as above the law.

Characteristics of Bad Government

Machiavelli agreed with Confucius' warning that too much spending would destroy a government:

A prince ... must not, if he be prudent, object to be called miserly. In course of time, he will be thought more liberal, when it is seen that by his parsimony, his revenue is sufficient, that he can defend himself against those who make war on him, and undertake enterprises without burdening his people, so that he is really liberal to all those from who he does not take, who are infinite in number,

---

[347] President Barack Obama, *New York Times* quote of the day, Feb 4, 2009

and niggardly to all to whom he does not give, who are few.[348]

The Bible explains how God punishes bad government:

> Woe to them that devise iniquity, and work evil upon their beds! when the morning is light, they practise it, because it is in the power of their hand. And they covet fields, and take them by violence; and houses, and take them away: so they oppress a man and his house, even a man and his heritage. **Micah 2:1-2**
>
> And I said, Hear, I pray you, O heads of Jacob, and ye princes of the house of Israel; Is it not for you to know judgment? Who hate the good, and love the evil; who pluck off their skin from off them, and their flesh from off their bones; Who also eat the flesh of my people, and flay their skin from off them; and they break their bones, and chop them in pieces, as for the pot, and as flesh within the caldron. **Micah 3:1-3** ~750 BC

God destroys society when government becomes too corrupt:

> Hear this, I pray you, ye heads of the house of Jacob, and princes of the house of Israel, that abhor judgment, and pervert all equity. They build up Zion with blood, and Jerusalem with iniquity. The heads thereof judge for reward, and the priests thereof teach for hire, and the prophets thereof divine for money: yet will they lean upon the LORD, and say, Is not the LORD among us? none evil can come upon us. Therefore shall Zion for your sake be plowed as a field, and Jerusalem shall become heaps, and the

---

[348] Machiavelli, *The Prince*, Of Liberality and Niggardliness

mountain of the house as the high places of the forest. **Micah 3:9-12** ~750 BC

Farmers understood that a shepherd had to serve his sheep to keep them alive. It worked best if the shepherd loved the sheep and served willingly. Sheep are sensitive to emotion and wouldn't cooperate with a shepherd who didn't love them. The Bible refers to rulers as "shepherds." This echoes Confucius' teaching that government had to be genuinely concerned for citizens' welfare:

> And the word of the LORD came unto me, saying, Son of man, prophesy against the shepherds of Israel, prophesy, and say unto them, Thus saith the Lord GOD unto the shepherds; Woe be to the shepherds of Israel that do feed themselves! should not the shepherds feed the flocks? Ye eat the fat, and ye clothe you with the wool, ye kill them that are fed: but ye feed not the flock. The diseased have ye not strengthened, neither have ye healed that which was sick, neither have ye bound up that which was broken, neither have ye brought again that which was driven away, neither have ye sought that which was lost; but with force and with cruelty have ye ruled them. And they were scattered, because there is no shepherd: and they became meat to all the beasts of the field, when they were scattered. My sheep wandered through all the mountains, and upon every high hill: yea, my flock was scattered upon all the face of the earth, and none did search or seek after them. **Ezekiel 34:1-6** ~587 BC

There are practical consequences for unjust government – tax revenue suffers when citizens either cheat the government by evading taxes or won't work hard because they fear they'll be robbed by corrupt officials. Some national leaders understand this:

No business wants to invest in a place where the government skims 20 percent off the top, or the head of the port authority is corrupt. No person wants to live in a society where the rule of law gives way to the rule of brutality and bribery. That is not democracy, that is tyranny, and now is the time for it to end.[349]

Most people recognize that non-virtuous behavior at the top harms society over time. The temptation to abuse power is firmly rooted in human nature. Confucius observed that societies fail when corruption becomes excessive.

Duties of Citizens to Each Other

Government employees aren't the only group who must behave virtuously towards other people. The Bible states that individual citizens have a duty to look out for each other regardless of what government does. Bosses must look out for their employees; everyone must look out for friends, relatives, and neighbors.

The Bible addresses citizens in general and outlines their responsibilities to each other:

And as for you, <u>O my flock</u>, thus saith the Lord GOD; Behold, I judge between cattle and cattle, between the rams and the he goats. Seemeth it a small thing unto you to have eaten up the good pasture, but ye must tread down with your feet the residue of your pastures? and to have <u>drunk of the deep waters, but ye must foul the residue with your feet</u>? And as for my flock, they eat that which ye have trodden with your feet; and they drink that which ye have fouled with your feet. Therefore thus saith the

---

[349] President Barack Obama on the need for government reform in Africa, *New York Times* quote of the day, July 12, 2009. It's needed here, too.

Lord GOD unto them; Behold, <u>I, even I, will judge between the fat cattle and between the lean cattle</u>. Because ye have thrust with side and with shoulder, and pushed all the diseased with your horns, till ye have scattered them abroad; Therefore will I save my flock, and they shall no more be a prey; and <u>I will judge between cattle and cattle</u>. **Ezekiel 34:17-22** ~587 BC

The phrase "judge between the fat cattle and between the lean cattle" means that our obligations extend to all others regardless of wealth or social class. The Bible states that God Himself judges people on how they treat each other. This idea is similar to Confucius' definition of societal virtue.

Confucius' ideas go far beyond Chinese philosophy. His ideas are rooted in an astute understanding of human nature; that's why they have been echoed by other thinkers down through the centuries who never heard of Confucius but were intimately familiar with the people of their own time and place.

In the next and last chapter, we'll explore these ideas in electoral, political, and most of all, practical terms.

15 - Turning Back From the Abyss

A little girl once asked, "Grandma, do all fairy tales begin 'Once upon a time'?" Grandma explained that modern fairy tales start, "If elected, I promise..."

Free societies can, in theory, change course by "voting the bums out," but harsh experience means that, today, no one trusts the new guys to do any better than the old ones. Do we go with the devil we know or the devil we don't know, and in the end, what difference does it make?

Political lying and duplicity have gotten so bad that voters can't tell if the politician himself knows he's lying. Someone who tells us that $2 + 2 = 5$ is lying only if he knows it's false. If he truly believes that $2 + 2 = 5$, he's wrong; he's not lying.

Maybe our politicians aren't lying when they talk about all the wonderful benefits we'd get if only we'd let them start their programs. Our government spends so much money taking very good care of politicians that they may actually believe that government programs work because it takes care of them.

So we're left stuck with liars and hypocrites; and with government-really-is-better do-gooders like Hillary Clinton, who've never personally experienced life as a peasant.

Voting is, ultimately, the only answer we have besides armed rebellion, which nobody wants. Alas, the election process hasn't been working all that well lately.

In order to avoid the disastrous tail end of the Confucian Cycle, we need to urgently ask: Where do elections work? Where do they fall short?

There are many suggestions floating around, but the most common ones have serious weaknesses. If all outside donations are removed from campaigning, only rich people or incumbents will win. Do we want that?

If signs, ads and marketing materials are banned or regulated, only well-connected and already-famous people will win. Do we want that?

All election laws are designed to favor those who are already in power because they're the ones who write the laws. If we decide on public financing of political campaigns, incumbents will write the rules to favor themselves, of course, and no challenger will ever have a chance to displace an incumbent. Do we want that?

You may very well be thinking, "We've been holding free and fair elections for well over two centuries now, and this book has shown that our government just keeps getting worse and worse. Why would we expect anything different in the future?"

If nothing changes, then, yes, our fate is sealed, and the Confucian Cycle will play out in the United States. However, there are several specific steps we can take, and which in fact are being taken in many parts of the country, that may turn the tide.

Jungle Primaries

In a country as large as the United States, there will naturally be a great deal of political diversity. Our Founders knew and expected this, which is why they designed a federal system with the idea that the central government would have strictly limited powers while individual states would be free to allow a wide range of diversity. Citizens would indicate support for one state's ideas over another by moving to a state that treated them better. This has been called the "laboratory of democracy."

One of the most noxious effects of our two-party system – which our Founders foresaw and decried but couldn't think of a way to avoid – is that, since the parties are national, politicians in every state almost always gravitate towards one or the other. In a state that tends towards the right, most successful politicians will be Republican; in left-leaning states, Democrats have a lock on the major offices.

Politicians elected in, say, Massachusetts or California, do have a democratic mandate. Because the Democrat is almost always a shoo-in, however, any voters who lean more towards Republicans are disenfranchised. They can't vote in the Democrat primary since they aren't Democrats, and while they can vote for the Republican there's rarely any real hope of victory. So they can be safely ignored by the people supposedly elected to serve them.

With this insulation from effective opposition, politicians become ever more corrupt. Our big cities, most of which haven't seen Republican administrations in living memory, are infamous for waste, fraud, theft, and every other governmental ill. Yet nothing can be done about it because there is no real competition.

But the problem can be solved!

The solution, which can already be seen in places like Louisiana, Washington state, and even California, is called a nonpartisan blanket primary, or more vividly, a "jungle primary."

In a jungle primary system, instead of having two different primary ballots for the Republican and Democratic Parties, you have one list of everyone who's running regardless of their party if any. Any candidate who wins a majority of all the primary votes cast wins the office immediately without having to contest the election.

More often, though, nobody wins a majority at the primary stage. In that case, the top two candidates compete in the general election and the winner of that contest takes office.

Why does this matter? Consider the situation of a Republican in Massachusetts if that state had a jungle primary. Presumably he'll vote for the Republican candidate in the jungle primary even though the Republican has no hope of winning.

He gets another chance to vote, however, because there are usually several Democratic candidates, none of whom wins a majority on the first round. The top two candidates, forced to rematch, need to appeal to all voters and not just to Democrats.

So a conservative, fiscally prudent, honest Democrat can appeal to the minority of Republicans to give him victory over a corrupt machine politician. If the conservative Democrat wins 40% of the Democrat votes and all of the Republican votes, he'll win.

Jungle primaries provide an essential check-and-balance in states that are heavily tilted to one party. This leads to better governance, more honest dealings, and indeed, better politicians who learn how to appeal to the center or even the opposition's voters.

Best of all, no Constitutional amendment is required. Article I of the Constitution grants states the authority to decide how their elections operate; Louisiana's system has proven both constitutionally valid and effective. Any other state can implement the same thing by an act of the legislature, or in about half of the states, by a popular referendum as did California.

Implementing jungle primaries is a systemic change that is known to work; it just needs wider use.

Gerrymandering

Politicians strive to accumulate and keep power. There are many paths to attaining power in the first place, but once you're in office, the easiest way to stay there is to carefully select your voters. American politicians have done this for two centuries through the abuse of redistricting.

The Constitution requires a national census every 10 years; Congressional districts and seats are allocated on the basis of the results, and most states also adjust the districts for state elections using this data as well.

The idea is that districts should contain roughly the same population so each vote counts somewhat the same. This "one man, one vote" principle is generally followed within states, but there's a great deal of room for shenanigans.

The first master of this art was Gov. Elbridge Gerry of Massachusetts back in 1812. He carefully drew a district so complex and sinuous that, according to a local editorial cartoonist, it resembled a salamander – hence the name "gerrymander" that we use to this day.

Gerrymandering is bipartisan, and can benefit the minority party just as much as the majority. California has been Democrat for a generation, but in a state so large, there are quite a few Republican voters. California legislators of both parties have set up the districts so that most of them are "safe" seats for whichever party holds them at the moment. This leads directly to the problem of polarization and corruption which is addressed by the jungle primary.

The voters of California finally rejected this corrupt system. They started in 2008 by passing Proposition 11 which stripped redistricting from the corrupt legislature and placed it in the hands of a separate 14-member commission. This wasn't enough, so they instated jungle primaries via Proposition 14 in 2010.

The California Citizens Redistricting Commission must include 5 Democrats, 5 Republicans, and 4 members from neither party. They're picked, not from serving politicians, but from a pool of applicants who are registered voters! What's more, implementing a new district map requires a supermajority of votes on the commission, thus preventing a stitch-up by Democrats conspiring with Republicans.

Has this eliminated safe seats in California? No, but according to various studies, it has definitely increased competition[350] and shaken up long-serving politicians. Over time, California's legislature can be expected to become more responsive to the voters and more honest since voting out bums is so much easier.

Again, redistricting reform is a system change that almost any state can implement. In many cases the people can do it over the opposition of the sitting politicians as in California. The ultimate solution might be to have no human being draw up the districts at all – simply feed the population data and locations into a computer,

---

[350] Eric McGhee; Daniel Krimm (September 2012). "Test-driving California's Election Reforms". Public Policy Institute of California. Retrieved 26 September 2012

and have a program that draws up districts with the geographically shortest total borders. It's simple, fair, entirely nonpartisan, and utterly devastating to unresponsive machine politics.

Spread Out the Electoral College Vote

American minority-party voters are also disenfranchised by the way Electoral College votes are distributed in Presidential elections.

Except for Maine and Nebraska, all states use a winner-take-all method. So, for instance, whichever presidential candidate wins Texas overall – generally the Republican – collects all 38 of its electoral votes.

In reality, of course, a lot of Texas voters preferred the Democrat: in 2012, for instance, Mitt Romney won with 57.17% of the vote. Barack Obama garnered 41.38%[351], yet he got nothing for his efforts. The same thing happens in the opposite direction in California and New York.

The result is that presidential candidates only spend time in swing states. Yes, the Republican might swing by California to collect money from rich donors in Orange County, but he isn't going to bother doing any rallies or voter outreach since there's no way he can benefit by it. The same goes for Democrats in Texas.

Instead, both parties send their heavy hitters to Ohio, New Hampshire, Florida, Virginia, and a handful of other swing states because both parties view those states as potentially winnable.

That's lots of fun if you live in New Hampshire, where a voter can say with perfect honesty and plausibility, "I haven't made up my mind because I haven't met all the candidates yet." For most everyone else, however, you get passed over come Presidential election season.

There's a solution to this problem, which Maine and Nebraska have had for many years: distribute electoral votes by Congressional

---

[351] Wikipedia: United States presidential election in Texas, 2012.

district. Whichever candidate wins in each district gets one electoral vote, and then the overall winner gets a "bonus" of the state's other two electoral votes.

With this change, it would make sense for Republicans to campaign in California and Democrats to make an effort in Texas. As with our other changes, proportionate distribution of electoral votes would force national candidates to truly care about the people of every state in the Union, not just the swing states.

As with the other changes, this one is perfectly feasible: the Constitution gives each state the right to determine how its electoral votes are allocated. Maine and Nebraska have established a precedent of long standing that their method is acceptable and fair.

There have been movements in Pennsylvania, Michigan, California, and elsewhere to implement proportionate distribution of Electoral College votes. Those would be a great start, and once the bandwagon starts rolling, other states would make the change too.

A New Dawn in America

Confucius predicted an irreversible decline when people found that government exploited them instead of serving them. As people lost confidence in their rulers, tax revenue suffered. In the end, the people rebelled or the barbarians swept in. Either way, the bureaucracy was forcibly reset to zero and started over.

As this book has shown, America is clearly in this dangerous condition. Nearly two-thirds of Americans believe that our country is on the wrong track, and more frightening still, it's been that way for over a decade.[352]

---

[352] http://blogs.wsj.com/washwire/2014/10/20/americans-gloom-marches-into-second-decade/

As if that isn't bad enough, fully three-quarters of Americans believe that their children will be worse off than they are.[353] This is the first time in all of American history that so many people have been so deeply depressed and pessimistic.

Confucius would look at our leaders and our government and predict a revolution in the very near future. He believed that virtue came down from the top; goodness knows we haven't had any top-down virtue in a long, long time!

Aside from violent revolution, Confucius didn't believe in the possibility of virtue coming up from the grass roots. In his world, this simply wasn't possible for reasons political, economic, cultural, and technological.

Thanks to the hard work, sacrifice, and historical brilliance of Americans past, we don't live in Confucius' limited world. Unlike the ancient Chinese, we have the ability to change our fate.

We have the liberty to propose, debate, and enact solutions.

We have the flexibility to try different things in different states while still remaining part of the same country.

We have new, potent communications networks and, yes, even still, enough education to perceive and understand the lessons of these experiments.

A famous quote, often mistakenly attributed to Thomas Jefferson, reads:

> "Where the people fear the government you have tyranny. Where the government fears the people you have liberty."

Confucius couldn't imagine any alternative to the people fearing government; in his view, that's what governments are *for*. Our current leaders, all too many of them, clearly feel the same way.

---

[353] http://www.washingtonpost.com/blogs/the-fix/wp/2014/08/06/the-single-most-depressing-number-in-the-new-nbc-wall-street-journal-poll/

Unlike the peasants of Confucius' day, we have the power to turn things around and put some of the fear of voters – if not of God – back into our elected leaders. Let's get out there and make it happen!

If we don't, Confucius will be proved right in the worst possible way, and it will be nobody's fault but our own.

Index

5

D

Daschle, Sen. Tom, 195, 250
David, King, 286, 288
Declaration of Independence, 191, 211, 284
Decline and Fall of the Roman Empire, 2
democracy, problem with, 46
desperation doctor, 184
Dewey, John, 246
Diocletian, Emperor, 38
discovery, 202
Dodd, Sen. Chris, 71
Dragon Ships, 125, 135
Durant, Will, 33
duty of marriage, 244

E

Eastern Airlines, 163
eight virtues, 80
Electoral College, 300
Elizabeth I, Queen, 117
Emperor
    example, 16
    joking, 14
    miscreant, 18
Equal Credit Opportunity Act, 69
equality before the law, 193
Erie Canal, 107
examination, 189

F

FDA, 170
Federal Deposit Insurance Corp, 66
Federal Register Act, 54
Federal Trade Commission, 54
FHBLB, 63
Fiddler on the Roof, 244
Filburn, 214
FMSF, 233
Food Pyramid, 169

Forbidden City, 78
Ford System, 128
Ford, Henry and divorce, 266
Fouquet, Nicholas, 90
Four Freedoms, 200
Frank, Rep. Barney, 72
Franklin, Benjamin, 196, 241
full pay 'til the last day, 163
functional foods, 167

G

Galbraith, John Kenneth, 68
gao kao annual examinations, 190
Gates, Bill, 3, 49
Genghis Khan, 198, 256
George III, King, 211, 285
Gerrymandering, 298
Gibbon, Edward, 2
Giuliani, Rudy, 202
goiter, 183
Grand Canal, 33, 43, 95
Great Wall of China, 7, 51
guilty mind, 209
Gutenberg, Johannes, 115

H

hard lemonade, 24
Havel, Vaclev, 30
Helmsley, Leona, 193, 195
Heritage Foundation, 4
Honda, 9

I

immunity letter, 203
Impeach Earl Warren, 189
income tax, 216
Industrial Revolution, 115
injustice, bureaucratic, 21
interesting times, 92

William Taylor

William Taylor's parents were American missionaries to Japan right after the Second World War. The Japanese had learned the secrets of civilization from the Chinese, so Confucian ideas were thick on the ground. Until he entered MIT in 1963, Mr. Taylor watched the Japanese use Confucian virtue to bootstrap themselves to first-world status. There were no Japanese cars on American roads in 1963 and next to no cars on Japanese roads. Cars move faster than bicycles; he was hit by cars 3 times his first year at MIT.

After studying computer technology at MIT and graduating before "computer science" had been invented, Mr. Taylor worked for truly monster societies such as the US Navy, General Motors, Ford, and Chrysler; middle-sized business cultures such as IBM, the *New York Times*, the First National Bank of Chicago, NASA, and the MIT Draper Lab; and tiny startups you've never heard of.

In many situations, he observed organizational dynamics which were dysfunctional to the point of incomprehensibility. Containing his incredulity so as not to get fired, he collected data.

It finally became clear that even the medium-sized organizations had enough employees to constitute a pseudo-nation, or society, or civilization within the greater American society. Groups of employees within these "nations" operated internally according to Confucius' rules whether they knew it or not.

Most job growth comes from small businesses because bigger businesses have enough employees to become pseudo-nations which lose virtue and start on the downward path of the Confucian cycle. Most such businesses die; very few of the Fortune 100 of 50 years ago are still on the list or even exist. Fortunate tribes such as IBM and Chrysler under Lee Iacocca have been rescued by leaders of extraordinary Confucian virtue who inspired virtuous behavior in the employees, but such leaders are few and far between.

This book was written out of concern for the author's grandchildren. What sort of society will they inhabit? Will America remain a first-world, peaceful society, or will it descend into the Confucian abyss of chaos, feudalism, and warring gangs? America has an advantage that businesses in jeopardy do not - elections. American voters can force virtue on their rulers by voting against non-virtuous candidates. American voters can save their civilization, but will they? This book is an attempt to help them do it.

Mr. Taylor is currently a vice president at a Fortune 50 financial services firm.

Kenneth R. Taylor

Growing up with well-educated parents of wide-ranging, eclectic experience and interests, Kenneth Taylor was exposed from an early age to a variety of cultural touchstones.

With his father working in the world of tech startups, he had a ringside seat to watch many of the principles discussed in this book illustrated in living and sometimes garish color.

Working for a Japanese tech company in the mid-1990s presented a unique view of modern Confucian management. At the time, most Japanese employers were very large, very old, or both. The Japanese had recovered from the destruction of WW II by learning from other countries. Having caught up with the West, they now had to discover new ideas on their own to keep their economy growing.

Mr. Taylor's employer had founded by a Japanese graduate of Tokyo University who'd been sent through MIT by a monstrous Japanese conglomerate. They expected him to work for them until he died so that they could recover their investment in his education; instead he founded a startup like so many in America at the time.

During his time there, Mr. Taylor found that the startup exhibited Confucian virtue. The boss took very good care of his employees, encouraged them to learn new skills, and shared the proceeds with them. Unfortunately, the company lacked the financial resources to survive the economic shock of the Tokyo property crash, and the firm went under.

Back in the United States, Mr. Taylor joined, ran, and founded tech startups in the Northeast, experiencing the economic shocks of 9/11, 2008, and following. These traumas and simultaneous loss of societal virtue led to the question: is America entering the final stage of the Confucian cycle; and if so, what can we do about it? His quest for the wisdom of history and for comparing the past to the present evolved into many articles on Scragged.com which became the basis for this book.

In addition to research and opinion writing, Mr. Taylor is currently involved in technology in the government sector as well as several other private-sector ventures.

CPSIA information can be obtained
at www.ICGtesting.com
Printed in the USA
LVOW12*0030300616

494666LV00001BA/3/P